Mental Health Policy in Britain

D0301153

* 000111021 *

Also by the same authors

Experiencing Psychiatry: Users' Views of Services (with Ron Lacey)

A Sociology of Mental Health and Illness

Mental Health Policy in Britain

A Critical Introduction

Anne Rogers

and

David Pilgrim

First published in Great Britain 1996 by
MACMILLAN PRESS LTD
Houndmills, Basingstoke, Hampshire RG21 6XS
and London
Companies and representatives
throughout the world

A catalogue record for this book is available
from the British Library.

ISBN 0–333–61392–9 hardcover
ISBN 0–333–61393–7 paperback

First published in the United States of America 1996 by
ST. MARTIN'S PRESS, INC.
Scholarly and Reference Division,
175 Fifth Avenue,
New York, N.Y. 10010

ISBN 0–312–16069–0

Library of Congress Cataloging-in-Publication Data
Rogers, Anne.
Mental health policy in Britain : a critical introduction / Anne
Rogers and David Pilgrim.
    p.   cm.
Includes bibliographical references and index.
ISBN 0–312–16069–0
1. Mental health policy—Great Britain.   2. Mental health policy–
Great Britain—History.   3. Mental health services—Great Britain.
4. Mental health services—Great Britain—History.   I. Pilgrim,
David, 1950– .   II. Title.
RA790.7.G7R645   1996
362.1'0941—dc20   95–51522
                                                                    CIP

10   9   8   7   6   5   4   3   2
05   04   03   02   01   00   99   98   97

Printed in Hong Kong

In memory of
Richard Marshall (1945–95)

Contents

List of Figures and Tables

Figures

Tables

Preface

This book provides a critical introduction to mental health policy and practice in Britain. It is written primarily with two audiences in mind: social science undergraduates and trainee mental health professionals. There are a number of excellent pieces of work on our topic, which we draw upon or summarise at times, but they tend to be about particular periods or particular aspects of British mental health policy. Our goal is to provide an analysis of the history and genesis of the current character of this topic. We will endeavour to relate policy not only to services but also to versions of knowledge about mental abnormality and their associated professional and other interests, which have shaped current mental health provision.

Texts on health policy tend to emphasise legislative changes but go into little detail about the stakeholders and controversies surrounding mental health policy or psychiatric knowledge. This tendency is even stronger in popular social policy textbooks, where mental health is dealt with superficially or omitted from consideration. Texts covering social policy usually have a remit which includes health, education, housing, urban planning, income maintenance and personal social services. Within this coverage mental health often has a marginalised status. Given the current controversies surrounding mental health issues for both local and central government, we hope that this book will help to rectify this imbalance.

In the light of the mixed audience we anticipate and the complexity of the issues entailed, we have tried to provide a set of building blocks of understanding. In the first half of the book, the chapters provide an introduction for newcomers to the field of mental health (or to areas within it). These chapters are necessarily descriptive and so may contain some material which is well known to those working as practitioners. However, working in contemporary services guarantees no historical knowledge and so chapters are included which trace the roots of current service configurations. We hope that social policy students unfamiliar with services may find the material describing them useful.

The second part of the book then presupposes that the reader has a basic understanding about stakeholders, policy formation, and current services and their history. This allows us to move into a set of understandings in more detail. These include the role and aspirations of mental health workers, the effectiveness of services, issues about mental health promotion, prevention and primary care and the recent impact of consumerism and service user criticisms.

By the final chapter, the understandings introduced in the early chapters, and the more detailed explorations thereafter, are rounded off by a discussion of the challenges facing policy-makers about mental health. Here we are more explicit about our value position and less concerned to simply summarise evidence and document debates. This is why we have sub-titled the book 'a *critical* introduction'. Our assumption is that it is not sufficient to accept official accounts of dominant interest groups (politicians, civil servants and psychiatrists), which tend to describe a series of honourable acts and incremental progress. Instead, we assume that mental health policy was and still is a contested issue, which contains silences about the problems created, as well as appropriate boasts about those solved, by 'progress'. There was and is more than meets the eye about the assumed success of the philanthropy and humani–tarianism of reformers and the public service and technical expertise of those working in the mental health industry. A neat ascending line cannot be drawn which suggests that, over time, sustained progress has been achieved in societal, governmental and professional responses to people with mental health problems. Apart from a variety of interests operating which are not those of these people, there remains under-stated ignorance and disagreement about how to conceptualise, explain and respond to mental abnormality. This is why by the end of the book we attempt to introduce a healthy scepticism about current mental health policy on a number of fronts.

In the first two chapters, stakeholders and their views are introduced and current services outlined. We also introduce models of policy formation. Easton (1953) succinctly defined policy as 'a web of decisions and actions which allocate . . . values'. Ham (1985, pp. 94–5) makes a number of useful clarifying points when reacting to this definition, which we will see have relevance when we look at mental health policy:

- Decisions do not always lead to actions.
- Policy is not about one decision but many.
- Policy is not static – it changes over time.
- Policy is also about inaction – much political activity is about maintaining the status quo.

- In practice, actions may occur in the absence of formal decisions which then constitute an aspect of policy – custom and practice 'on the ground' may emerge independently of central government decision-making.

This complexity about social policy, which Ham appropriately highlights, is compounded further by the particular ambiguities which surround our topic. For example, the term 'mental health' has crept in in recent years as a substitute for, or alternative to, the term 'mental illness'. More typically at present the terms co-exist. For example, NHS managers and clinicians quite happily talk of 'mental health services' in one breath and 'people with a severe mental illness' or 'with an enduring mental illness' in the next. In part, this shift in terminology reflects changes in the balance of interests, values and beliefs about mental health provision which we address throughout this book. Despite this new preference for prefixing 'policy' and 'services' with the term 'mental health', which for simplicity we conform to in the title and the text of this book, it is important to recognise that both policy and services have overwhelmingly been about people with a diagnosis of 'mental illness'. As we note in Chapter 8, mental health promotion still only constitutes a small part of the contemporary mental health policy agenda. Currently there is little consensus amongst professionals or lay people about what constitutes a positive notion of mental health. There is also confusion about how to promote the latter.

Apart from the conceptual problem about mental health, there are also unresolved philosophical questions when we start to explore what constitutes a 'mental health problem'. Whilst each society has some notion of sadness, fear and unintelligibility there is no universal and trans-historical agreement on the definition of these states, how they are caused or how they should be responded to. The dominance of medical notions over the past two hundred years in Western societies has not resolved these questions. Medicine offers no certain answers to the question of causality in most cases of diagnosed mental illness. What we are offered instead is a whole range of biological, psychological or social possibilities. Sometimes these are pitted against one another. Sometimes they are blended together in some eclectic portmanteau model, such as the 'biopsychosocial' model, which currently finds favour in many training courses for mental health professionals. At other times, as in the case of 'schizophrenia', a genetic, biochemical or neurological explanation remains elusive. For some this signals the failure of medical explanations for madness. For others it inspires a redoubling of research efforts. What is clear is that given the contested status of medical research into mental abnormality, in this part of health policy, more than most, the views of psychiatric experts need to be addressed in a challenging and critical way. We will return to the problem of a reliance on medical knowledge in mental health policy in Chapter 10.

And then there are the particular moral questions which surround mental abnormality. How much should madness be tolerated or valued? Whose civil rights should be privileged – the mad or those they disrupt, exasperate, embarass, perplex, scare or threaten? Paternalism, backed up by legislative powers to segregate and 'treat' madness as an illness, is the policy solution to which we have become accustomed, even though the latter is sited more in the community than it was in the past. But such a working formula does not resolve difficult moral questions, any more than the technical means and the legislative framework to carry out abortions resolves the arguments about the competing rights of women and foetuses.

Thus mental health is a contested field in more ways than one. Despite this, politicians pass laws about and professionals provide services in response to individuals with a range of personal difficulties. For this reason, the book will take into consideration and explore controversies, but it will also deal with the current dilemmas facing policymakers and professionals about developing and assessing the effectiveness of services. The current debates around effectiveness of services and treatments and the push for a health service planned on knowledge about the outcomes of health technologies and interventions make it particularly necessary for this book to deal with these questions (Chapter 7). Before that there will be an historical focus (Chapters 3, 4 and 5). This is designed to illustrate the connections between the rise and decline of the asylum and contemporary 'community care' policies. In this regard the history of the present policy dilemmas can only be understood with reference to the all-embracing influence and longevity of the Victorian asylum system. The rest of the book will describe and critically analyse current policies and services.

In the United States, Rochefort (1988) has pointed out that mental health policy formation goes in cycles, with peaks of activity and troughs of stagnation. The same is true of Britain. The chapters about history, and those describing more recent times, will report this cyclical pattern, which contains a connecting thread of ambivalence. On the one hand, there was and remains a clear impulse of exclusion – people with mental health problems are not 'us' but 'them', not benign but dangerous, not citizens but patients. On the other hand, increasingly during this century there have been many lobbies which consider that all people have more in common with their fellows than they have features which distinguish them as a separate category of human beings. The current policy of community care offers the possibility of inclusion. However, as we will see in relation to recent forms of community surveillance, the process of exclusion remains powerful at the end of the twentieth century.

To summarise, because of the particular controversies surrounding the topic of this book, we will be concerned to do more than describe a series of legislative events and their service implications. We will also attempt to relate these to the moral and epistemological uncertainties which are present, sometimes in the foreground but always in the background, about mental health. The book intends to offer the student some food for thought about the complicated relationships which exist between policy formation, services, and stakeholder interests.

Finally, we note a limitation on the scope of the book. It focuses on the policies and services developed in the main for people in young and middle adulthood. Space does not permit an examination of two groups – children and older people with mental health problems. Each of these, with its peculiar policy implications, could be the basis for other books.

ANNE ROGERS
DAVID PILGRIM

Acknowledgements

We would like to thank Catherine Gray, Steven Pilgrim, Keith Povey and Diane Taylor for their editorial advice and technical help with the manuscript. The feedback we were given by the two anonymous reviewers from Macmillan was invaluable. Thanks are due also to Bonnie Sibbald, Geraldine Strathdee and colleagues at North West Regional Health Authority who have offered views and advice during the book's preparation.

ANNE ROGERS
DAVID PILGRIM

1

Stakeholders and Their Views

Introduction

This first chapter will introduce the views of different parties with an interest in mental health policy and services. Are people mad, frightened and sad? Are they suffering from a 'mental illness'? Why are some people who offend everyday morality and break the criminal law sent to prison, whereas others committing identical offences are placed in mental hospitals? If the latter entails 'mental disorder', how is this different from 'mental illness'? These simple questions highlight the problem of understanding both mental abnormality and the way that citizens, professionals and politicians respond to irrationality in society.

The debate about whether we should use competing terms such as 'madness', 'mental illness', 'mental distress', 'mental health problems', 'freaking out' and 'mental disorder' is not only about semantic disagreements. These terms are products of different stakeholder or interest groups. For example, 'mental disorder' is essentially a legal category, whereas 'mental illness' is a medical one. For now we will clarify why they are different and to what degree they are compatible. More will be said in Chapter 6 about professional knowledge. Below, the latter will be briefly noted alongside other perspectives.

The mental health care policy arena, like other areas of health and social care, involves a number of stakeholders who at times hold different sets of interests. Williamson (1993) provides a definition of interests and 'stakes' which can usefully be applied to the structure and organisation of mental health provision:

Interests are to do with advantage and detriment to individuals and to groups. Interests ... are something in which a stake is held; a

personal or group resource or means to protect or enhance a resource. Everyone has interests in resources like influence, power,
time, money, knowledge, the way situations involving themselves
are defined. (Williamson, 1993, p. 3)

There are diverse stakeholders in our field of interest who have different degrees of power and influence. These are not static but change
over time and according to the issue. Some groups have a defined
occupational interest in framing mental health problems in certain ways.
These 'dominant' interests tend to predominate over those of other
stakeholders. For their part the other groups are not disinterested. They
are less preoccupied about occupational status and salaries except as a
possible target of criticism and more concerned about the sources of
their own mental disability or the offence, burden or disruption caused
by others. Some, like the police and those working in the criminal
justice system, also have to deal with mental health problems and so
have a perspective to be noted. This is true also of the managers and
commissioners of services. These have considerable influence over mental health service provision but lack a distinct coherent disciplinary
notion of mental health. Let us look at these stakeholders and their
perspectives in a little more detail.

The Mental Health Specialists

The occupational groups that claim an expertise in mental health are
sometimes called the 'psy complex', which includes psychiatrists, clinical
psychologists, psychiatric social workers, psychiatric nurses, psychoanalysts, psychotherapists and counsellors. In Chapter 6 we will go
into more detail about the relationship between the state and the different mental health occupations. Here the perspectives held by different expert groups will be noted.

Psychiatrists

Psychiatrists are trained in medicine and so they tend to emphasise
diagnosis, treatment, prognosis (predicting the outcome of an illness)
and aetiology (speculating about its cause). In the latter regard, the
bodily emphasis of medical training and its social history ensure that
biological/chemical or physiological causes have been privileged. This
has led, in the main, to treatment approaches dominated by drugs and

other somatic interventions. In the nineteenth century biological theories of madness prevailed and this has left a strong impact on psychiatric thinking even a century later (see Chapter 3). In the twentieth century, psychiatrists have become more eclectic in their etiological theories. Many of them now accept social and psychological causes of mental illness, as well as biological ones. They also use psychological as well as somatic treatments, although the latter still predominate. The new eclectic psychiatry emphasises all three sources of causation in its 'biopsychosocial' model (see, e.g., Falloon and Fadden, 1993). The dominant role of psychiatrists in services is reflected in the terms 'psychiatric hospital' and 'psychiatric nurses' and 'psychiatric social workers'. Indeed, until recently the term 'psychiatry' had become a catchall phrase to include not just a medical specialty but its associated facilities and subordinated occupational groups. More recently Community Psychiatric Nurses have dropped the term 'psychiatric' for the preferred 'Community Mental Health Nurse', signalling perhaps a dilution of the impact of medical authority.

Clinical psychologists

Clinical psychologists are a relatively new group. Their occupation was officially recognised by the title of 'clinical psychologist' with the introduction of the NHS (Dabbs, 1972). They hold a variety of theoretical positions, which reflect competing models in their academic discipline. Thus psychoanalysis, behaviourism, humanistic psychology and cognitivism are all represented in the work of clinical psychology practitioners (Goldie, 1974; Pilgrim and Treacher, 1992). These are divergent and often antagonistic models of human functioning. Consequently, 'psychologically-orientated' mental health work has no coherent and agreed way of theorising the problems of service recipients.

Psychoanalysis and other forms of depth psychology emphasise the role of the unconscious mind. By contrast, behaviourism only considers external aspects of conduct to be amenable to scientific description and systematic and measurable modification. Humanistic psychology emphasises subjectivity and the potential of human beings to grow, given the correct personal circumstances. Like psychoanalysis this implies the provision of some form of psychotherapy. Cognitivism emphasises the role of thought processes in human functioning. Whereas behavioural treatments (such as the use of 'token economies') emphasise changing outer behaviour, cognitive therapies emphasise the modification of thought processes. Despite this plethora of apparently contradictory theoretical positions, clinical psychologists have developed an array of hybrid and eclectic mixtures for themselves in their assessment techniques and therapeutic practice.

Unlike GPs, psychiatrists, nurses, social workers and police officers, psychologists hold no legal powers of detention under mental health legislation. For this reason, in comparison with the other mental health occupations the influence which they exert flows more from their theoretical knowledge and therapeutic credibility, rather than from their organisational power or position.

Psychiatric nurses

Compared with psychiatry and psychology the knowledge base of nursing is less well developed. As in other branches of nursing, psychiatric nurses have traditionally been subordinate to medicine. Consequently, they have not developed a separate body of knowledge. In practice they follow the contours of more academically based disciplines (psychiatry, clinical psychology and sociology). More recent changes in the curriculum of psychiatric nurse training suggest that reactions against medical theory (embracing more social and psychological models) have been associated with attempts to shift towards greater professional autonomy. The practice of psychiatric nurses is discussed in detail in Chapter 6.

Social workers

Social workers who are specially trained to fulfil their duties under the 1983 Mental Health Act are more likely to import a social perspective into mental health work. In part this stems from their different occupational roots. Psychiatrists, clinical psychologists and psychiatric nurses arose within, or as a result of, the asylum system. The modern occupational location of social work is different. Its recent development is embedded in local authority social services structures with a focus on 'community' working and links. However, this does not necessarily imply a coherent theoretical approach to social work. Social science itself is internally divided about the topic of mental abnormality. Two broad strands of sociological thought can be identified as having influenced social work training and practice in mental health. First, a social causation approach accepts the existence of mental illness but seeks to identify its social determinants, e.g. the stresses of poverty or racial or sexual disadvantage. Second, social reaction or labelling theory emphasises the role of the reactions of others to deviance in its maintenance and amplification (Scheff, 1966). Whilst a social focus is often referred to in social work theory and training, in practice social workers often follow a medical model of mental illness in their every-day work (Goldie, 1974; Bean, 1979). Psychoanalytic ideas have also been influential in case work in and outside of mental health work.

Psychoanalysts

Psychoanalysts are drawn from a number of occupational groups but psychiatrists tend to dominate their training institutes. (Non-medical practitioners are still called 'lay analysts'.) Psychoanalysis was invented by Sigmund Freud but his modern-day followers are divided into those following his ideas, those of Melanie Klein, and others who draw eclectically from these two main sources. Freud focused on explaining the unconscious basis of neurotic symptoms and later analysts exam-ined the early infantile sources of depression (Bowlby, 1969) and psy-chosis (Winnicot, 1958; Laing, 1967). This spread of interest within psychoanalysts reflects theoretical splits about both the age at which mental health problems are assumed to begin and also the role of the instincts versus quality of parenting.

Psychoanalysts conceptualise mental health problems in terms of a hierarchy of fixation at, or regression to, earlier forms of psychological functioning in a person's life. Neurotic anxiety for instance might be seen as an outcome of unresolved sexual feelings about a parent. De-pression might be understood as resulting from early difficulties around separation from a parent. Psychosis could be understood as a failure to be nurtured and made secure in the very earliest months of a person's life. Over the last fifty years psychoanalysis as a body of knowledge has had considerable influence on social, and mental health policy and practice. This has been seen as having both a positive and negative effect. Comments by two of the leading social policy analysts, Richard Titmuss and Barbara Wootton, writing in the 1950s, illustrate the point. Titmuss writes of psychoanalysis in almost messianic terms:

> the work of Freud and his successors has been of revolutionary im-portance to medicine; it has changed our attitudes to the mentally ill, it has at least helped towards the alleviation of mental suffering, it has enlarged the possibilities of preventative therapy, and it has given us new ways of looking at the growth of personality and the origins of illness . . . it has for, doctors and laymen alike, under-mined our psychological innocence, sensitised us to an inner world of reality, and made us see all sickness, in whatever guise, as part of a psychological continuum. (Titmuss, 1958, p. 187)

By contrast, Wootton expresses dismay and contempt at the end of
a discussion about the pervasiveness of psychoanalytical ideas in social
work texts, which she views as a trend which disguises the social and
economic root of peoples' social problems:

> Happily, it can be presumed that the lamentable arrogance of the
> [psychoanalytical] language in which contemporary social workers
> describe their activities is not generally matched by the work that
> they actually do: otherwise it is hardly credible that they would not
> constantly get their faces slapped. Happily, also, the literature of
> social work is not generally read by those who receive its adminis-
> trations. Without doubt the majority of those who engage in social
> work are sensible, practical people who conduct their business in a
> reasonably matter-of-fact basis. The pity is that they have to write
> such nonsense about it: and to present themselves to the world as so
> deeply tainted with what Virginia Woolf has called 'the peculiar
> repulsiveness of those who dabble their fingers self approvingly in
> the stuff of others' souls'. (Wootton, 1959, p. 279)

Psychotherapists and counsellors also work in statutory and voluntary
educational and health settings. Their theoretical approaches may be
drawn from psychoanalysis, behaviourism, cognitivism or humanistic
psychology. The latter (for instance following the work of Carl Rogers)
has been particularly influential in voluntary sector mental health services
such as The Samaritans and Marriage Guidance (now Relate).

Given the wide divergence of theoretical perspectives within the occupational groups described above, it is clear that collectively they share
no common theory of mind and behaviour. It is not as if there is a
broad consensus which contains conflicts of opinions. Instead, theoretical polarisations can be identified about a number of issues. In particular, splits occur between:

- Those emphasising biological or inherited tendencies towards mental abnormality versus those emphasising environmental factors.
- Those emphasising internal events (thoughts and feelings) and those
emphasising behaviour.
- Those emphasising causes and those emphasising consequences of
mental abnormality.
- Those emphasising an eclectic inclusion of biological, psychological
and social factors versus those privileging one group of these factors.

A practical consequence of this mixture of ideas is that service recipients encounter a wider range of interventions, which sit more or less easily together. For example, in relation to rehabilitation, Bean and Mounser (1993) describe a typical treatment approach thus:

A man being resettled after developing schizophrenia may receive medication (medical model) in a hostel run on therapeutic community lines (social model) whilst receiving social skills training (behavioural model). (Bean and Mounser, 1993, p. 31)

The Impact of Professional Knowledge Claims on Policy Formation

The knowledge produced and used by professionals is not comprised of static entities divorced from policy formation processes. Rather, professional ideas about the nature and treatment of mental health problems impact on policy formation which in turn feeds back into professional knowledge. For example the differentiation of services for different groups in the nineteenth century is related to different notions about emotional and intellectual deviance. Prior to the 1890 Lunacy Act an elaborate network of asylums had been built (see Chapter 3) which contained 'aments', now known as people with learning difficulties or disabilities, as well as 'dements' or 'lunatics'. As 'mental illness' and 'mental handicap' came to be seen as the separate specialisms with distinct bodies of knowledges so these were distinguished from one another in policy legislation and provision. The advent of community care policies has also heralded changes in the conceptualisation of disease categories within psychiatry, which have made the task of detecting and managing madness in non-institutional settings by psychiatry easier. New models of schizophrenia have recently begun to emerge. Positive symptoms which were once important in deciding whether hospitalisation should occur are now displaced by an elevation of the importance of so-called 'negative symptoms':

delusions and hallucinations, although easier to define reliably, are not the most important characteristic, or crippling symptoms of schizophrenia. (Andreason, 1989)

Within this scheme, aspects of 'schizophrenic' behaviour which fail to meet criteria of self-motivation and self-surveillance within a domestic

context are emphasised. Negative symptoms like 'avolition . . . mani-
fests itself as a characteristic lack of energy, drive and interest', which
often leads to 'severe social and economic impairment' (ibid). Accordingly, psychiatrists now recognise aspects of a 'schizophrenic's' personal life which they are deemed not to be able to manage themselves
– such problems include: irregular attendance at work, carrying out
employment and domestic tasks in a disorganised and half-hearted manner, the lack of the pursuit of pleasure ('ahedonia') and a disinterest
in sex.

Other Stakeholders

The 'paraprofessional' perspective

De Swaan (1990) has pointed out that a layer of professionals exists
outside of the psy complex, including GPs, the clergy and the police,
who make decisions about mental health problems and may play a
temporary or partial role in actually working with psychiatric patients.
From what we know about this group they seem to form a bridge
between mental health experts and patients and the general public.
Consequently, their theories are a mixture of ordinary and expert
understandings. For instance, a study of the understanding that the police
have about mental health problems when operating Section 136 of the
Mental Health Act suggests that they use commonsense judgements
about people they deem to be mad in public places (Rogers, 1990). As
evidence of the proximity of the lay discourse to judgements made by
psychiatrists, this study showed that the police were as reliable in their
judgements, as experts, about the presence or absence of mental illness, as confirmed by psychiatric diagnosis after a police referral.

   This suggests that ordinary conceptions of madness or unintelligible
conduct may approximate to psychiatric diagnoses of psychosis. Coulter
(1973), in his study of everyday judgements about madness, pointed
out that lay people are involved in making decisions about mental illness
which are then rubber-stamped as formal diagnoses by professionals
called in to deal with crises. However, as we will see below, experts
and non-experts making judgements about mental abnormality may not
always concur.

The legal perspective

Another example of theorising mental abnormality can be found in mental health legislation. The 1983 Mental Health Act, passed by politicians and drawn up by lawyers, has an explicit account of mental abnormality. However, in legal terms 'mental disorder' refers to more than 'mental illness'. The Act includes four types of mental disorder:

1. Mental illness – this is not defined.
2. Mental impairment – this refers to people with learning difficulties who are also deemed to be abnormally agressive.
3. Severe mental impairment – this refers to people with severe learning difficulties who are also deemed to be abnormally agressive.
4. Psychopathic disorder – this refers to anti-social individuals who are 'abnormally aggressive' or who manifest 'seriously irresponsible conduct'.

Thus, the legal perspective offers four explicit categorisations of mental abnormality but offers little beyond that given by psychiatric experts. Mental illness is not defined, so its existence in law must remain parasitic on the views given by psychiatrists. Similarly, the third and fourth categories rely on an expert (psychiatric or clinical psychological) view about learning difficulty combined with a judgement about dangerousness. The final category is completely circular and so has little explanatory value. People are judged to be psychopathic because of their dangerous and anti-social acts, and they are deemed to be dangerous and anti-social because they are suffering from a psychopathic disorder. This would seem to offer little improvement on the explanatory power of the notion of 'evil'.

Whatever the theoretical weaknesses of a legal view about mental abnormality it has great practical significance. As we will see in later chapters, the courts have been involved in admitting people to psychiatric facilities over a long period. Since 1959 those powers have been substantially reduced, but even today the courts are still involved where judgements are made about mentally disordered offenders. Also, lawyers are involved on Mental Health Review Tribunals, when decisions are made about the discharge of both offender and non-offender patients held under varying sections of the Mental Health Act.

Politicians and service managers

The legal and medical perspectives are endorsed by parliamentary politicians and subsequently by civil servants serving government. They
also provide a framework of duty and constraint for mental health service
managers. Politicians creating and changing legislation have wider powers
of influence over mental health than mental health legislation. Additionally, they are responsible for other legislation, for instance about
health care organisation, employment, housing and income maintenance,
which impinge on mental health care service users. Recently, the 1983
Mental Health Act has probably had less of an influence on service
development than has a different piece of legislation, the 1990 NHS
and Community Care Act.

The recent views of service managers and the governing politicians,
to which they are ultimately accountable, have been researched very
little. However, Ramon (1985) documents the views of politicians about
mental health legislation in the 1920s and 1950s. A number of features were present which are likely to be relevant considerations still
today:

- Mental health is not a high priority for most MPs.
- Views about the topic do not always fall neatly into party political
  perspectives. A recent example of this is in relation to civil liberties, with right-wing Conservatives and their traditional opponents
  occasionally sharing a common libertarian concern in debates.
- MPs are sensitive to public opinion and prejudice. Whether this is
  about the wrongful detention of the sane or fears about dangerous
  patients in the community, it is clear that mental health policy may
  be shaped often by the proxy interests of a voting public, as interpreted by politicians.
- A minority of parliamentarians may become 'product champions'
  for mental health policy often because of their own personal experience
  or interests. Examples here are the Conservative Donald MacIntosh
  in the 1950s who was not only a doctor but also an ex-mental patient.
  More recently (1992) Ian McCartney, a Labour MP, whose partner
  is a psychiatric social worker, was instrumental in setting up a policy review of mental health as a priority area of health policy by
  the Parliamentary Labour Party. Tessa Jowell, another Labour MP
  and ex-training and education director for MIND, has also recently
  sponsored a private members bill in response to government pro-
  posals for supervised discharge orders. The former Secretary of State

for Health Virginia Bottomley was an ex-psychiatric social worker and this was a relevant influential factor in some recent debates about mental health policy and services.

- People with mental health problems are themselves a minority voting group. This is a relatively new phenomenon. Patients in psychiatric hospitals did not have the vote prior to the 1983 Mental Health Act.

Below politicians are groups of civil servants who also may define or shape policy in their advice to Ministers. A sub-group of these will be indirectly representing professional interests as they are appointed as medical or nursing officers in the Department of Health. To complicate matters, there now exists a range of purchasing and provider managers in each locality. These will have a variety of personal and professional experiences of mental health services. They are constrained by central government policy but also can exercise considerable discretion about engendering or retarding local policy initiatives. Purchasing managers set and monitor the performance of provider units by their specifications in contracts. This contractual control allows purchasers to import expectations about service type in a locality. They may also exercise discretion over the types of service which are bought within their allocated budget. For this reason, purchasers have become an important countervailing power to that of local clinical interests within the NHS. As well as having their own pre-existing views about what should constitute a good local mental health service, they are open to local lobbies, such as advocacy and self-advocacy groups.

The lay perspective

The gap created by the absence of a legal definition of mental illness has led to variable outcomes in court decision-making and rulings about mental disorder in society. For instance, expert witnesses for both the defence and prosecution examining Peter Sutcliffe ('The Yorkshire Ripper') agreed that he was suffering from paranoid schizophrenia when he murdered a series of women. However, the jury of lay people found him guilty of malice aforethought and he was sent to prison, not a secure hospital. (After the judgement he was transferred from prison to a Special Hospital.) In the case of Dennis Nilson who killed, dismembered and stored fifteen young men in his flat, the defence expert witness argued he suffered from a psychopathic disorder but the one for the prosecution did not. He was also sent to prison by a jury. These examples demonstrate that lay people are in a position to overrule

expert judgements about mental disorder. Moreover, as an indication
of the difficulty the criminal justice system has in making distinctions
between mental normality and abnormality, here is an example of an
opinion given by Judge Lawton in 1974. He said that the words 'mental illness' are 'ordinary words of the English language. They have no
particular medical significance. They have no particular legal significance.' Lawton refers back to a ruling given by Law Lord Reid who
was talking of an offender whose sanity was in doubt:

> I ask myself what would the ordinary sensible person have said about
> the patient's condition in this case if he [*sic*] had been informed of
> his behaviour? In my judgment such a person would have said 'Well
> the fellow is obviously mentally ill.' (Cited in Jones, 1991, p. 15)

Hoggett (1990) points out that this has been called 'the man (*sic*)-
must-be-mad' test. In other words, in order to carry out act X, the
person must have been crazy. This might highlight what is at the heart
of lay judgements about madness – the unintelligibility of acts. What
Lawton may have been trying to express by his use of the word 'significance' was really 'validity' or even 'utility', when the term 'mental illness' is used. In other words, the term 'mental illness' gets us
little beyond the situation that when a person's conduct in its context
cannot be understood, this leads to a judgement that the action is 'mad'.
A diagnosis of mental illness merely puts a technical gloss on this lay
judgement. This returns us to the analysis given by Coulter (1973)
noted above.

However, there are two cautions against conflating lay judgements
about madness and psychiatric diagnoses. First, as we have already
noted in the cases of Sutcliffe and Nilson, lay people may believe
someone to be sane when psychiatrists believe them to be suffering
from mental illness (or psychopathy). Also at times the reverse may
apply. Bean (1979) found that psychiatrists sometimes will disagree
with relatives who insist that a person is mentally ill. Second, lay people
seem to hold a much narrower view about what constitutes mental
illness than do psychiatrists. Studies of stereotypes about mental illness (Jones and Cochrane, 1981) show that lay people mainly focus
on florid psychotic symptoms, bizarre behaviour, delusions and hallucinations but ignore the commonest of all psychiatric conditions –
depression.

The association between violence and mental illness made by lay
people is well known. This is both reflected in and reinforced by journalistic accounts of mental illness. It is also discernible in government

action and policy statements, and is an association that is pointed up during political debates about the availability of services, indicating the sensitivity of mental health policy-makers to this public concern.

Finally, we should note that lay people themselves may hold different views according to their circumstances. The parents of a disruptive adolescent with a diagnosis of schizophrenia may seek response from mental health practitioners that differs from the response sought by the identified patient. This is shown up at the collective level by the conflicting demands about services made by organised interest groups. Groups which have tended to see themselves as mainly representing relatives' and carers' interests (like SANE – Schizophrenia a National Emergency – and the NSF – National Schizophrenia Fellowship) have tended to focus on the need for hospital beds and for interventions to be imposed more frequently against resistant patients. The reverse can then be found in the demands of service user groups like Survivors Speak Out. They want less coercion, less inpatient facilities and more social support and help in ordinary environments. The recent trend of consumerism in health care has increased the credence of such views (see Chapter 9).

People with mental health problems

It not an easy matter to specify which people in society constitute those with a mental health problem. In the next chapter we recognise diversity, to some extent, by listing a wide range of services, from primary care to secure psychiatry. However, this definition by service contact only captures a group of people with mental health problems who enter the role of patient. In this regard, mental health and physical health are similar. Community surveys point up a 'clinical iceberg' (Hannay, 1979) with many more people experiencing symptoms than are diagnosed by professionals. For example, Goldberg and Huxley (1992) suggest the prevalence levels shown in Table 1.1.

This model of prevalence attempts to use diagnosed and undiagnosed groups in society to define those with mental health problems. Those objecting to psychiatric diagnosis on moral or scientific grounds may be uneasy with this formulation (see Chapters 9 and 10). Nonetheless, it is a starting point to think about the scale of mental distress and oddity in society. Unfortunately, even those committed to a medical diagnostic or epidemiological framework offer no certain consensus about prevalence. Prevalence refers to the number of people with a particular illness at a point in time in a population. Incidence refers to new cases. Within a psychiatric epidemiological framework, results

TABLE 1.1 *Five levels and four filters, with estimates of annual point prevalence rates at each level*

Level 1   The community
                   260–315/1000/year
.... 1st filter
                                                        (Illness behaviour)
Level 2   Total mental morbidity – attenders in primary care
                   230/1000/year
.... 2nd filter
                                                (Ability to detect disorder)
Level 3   Mental disorders identified by doctors ('Conspicuous Psychiatric Morbidity')
                   101.5/1000/year
.... 3rd filter
                                        (Referral to mental illness services)
Level 4   Total morbidity – mental illness services
                   23.5/1000/year
.... 4th filter
                                        (Admission to psychiatric beds)
Level 5   Psychiatric in-patients
                   5.71/1000/year

Source: adapted from Goldberg and Huxley (1992).

of prevalence studies differ greatly. For example, in relation to 'schizophrenia', estimates vary from rates of 1:2,000 to 1:100 adults. Variations are due to differences in diagnostic practices of psychiatrists, but also to social and environmental factors (Warner, 1985). More recently psychiatric epidemiology has used symptom-based measures rather than relying on simplistic diagnostic categories to assess the levels of mental health problems in populations. Results from a survey sponsored by the Department of Health carried out at the end of 1993 (OPCS, 1994) provides a recent picture of the prevalence of mental health problems of adults aged between 16 and 64 living in British households. The main findings were:

1. The prevalence of neurotic disorders is estimated at 156 per thousand. Women were far more likely to experience neurotic symptoms, and younger women were more likely to experience depression and anxiety than older women. The most common neurotic symptoms were fatigue, sleep problems, irritability and worry.
2. Psychotic disorders were estimated to affect four people in every

thousand. Alcohol problem prevalence was estimated at 47 per thousand and drug dependency as 22 per thousand. Men were three times as likely to experience such problems as women and they were most prevalent amongst young men.

As well as the question of how frequently mental health problems occur being a basis for defining a population, we can also consider other social indicators. For example, whilst all mental health problems, whether defined by diagnosis or by lay accounts of distress and oddity, occur across society, the spread is not random nor is it even. Prevalence is associated with marital status, rural/urban location, class, gender, age and race. We have examined this point in relation to age, gender, race and class in some depth elsewhere (Pilgrim and Rogers, 1993). Here we summarise some relevant points and give a few examples.

Age   About 5 per cent of the child and adolescent population are deemed, by standard psychiatric criteria, to be suffering from conduct or emotional problems (Harrington, 1993). The probability of being newly diagnosed as schizophrenic is relatively high in young adulthood but very low in childhood and old age. Organic changes to the brain increase the probability of a diagnosis of dementia with increasing age. Predictions are that the numbers of those suffering from dementia will increase dramatically in the future. The number of people over 75 years old has increased in the general population by 30 per cent since 1976. Age is also relevant in relation to the correlation between sexual abuse in childhood and the raised probability of mental health problems in later years.

Gender   Women receive a psychiatric diagnosis more frequently than men. The bulk of this difference is accounted for by the higher rates of diagnosis in women of depression. Men receive a diagnosis of personality disorder and commit suicide more often than women and are over-represented in secure psychiatric facilities.

Race   African Caribbean people in Britain are disproportionately diagnosed as suffering from schizophrenia. Irish people are over-represented in all diagnostic groups. (See Chapter 7.)

Class   People with a diagnosis of schizophrenia are disproportionately likely to be poor, although the relationship between cause and effect here is still contested. Some argue that becoming mentally ill creates downward drift in society. Others emphasise that the stress of poverty increases the probability of morbidity.

If we take these variables together, they point to a direct correlation between mental health problems and social disadvantage. As with the note about the clinical iceberg, this correlation is also true of physical health problems. The interaction of the variables can also be noted. The mental health of rich people tends actually to increase in old age, whereas the opposite is true of poor people (Blaxter, 1990). Women live longer than men, on average, and so have a higher probability of suffering from senile dementia. At least some of the raised levels of severe psychiatric morbidity in black people could be attributed to the combined stress of racism and poverty. However, this claim applies more to African Caribbean people than to Asian people in Britain.

Despite these complex interactions and difficulties in tracing cause and effect, it is possible to draw three conclusions about mental health problems and disadvantage. First, people who are already disadvantaged or oppressed have a greater probability of having to contend with the extra burden of mental health problems – the experience of distress and the loss of social credibility associated with a loss of reason. When and if they enter the role of psychiatric patient, they will import all the vulnerabilities of their race, class and gender background. These multiple sources of disadvantage may account for why psychiatric patients have been treated so oppressively within services.

Second, people with mental health problems are more likely to have to contend with additional sources of disadvantage, such as racism, sexism and unemployment, when they attempt to live independently of specialist services. These compound the process of social exclusion resulting directly from the stigma associated with psychiatric diagnosis ('mentalism'). Thus, psychiatric patients suffer disadvantage both inside and outside the services they receive. The protection of class privilege may mitigate, but not eliminate, this double disadvantage, for instance by having a choice of paid therapists and by being able to be unemployed without being poor.

Third, at times the way in which psychiatry and psychiatric researchers have conceptualised the relationship between disadvantage and mental health has militated against an analysis of mental health problems and policy initiatives which tackles the causes and effects of such disadvantage. There has for example been a longstanding interest in the relationship between *homelessness and mental health*. Traditionally social scientists have placed the root of the problem of homelessness in the context of poverty, economic disadvantage and social upheaval. From his experiences of being 'Down and Out' George Orwell vividly depicted the effects on mental health in describing homeless people as those 'who have fallen into solitary half-mad grooves of life and given up trying to be normal or decent. Poverty frees them from ordinary standards of behaviour, just as money frees people from work' (Orwell, 1986). Yet rarely has traditional psychiatric research put poverty centre-stage in examining mental health and homelessness or seen mental distress as a response to homelessness. Rather, a lack of a home has frequently been viewed as the by-product of the personality defects of individuals. A relatively early study (Whiteley 1955) described the central problem of 'down and outs' who presented at a London observation ward as personality defects which made the development of a therapeutic relationship difficult in a hospital environment. The lack of sensitivity of this psychiatric researcher to the plight of being without a home is summed up in the suggestion that an appropriate response was that 'a psychiatrist may be able to help these men by holding counselling groups in their *residential* [our emphasis] setting' (Hamid, 1991).

Since this study in the 1950s there has been a plethora of psychiatric research which has attributed high rates of mental illness to homeless populations both here and in the United States. Some studies have estimated prevalence rates of over 90 per cent (Bassuk *et al.*, 1984). However, the emphasis has remained on 'maladaptive behaviour' psychiatric symptomatology and 'social functioning' of homeless people.

Whilst on the face of things this appears to be an 'interest free' area of research, albeit one that pathologises individuals, some commentators have suggested that professional interests are important in understanding the construction of mental illness and homelessness as a psychiatric problem. Snow *et al.* (1986) undertook ethnographic fieldwork to assess the mental health status of homeless people in the United States. They found that only 15 per cent of the 911 homeless people the researchers had contact with could be considered as 'mentally ill' (based on criteria of prior institutionalisation, peer identification and observed bizarre and inappropriate behaviour). The authors of the study consider the high prevalence rates previously recorded as in part due to a desire to medicalise problems.

Certainly, in Britain a catastrophic discourse about homelessness and mental health problems can be identified in the context of discussions about community care. At times this appears as little more than a thinly veiled attempt to promote the advantages of the Victorian asylums by vested psychiatric interests with not so much as a passing wave to the social disadvantage and needs of homeless people themselves.

Given this picture of disadvantage, it is not surprising that many of the social policy debates about mental health are not only about the provision of specialist services but impinge on much wider questions about citizenship. We return to these questions in Chapters 7, 9 and 10. The picture of disadvantage also explains, to some extent, why some mental health service recipients become politicised about their oppression and campaign to abolish or reform psychiatry and reverse social exclusion (see Chapter 9).

Conclusion

This first chapter has introduced a variety of interests in the field of mental health. Competing stakeholder perspectives are more common here than elsewhere. For example, whilst medical knowledge in general is contested by academic sociologists, only a few specific areas of medical practice have evoked a passionate and articulate lay critique, one such area being women's health (particularly about obstetric care) and the other, mental health. These share particular common features about power and control over the body and the self, and sensitivities about privacy and individuality.

As we have noted in this chapter and will revisit in Chapter 4, politicians are particularly sensitive about their reading of public fears about mental abnormality. At the same time they do not prioritise mental health as an issue overall. Whereas the public's view on the general state of funding and viability of the NHS has been a focus of political concern in recent years, few specific topics have been debated with as much passion and prejudice as mental health. Having introduced the importance of stakeholder perspectives about mental health policy, in the following chapter we will begin to describe mental health services.

2

Policy Formation and Mental Health Services

Introduction

Allsop (1984) has suggested that there are two ways of approaching the question of policy formation. The first is to examine statements of intent and their implementation. The second is to examine policy-making as the outcome of a process of implementation. Of course both of these are possible, with the second being a check on the first – i.e. what were the intended and unintended outcomes of a policy, and did stated intentions lead to inaction or action? In the rest of this book we do, where relevant, take the statements made by government and other agencies as a benchmark for examining particular issues (e.g. in relation to mental health legislation). This however is given less salience than 'the policy as process' focus, which looks to the actions of groups of actors to explain the implementation of policy and configuration of service provision. Policy formation is not as centralised as it sometimes appears but is often shaped by specific local factors and stakeholder perspectives.

When discussing health policy in general, Palmer and Short (1989) draw attention to four major policy perspectives:

- Economic
- Political science
- Sociological
- Epidemiological and public health

Here we will check the extent to which each of these perspectives can explain how and why mental health policy has developed.

The Economic Perspective

This centres on two main concepts: supply and demand. The former refers to the quantity of a commodity that providers are willing to offer for sale at a price, and the latter refers to the quantity of the commodity that consumers are prepared to buy at a specified price. This market-focused model has severe limitations in relation to health care service users in general and those using mental health services in particular. Here are some examples:

(1) Only some people with mental health problems can be described unambiguously as 'consumers'. The term applies only to those using private therapists voluntarily. In other words, an economic model assumes that patients are purchasers. In fact, even when they do buy therapy it is not a tangible product (like a washing machine) but an intangible expectation that their psychological well-being will be improved or their distress ameliorated.

(2) In recent times with the introduction of market principles in the NHS the term 'purchaser' has indeed been introduced. However, it does not mean individual patients (an individual 'shopper') but commissioning authorities or GP fundholders which buy services on behalf of local groups of patients. Thus the notion of demand being individual–consumer linked in general economics does not apply to publicly provided mental health services.

(3) In the ordinary market-place consumption takes place on the basis of choices being available. With the exception of that minority of patients rich enough to shop around for private therapists, most NHS patients have to accept what is given in their locality. Clinical professionals are monopoly suppliers of services. General practitioners control who the person is referred to and the specialist then determines what treatment is given. This context tends to produce services which are limited in range by the pressures of a professional monopoly of supply plus resource constraints. These twin processes militate against the individual patient having choice.

(4) The market model also has a clear definition of the client. As well as the term 'purchaser' not applying to individual patients, there is a further ambiguity about who is the client of psychiatric services. Mental patients themselves are arguably only the client when they opt to approach services for help. But there are a variety of other circumstances in which people become mental patients. In private dwellings their relatives may summon help with a crisis. If, subsequently, the patient is forcibly taken away and treated by psychiatric staff, when it

is the relatives and not the identified patient who are the clients of psychiatry. Therefore, they, not the labelled or identified patient, are having a 'service' provided for them. Similar arguments apply to the removal of patients from a public place to a place of safety by the police for a psychiatric assessment. In these circumstances arguably the police and the complaining public, not the patient, are the clients. Whenever patienthood is imposed on a person (by involuntary detention or treatment) it is clearly nonsensical to construe them as a 'customer'.

(5) Everyday choices in the market place entail the purchaser of goods being able to understand clearly what they want (e.g. a machine that efficiently washes their clothes). This is less clear in health services, which entail a knowledge imbalance between patients and professionals. In relation to psychiatric patients there is the additional common assumption operating around them that due to lack of insight they do not appreciate what they need. Thus 'need' is defined by suppliers of mental health services, whereas in the market place it is defined by the consumer (though the latter's view can be shaped by sales talk and advertising). We return to the question of need in Chapter 9.

Thus, the market-focused model of traditional economics can be applied only very inadequately to mental health services. Indeed, the latter term implies that providers are 'at the service' of patients. This view finds little endorsement from surveys of users of mental health services (Rogers *et al.*, 1993). However, *because* the model fails to work as a basis for explaining service policy development, the contradictions it sets up (i.e. the limitations listed above) provide us with some interesting critical questions about why 'services' fail in their own terms. That is, they highlight why the term 'mental health services' is problematic. What evidence is there that they promote or improve mental health, as their name implies? Also, in what sense are they 'services' – services to whom and to what end? In the first regard, surely it is mental illness which is being treated and not mental health facilitated. In the second regard, we can see that psychiatry has many potential clients beyond the patients it labels. It operates as much to control disruptive conduct and bring to an end social crises, as it does to ameliorate mental distress.

However, whilst standard economic formulae about supply and demand have a limited value for policy analysis, health economists have provided rich conceptual tools for analysing the utility and effectiveness of services. There are four main economic methods of analysis in this regard:

- *cost–benefit*, i.e. measuring how much interventions cost against the economic benefits they generate (e.g. the price of treating disability against savings on social security payments)
- *cost-minimisation*, i.e. comparing different interventions with equal claims of efficacy to check which is the cheapest
- *cost-effectiveness*, i.e. extending cost–benefit analysis to look at say the (quantified) extension of life by an intervention
- *cost–utility*, i.e. extending the above to look at the improvement in quality of life for patients created by an intervention.

Each of the four forms of analysis have their strengths and weaknesses when investigating the utility and effectiveness of medical interventions with physically ill or disabled people. When the latter are *psychiatric* interventions the forms of analysis become particularly problematic.

Given the confusion about the purpose of psychiatry and whom it is serving (see above), what is to be investigated by health economists? Is it the improvement in the quality of life of patients or of their relatives? What if these are at odds with one another? What if some interventions are highly effective at suppressing disruptive conduct but have profoundly disabling and distressing effects on their recipients? Whose word is privileged about improvement following an intervention? Is it the word of the patient, or their relatives, or their treating professionals? When some drugs (like anti-depressants) are cheaper than labour-intensive psychological interventions, and just as effective at reducing depressive symptoms, should the latter be abolished in favour of the former? What happens though when these drugs are sometimes used for self-poisoning to commit suicide? What if some patients demand the more expensive (psychological) intervention on grounds of quality of life? In these circumstances is there a tension between cost–benefit, cost-minimisation, cost-effectiveness and cost–utility analyses?

Thus, even if the modified health economic model, which is more sophisticated than the crude market model, is utilised, it does not give us simple answers to the complex questions and controversies surrounding mental health policy. However, it can provide some interesting data to contribute to those controversies. It also might clarify the relevant *questions* to ask about services and the policies generating them. For instance, as we will see in Chapter 4, during this century politicians have tended to naively assume that psychiatric interventions are effective and useful. The four types of health economic analyses listed above, if pursued systematically, would bring such naive trust into question.

The Political Science Perspective

The work of political scientists forms a bridge between economic and sociological models of policy formation. Health policy analyses by Alford (1975) and Marmor (1973), focusing on the US health care system, have been generalised to other mixed economy capitalist systems, for example in Britain (Allsop, 1984; Ham, 1985) and Australia (Palmer and Short, 1989).

Alford emphasises the tensions which exist between three major structural interests in health policy. Each of these contains stakeholders who gain or lose from policy developing in this or that direction. The groupings Alford describes are:

- *Professional monopolists* – mainly the medical profession and its beneficiaries like the drug industry. This alliance would also include those members of the public persuaded by the unique authority of medicine as a profession.
- *Corporate rationalisers* – these are planners, health administrators and some health professionals whose interests are served by greater efficiency, effectiveness and equity in health care delivery.
- *Community interests* – these are community groups representing or being constituted by service recipients and their relatives.

The group superordinate to, and lobbied by, all three – the group with the power to make and implement policy (politicians) – is missing from Alford's model. If this fourth group were added then we can see that this framework would be a useful way of understanding the current negotiations and shifts around different lobby groups: the Department of Health, psychiatrists, NHS managers, users' groups, relatives' groups, which we discussed in Chapter 1.

Marmor considers policies as political goods which are traded in a political market place in exchange for financial backing and votes. (Note this is an economic metaphor not literal economics.) Marmor then emphasises that the key bargainers in this market place are government, health care professionals and service recipients. Governments seek to provide policies which are affordable, efficient and popular (to catch votes). They may vary ideologically, though, in their position on equity (as tensions in the UK show between Labour and Conservative policies on health). Providers seek to maximise their status and salaries. Recipients seek to influence policies to improve their access to, choice about and experience of services. Changes in policy and barriers to that change can be understood within this model as outcomes of power exchanges between the three key players.

One problem with this model is that it contains internal contradictions and tensions: the middle group of providers has conflicts between clinicians and bureaucrats. As we will see later in the book, the purchaser/provider split has introduced a further complication to this picture, with managers and clinicians (and their interests) being present on both sides of the divide. The recipient group is ambiguous in the field of mental health because it contains those dominated by patients and those by their relatives. A second problem is that the power emphasis may not always explain why some very powerless groups can sometimes accrue apparent benefits (in terms of policy outcomes and resource allocation). In the case of psychiatric patients this might be explained by two factors: the need to allocate funds for their social subsidence and the genuine paternalistic desire on the part of other players like bureaucrats and politicians to improve the lot of vulnerable and disadvantaged groups.

Let us turn now to theories influenced by Marx's concept of political economy. Scull (1977 and 1979) argues that during the nineteenth century the capitalist economy necessitated the segregative control of deviant parts of the population which were disruptive or burdensome. Thus a network of workhouses, asylums and prisons emerged to contain pauper deviants. Scull goes on to argue that this segregative solution became too expensive during the second half of the twentieth century. At this point welfare capitalism entered a period of prolonged fiscal crisis. One cost-cutting policy prompted by this crisis was hospital closure ('decarceration'). We will examine this theory further in Chapters 4 and 5. Another political economy theorist, Warner, argues that fashions in psychiatric treatment have been relatively irrelevant in explaining service utilisation. Instead, he suggests that unemployment levels have been a good predictor of recovery rates for schizophrenia, with the Great Depression of the 1920s and 1930s being a period when recovery rates were at their lowest (Warner, 1985).

Sociological Perspectives

The relevance of social theory is that it can explain differences of both ideology and emphasis in different forms of policy analysis. The example of the differing works of Kathleen Jones and Andrew Scull is a case in point. Jones has developed a form of policy analysis which is, by her own admission, anti-theoretical (Jones, 1972, p. xiii) and therefore uncritically accepting of the views of dominant interest groups like the psychiatric profession. Consequently, her work offers an account of policy development which endorses a public relations view of psychiatric history – one of nineteenth-century humanitarianism (Jones, 1960, p. 149) and twentieth-century technical breakthroughs, like the introduction of major tranquillisers (Jones, 1988, p. 82). By contrast, Scull's work (1977 and 1979), based mainly on Marxian economic theory, as we have noted, offers a critical view of history and a cynical view of services.

But sociological theories beyond these positions of Jones and Scull can be identified. To start with Scull's Marxism – this is actually mixed with the views of Max Weber on professional dominance and social closure (Scull, 1979, p. 129). Weber and his followers (Freidson, 1970; Abel, 1988) place less emphasis on economics than Marxians and more of an emphasis on the negotiation of social status by different interest groups in society. Professionalisation entails some occupational groups like psychiatry cornering the market and protecting their boundaries from outside intrusion and scrutiny (social closure). In doing so, this allows professionals to exert power over their clients who do not have the same access to professional knowledge and over subordinate professionals who are not trained as extensively (professional dominance). This Weberian theory of professional activity allows us to understand some of the finer processes of negotiation on the part of stakeholders which take place in the policy formation process (following Alford and Marmor).

Interest-group work has also been analysed by neo-Marxians such as Habermas (1971). He emphasises that medical knowledge is not value free (or neutral) but that it reflects the cognitive interests of a professional group (doctors) in controlling and predicting disease. This is relevant to the policy-making process in terms of the confidence that other stakeholders have in the legitimacy of psychiatric knowledge.

In psychiatry more than other medical specialities (with the possible exception of obstetrics) there has been a legitimation crisis about the credibility of medical theory and practice. This is evident in the emergence of both 'anti-psychiatry' and a sustained and campaign-focused service user protest movement (see Chapter 9). It is in the context of this legitimation crisis that mental hospitals became discredited during this century. The work of Goodwin (1990) discussed in Chapter 4 places an emphasis within this neo-Marxian perspective on legitimacy, as well as economic factors, in explaining policy developments.

A contrasting theoretical current, influential recently in sociology, is that of Michael Foucault. His work on the beginnings of psychiatry (Foucault, 1964) was close to a Marxian emphasis on the need for social control. The difference was that whereas Scull emphasised the economic necessity of segregative psychiatry, Foucault emphasised the moral offence created by madness which led to its rejection by the non-mad in society. Later writers following Foucault suggested that after the segregative and coercive emphasis of early psychiatry, its field of interest broadened to include voluntary relationships in community settings (like psychological therapies) (Rose, 1990; Castel *et al.*, 1979). This marked a shift from an external form of regulation of the population to one which is based more on self-surveillance.

A final sociological theory which is relevant is that traceable to the work of Durkheim which is more appropriately addressed under the next sub-heading.

Public Health Perspectives and Epidemiology

What is unusual about mental health problems is that although no one has ever claimed or proved that they are transmissible like infectious diseases, they have been treated as if it were the case (Jodelet, 1991). Asylums and sewers were the first two main public health measures imposed by central government in the mid nineteenth century. This juxtaposition of sewerage and madness might suggest that lunatics were considered to be human waste. This is not such a fanciful notion when the emerging ideology for segregation is uncovered: eugenics. As we will see in the next chapter, late nineteenth-century asylum psychiatry was closely dependent on the underlying assumption that madness was biologically determined. In turn this was part of a wider assumption common in medical scientific (and governmental) culture that a variety of deviant states in the lower classes were a function of inferior inheritance.

This core assumption at the turn of this century about the genetic determination of deviance had two opposing consequences in Western psychiatry. On the one hand there were signs, in some countries in the first part of the twentieth century, that the eugenic position went into the ascendance and became more extreme in its policy consequences. The segregation of madness from society, and between the sexes within the asylums to minimise the inheritance of purported faulty genes, had been a convergent policy in Europe and North America. This measure was then amplified to include sterilisation of patients in Denmark and the US, and extended further in the 1930s in Germany when the German Medical Association proposed a policy of involuntary euthanasia for 'life devoid of meaning'. This meant killing people with learning difficulties, physical disabilities and those diagnosed as being mentally ill. Up to half a million patients in these categories were killed lawfully by German doctors between 1939 and 1942 in health settings. These killings were endorsed by Hitler but not proposed by him.

However, as we will see in Chapter 4, there was a conflicting consequence of nineteenth-century eugenics – its modification by a new environmentalism. This meant that biodeterminism remained as a common assumption in psychiatry but that it was joined by theories which emphasised environmental causes of mental illness.

A common feature of both biological and environmental versions of psychiatric theory is that they accepted that mental illness existed and that it had causes. The opposing theories differed only over the source of the latter. It is here that Durkheim's positivistic view about the reality of social as well as natural phenomena is relevant. It fed into a tradition in social science (traceable to the medical surveys in the eighteenth century) which were directed towards political intervention to prevent ill health (Rosen, 1979; Turner, 1990). Social medicine was the environmentalist tradition, associated with epidemiology, which was challenged by eugenics and a form of medicine emphasising the pathology within individuals in the late nineteenth century. However, whilst there was a eugenic emphasis in the theoretical developments of psychiatry by 1900, earlier, in the mid nineteenth century, both physical and psychological ('moral') causes were recorded about lunacy (Hunter and MacAlpine, 1964). Moreover, even though physical causes predominated in records, these were mainly ascribed to environmental not genetic events.

By the nineteenth century, decisions about regulating disease levels in the population by government policies were reliant on epidemiological data. The asylums kept detailed records of the conditions of inmates and their ascribed causes. This has had two important consequences for twentieth-century policy formation. First, data collection became an ongoing part of the state bureaucracy. Clinical professionals, hospital administrators, and civil servants spent (and still spend) much of their time recording and exchanging information about the prevalence and incidence of psychiatric diagnoses.

A second consequence was the continued legitimacy of a version of social medicine. In the case of psychiatry this meant the emergence of *social psychiatry*, a hybrid discipline of psychiatrists and social scientists. Sometimes medical and social scientists co-operated in large surveys (Hollingshead and Redlich, 1958) or in studying the environmental impact of different hospital regimes (Brown and Wing, 1962). This acceptance of the non-problematic reality of mental illness has entailed some social scientists using epidemiological methods to test theories about its social causation (e.g. Brown and Harris, 1978; Newton, 1988).

Epidemiology can provide data to make decisions about the organisation of psychiatry but it has no conceptual capacity (cf. the other sociological and political science approaches above) to deal with problems of legitimacy in psychiatric theory and practice. It also has nothing to say about stakeholders and the dynamics of their transactions. Its emphasis on measurement means that it offers precise information about the status quo, but it provides no necessary rationale about what to do with that information in the future. It can thus potentially be used or co-opted by all stakeholders involved in policy information. If epidemiology is an inadequate method for *explaining* policy information, it remains a central method for *contributing* to policy formation. It offers a tangible data base in the midst of ignorance and uncertainty in mental health debates. However, a final weakness to note about psychiatric epidemiology is that the epidemiology of *physical* disease includes data on the distribution of causes not just diagnoses in a population. Because the etiology of mental illness remains elusive or contested, psychiatric epidemiology is not able to include causal information.

It can be seen that the different approaches to policy formation described above can be useful in different ways to account for the development of mental health policy. Accordingly, in the following chapters, where appropriate these approaches will be revisited, but their specific shortcomings, in terms of explanatory power, will also be noted at times.

Services

The notion of 'services' is actually quite recent and emerged with the NHS in the mid twentieth century. Prior to that, there were 'hospitals' and 'clinics' and 'asylums'. As we note elsewhere in this chapter, the notion of 'service' may be particularly inappropriate or inapplicable at times in relation to the mental health industry. However, the term is commonly used and so we will retain it here to describe those facilities and organised professional activities directed at people with mental health problems.

The differentiation of services for this group really began in the wake of the 1890 Lunacy Act. Prior to that an elaborate network of asylums had been built (see Chapter 3) but they contained 'aments', now called people with learning difficulties or disabilities, as well as 'dements' or 'lunatics'. It was not really until the twentieth century that separate mental health services are fully discernible.

The Range of Current Services

It would be possible to limit this outline to those services which are formally described as 'mental health' (or 'psychiatric') facilities. Indeed, it is often the case that politicians, service purchasers and providers and even service recipients may have such a limited view. It is important though to make a distinction between *specialist* facilities for people with mental health problems and *non-specialist* facilities and services. The latter may have a significant influence on a person's psychological well-being and the probability of them returning to an inpatient role. Thus, the title we give them here does not imply their lesser importance.

As we will see later, current services are biased heavily towards inpatient work. For this reason, although it is important to describe the range of facilities organised or available for people with mental health problems, it is also important to recognise the imbalance in resources supplied to each part of the system.

Mental health researchers have an initial difficulty in actually defining a population which is within their field of interest. The reason for this is the wide range of people who are service recipients. At one extreme there is the mentally disordered offender, locked up for decades in a secure psychiatric facility, and at the other is a person visiting their general practitioner (GP) reporting an emotional problem for the very first time in his or her life. Thus the range of services which need to be considered for our purposes can be summarised as follows:

1. Psychiatric hospital beds
2. Community mental health facilities
3. Primary and social care
4. Psychiatric services in prisons
5. Secure psychiatric provision

1 Psychiatric hospital beds

From about 1890 to 1983, in excess of 95 per cent of psychiatric beds were in large institutions. By 1993 only 58 per cent of NHS provision was provided for in this way (Davidge *et al.*, 1993). The Hospital Plan set out by Enoch Powell, when he was Minister of Health in 1962, included a central judgement that the old Victorian asylums should be phased out and psychiatric beds relocated in District General Hospitals. This policy took considerable time to be initiated in practice. The first hospitals to fit the policy of leaving districts without a large mental hospital were Belmont (Merton and Sutton) in 1974 and Powick (Worcester) in 1989 (Davidge *et al.*, 1993). However, since then there has been a rapid programme of hospital rundown. Present estimates suggest that two-thirds will be closed by the mid-1990s (Seager, 1991).

The slow implementation of this major policy commitment reflects the lack of an overall mental health policy and the failure to act imaginatively in setting up alternatives. In 1984 a House of Commons Select Committee, examining the policy of hospital closure, were scathing in their criticism of central government failure to provide adequate funding arrangements or clear policy guidelines for achieving closure and the provision of alternative services:

> Any fool can close a long-stay hospital: it takes more time and trouble to do it properly and compassionately. The minister must ensure that mental illness or mental handicap provision is not reduced without demonstrably alternative funding being provided beforehand both for those discharged from hospital and for those who would otherwise seek admission. (HMSO, 1984–5)

The closure of the large Victorian hospitals has triggered a number of controversies which we return to later in this book. These include the loss of the residential function they provided, as well as their resource legacy or lack of it (a loss of income from the sale of asylum sites). Another controversy relates to whether or not they mark the end of services dominated by hospitals and whether adequate community provision has been forthcoming. The image that current policies are concerned with community care should not deflect from the evidence that services are currently still hospital-centred. As we will see in Chapters 4 and 9, the shift of focus for most psychiatric work in recent years has not been from the hospital to the community but from asylums to new District General Hospitals. The two decades up until the mid-1980s saw a growth of over 60 per cent in the number of small psychiatric hospital facilities (DHSS, 1987). The pattern and rate of bed use has altered as a result of this organisational and policy shift:

- The overall number of psychiatric beds decreased by about one-third, from 193,000 in 1959 to 108,000 in 1985 (DHSS, 1987). Bed occupancy in large hospitals has also decreased dramatically – between 1980 and 1990 alone it dropped by almost a quarter (HMSO Mental Health Enquiry 1986).

- The number of admissions to hospital and patient 'throughput' have increased. In 1982 there were 183,593 admissions to hospital compared with 192,600 in 1992 (DH, 1994a). The number of available daily 'mental illness' beds were 84 per thousand population compared with 47 in 1993 (DH, 1994a). Differences in patient activity and throughput has also been noted between the old asylums and general hospital-based provision. Patients are discharged more slowly from Districts with a large mental hospital and a greater proportion of patients are still resident one year after admission (Glover *et al.*, 1990). In Britain in 1992, 133,410 psychiatric patients left hospital after less than a month – representing 63.2 per cent of all patients leaving hospital that year. The increase in the number of short-stay admissions has led to the notion of 'revolving door' patients, who are admitted for a short period and then discharged only to be readmitted a short time later.

- Hospital outpatient activity has increased modestly. In 1982, 188,000 'new patients' were seen on an out-patient basis compared with 238 in the year 1992–3 (DH, 1994a). However, it is interesting to note that over the same period the number of total attendances increased only marginally, suggesting that contact for each patient is currently *lower* than a decade ago.

- The decrease in the number of beds has not led to any apparent significant increases in admissions to private nursing homes. In 1984 there were 5,045 admissions to authorised private mental nursing homes, and in 1990 there were 4,943 (Faulkner 1992). However, as discussed below, occupancy of private residential (not nursing) homes has dramatically increased.

The changing pattern of bed use needs to be seen in the context of the services available for people when they are not in hospital. This takes us to our next section.

2 Community mental health facilities

These include residential and day care, community mental health centres and crisis intervention services. We noted earlier that they receive poor levels of finance compared with hospitals. The running-down of hospital services and the development of community-based services has (particularly over the last decade) presented authorities with the financial and pragmatic difficulties of trying to run both services in tandem. In 1975 the White Paper *Better Services For the Mentally Ill* set out norms (which later became guidelines) for future community services. However, to date there are poor mechanisms for monitoring the wide range of community mental health services. In the absence of such data the impression has been given that there are few community facilities to replace the abolition of hospital beds.

There is some evidence to suggest that there has been greater success in providing numbers of residential places for people than in providing day care provision. The Audit Commission (1986), taking the norms set out in the 1975 White Paper as criteria of success, reported that 70 per cent of the hostel or homes targets were met but only 30 per cent of the day centres and 40 per cent of the day hospitals targets were achieved. One research study which followed up a cohort of former long-stay patients discharged between 1985 and 1989 showed that they were a residentially non-mobile group. However, in terms of quality of life, unmet needs included inadequate living space, and poor work and leisure opportunities. Less than half of the people followed up were in receipt of formal day care provision (O'Brien, 1992).

Whilst the role of the private sector in replacing hospital beds remains a marginal activity (discussed above), residential care is increasingly being provided by the private sector. This now constitutes the largest single provider of residential care for people with mental health problems (40 per cent of all provision). Private provision is distributed unevenly with a concentration in southern coastal towns and urban districts. Social services provision appears to be remaining static or declining in line with Social Services Department's new role as purchasers, rather than providers, of care. A survey in 1992 suggested that health authorities (alone or in partnership with voluntary organisations) were planning to double their residential provision (Faulkner, 1992).

A new feature of the 1980s was the expansion in community mental health centres. Sayce (1989) found that between 1977 and 1987 these leapt in number from 1 to 54. A related expanding phenomenon was the 'community mental health team'. These teams have developed unevenly, with some being attached to hospitals and others to community mental health centres. It has been recognised that within these types of service the optimal version should include a 24-hour, seven-days-a-week crisis intervention service. It was also acknowledged by the Royal College of Psychiatrists in 1993, when complaining about pressures on bed occupancy, that outreach work in the community can reduce the need for patients to be admitted. This was confirmed by Barnes *et al.* (1990), who found that the lowest rates of compulsory admissions to hospital were found in those localities providing a comprehensive crisis intervention service. Community orientated mental health professionals advocate that crisis intervention, residential alternatives to hospital and home-based care should be combined with supported primary care work to minimise the need for hospital admission (Stein and Test, 1980; Falloon and Fadden, 1993). If such blueprints were effected, they would help to invert the current resource allocation between hospital and non-hospital settings. The problem of resources currently being over-concentrated in hospital facilities will be readdressed in the final chapter.

3   Primary and social care

Many community mental health services are now jointly funded and managed initiatives between health and social services, although health services provision far outstrips that provided by local authorities. Bridging the gap between these two agencies has traditionally been difficult. Whilst policy-makers have often stressed the need for joint planning (as for example in the Nodder Report of 1980 discussed in Chapter 5), the successful co-ordination of services has proved elusive. A number of structural and other factors have contributed to social service input to, and responsibility for, community mental health work being problematic:

(1) Although local authorities, via their social service departments, are now responsible for co-ordinating community care (following the 1990 NHS and Community Care Act), the funding of core mental health services is via the NHS.

(2) The boundaries of responsibility between social and health care are often unclear, which can lead to patients being a focus of dispute between medical and non-medical workers. The reverse can also apply, with patients being neglected because each party in the social/health split may consider that the other is responsible for a service. A good example of this is the issue of aftercare under Section 117 of the 1983 Mental Health Act. If NHS staff fail to follow up patients after discharge from hospital and local social workers fail to provide for these patients properly, then they can 'fall between' the services.

(3) Chronic care groups like long-term users of psychiatric services living in the community may be not be welcomed by GPs. The latter deal with most cases of mental distress. Before hospital run-down, Goldberg and Huxley (1980) calculated that out of 230 people attending their GP with psychological symptoms, only 17 were referred to psychiatrists and only 6 admitted to hospital. With hospital closure this picture will change, adding more pressure on primary care services, with more ex-inpatient attendances. Whilst SSDs now have a formal responsibility for community care groups, they have no tradition of shaping or regulating the work of GPs, who have had their traditional autonomy augmented by fund holding.

(4) Social services are greatly under-resourced compared with the NHS. For instance, only 3 per cent of social service expenditure is currently allocated to mental health services.

In the last decade the involvement of primary care in mental health service provision has increasingly been highlighted. Researchers drew attention to the extent of psychiatric morbidity in the community (Goldberg and Huxley, 1980) and in particular to what has been termed the 'somatic presentation of psychiatric illness' in primary care settings (Goldberg and Bridges, 1988). Not only has primary care been a new site of activity for psychiatrists, but for other groups of mental health workers as well, such as counsellors, social workers and clinical psychologists.

Recently GPs have been the source of providing services which are independent of psychiatry. This has been stimulated by the new fundholding arrangements which have placed GPs in the position of purchasing their own services. Of most note in this regard is the rapid expansion of counselling services as a means of dealing with psychosocial problems in primary care settings. The role of primary care services, particularly their role in mental health prevention and gatekeeping to secondary services, is dealt with in Chapter 8.

4 Psychiatric services in prisons

When the National Health Services was introduced in 1948 the Prison Medical Service continued as a separate service under the jurisdiction of the Home Office, its full-time medical officers being civil servants; though in Scotland there is a greater reliance than in England and Wales on NHS staff for psychiatric work in prisons. Most of the work of prison psychiatrists is diagnostic not therapeutic – they provide reports about the mental state of remand and other prisoners. Prison doctors are also involved in negotiating transfers of prisoners to NHS facilities for psychiatric care. One hospital prison exists in England (at Grendon Underwood) run loosely on therapeutic community lines. There have also been some special therapeutic units for long-term prisoners (e.g. Wormwood Scrubs in England, and Barlinnie in Scotland which has been closed during the writing of this book).

Estimates of the prevalence of psychiatric difficulties in prisoners vary according to whether these are limited to diagnoses of psychosis. Taylor and Gunn (1984) found that 9 per cent of remand prisoners were psychotic. They also found 4 per cent to be alcoholic and 5 per cent drug dependent. As for psychopathy, we have already noted its circular definition under the Mental Health Act and so arguably most violent offenders could, theoretically, be described as being psychopathic (though in practice this does not happen).

Over the last two decades there has been what can be described as an endemic crisis in prisons relating to the levels of mental distress experienced by inmates and the way in which mentally disordered people are managed. The rise in the number of people deemed to be suffering from mental disorder in British prisons may be linked to a number of factors. Some have tried to link the closure of psychiatric hospitals with a rise in the number of people sent to prison (Weller and Weller, 1989). American research has found little evidence to support the contention that there is a valid connection between the policy of de-institutionalisation and the number of people sent to prison (Teplin, 1984). A further concern in the 1980s were the levels of distress and self-mutilation among women kept in confined conditions in Holloway Prison. The suicide rate of those on remand has also been a recurrent embarrassment to the Home Office.

In many respects the poor facilities in prison can be viewed as part of the larger crisis about overcrowding that has characterised British prisons in the same period. Several solutions have been suggested, one being the transfer of a greater number of prisoners out of prison to other forms of secure provision. Another policy option proposed by the Tumin Report (Wolfe and Tumin, 1990) has been the integration of the prison medical service into the National Health Service with adequately staffed psychiatric intensive-care wards to be provided inside prisons.

5   Secure psychiatric provision

In the UK these services include maximum secure ('special') hospitals
and medium secure psychiatric units. In the case of the former, England has three Special Hospitals (Ashworth, Broadmoor and Rampton).
In Scotland there is the equivalent facility at Carstairs State Hospital.
Wales and Northern Ireland have no maximum secure psychiatric facilities. Although these hospitals are supposed to be for offender patients, they also contain patients with learning difficulties who have
not committed offences. Such cases were usually transferred from open
facilities because they were deemed too difficult to manage. Because
the hospitals deal with all of the four categories of mental disorder
under the mental health act (see earlier) they are not only for those
diagnosed as being mentally ill.

The hospitals have been the focus of intense criticism in recent years.
Two of the worst mental hospital scandals exposed by media investi-
gations and confirmed by official inquiries emerged in 1980 and 1992
at Rampton and Ashworth respectively (DHSS, 1980a; DH, 1992). The
degree of brutality and neglect associated with these hospitals has meant
that there has been an ongoing campaign from their opponents for their
closure and replacement with a range of flexible smaller facilities in
each locality.

Turning to regional medium secure units, these were first mooted
shortly after the 1959 Mental Health Act, by a Ministry of Health
working party reviewing the changing emphasis on voluntary patients
in psychiatric hospitals in 1961. The subsequent recommendations for
secure units bore no fruit, in terms of buildings. This led to a growing
gap between the maximum secure and open psychiatric hospital provision, with the latter being more and more reluctant to take offender
patients under court orders. For instance, in 1966 open hospitals received 1,259 such referrals. This had dropped to 924 by 1972 (Bluglass,
1985).

According to Bluglass (ibid), in the early 1970s three factors pre-
cipitated further reviews of medium security: the open door policy of
ordinary hospitals; overcrowding in the Special Hospitals; and the pressure of abnormal offenders in prisons, 'who should not be there'. Two
reports ensued in this context in 1974, from the Butler Committee on
Mentally Abnormal offenders, and the Glancy Committee, reviewing
services for the non-offender but difficult-to-manage patient.

Conclusion

This chapter has introduced two major dimensions to mental health policy: policy formation and the organisation of services. Each needs to be understood in relation to the other. For this reason, it is tempting, faced with this complexity, to focus on only one dimension. The danger of this is that a partial or reductionist account would emerge, which we will try to avoid in this book.

The subsequent chapters, amongst other things, will explore two peculiarities about mental health policy and services. First, there is a lack of clear 'top down' policy guidelines governing the major structural changes, which have characterised recent British mental health provision. This lack of specificity had been exacerbated by the fact that much recent policy-making and implementation relating to mental health has been subsumed under legislation and policy for all groups requiring health and social support, such as the 1990 NHS and Community Care Act. Policies have not been designed specifically for those with mental health problems in mind. The advantage of this approach is that it means that those stigmatised with the label of mental illness have been considered to require social and health care alongside other groups whose association with stigma has been less (though by no means absent). The drawback has been that the specific problems that face mental health users have not always been taken into consideration.

A second peculiarity of mental health policy, services and their recipients is the extraordinary range of formal and informal decisions that are entailed or implicated in practice. People with mental health problems become identified in society via very diverse processes: self-referral to general practitioners; court 'disposals'; contact with voluntary services; strangers calling the police during mental health crises in public places; social work interventions; and relatives sending for medical help during domestic crises. No other patient group comes into being from such disparate sources. Moreover, this diversity is mirrored by the agencies implicated in responding to the needs of people with mental health problems, once they are expressed or defined: primary care; crisis intervention and outreach services; dental care; housing departments; welfare benefit offices; job centres; as well as a wide range of specialist mental health interventions from health and social service staff. This diverse and dispersed character of mental health problems, in terms of their definition, control and amelioration, makes the topic of this book peculiarly challenging. Virtually every central or local government policy and department can be implicated directly or indirectly in mental health and can make their presence felt much more acutely than in other areas of social and health care. For example, admission to a psychiatric facility, in contrast to other areas of medicine is not effected solely by medical practitioners. The courts and the police are able to order hospitals to accept patients for assessment or treatment. Whether such practical and political interdependence operates efficiently and in the interests of people with mental health problems is an issue which we will return to in the final chapter of the book.

So much of the twentieth-century mental health service configuration has been an extension of or a reaction against the asylum system developed in the last century. For this reason, we will now explore and summarise some of the historical roots of current services.

3

The Rise of the Asylum

Introduction

The bulk of this book is concerned with contemporary mental health policy. However, the latter, with its emphasis on mental hospital closure, can only be understood with reference to the massive warehousing of pauper lunatics prior to the twentieth century. The rise and dominance of the asylum will be explored by focusing on phases of development during the nineteenth century. Prior to that a brief note will be made of developments which preceded the emergence of the state asylum system. This picture will be built up by summarising some of the extensive work of psychiatric historians (Porter, Donnelly, Busfield, Scull and Skultans).

The English 'Great Confinement'

Foucault (1961) maintained that from the mid seventeenth century a 'great confinement' took place across Europe. The logic of enlightenment values with its emphasis on rationality meant that those that represented 'unreason' were stigmatised and separated from mainstream society. Deviancy of all types embodied in a variety of groups – the criminal, the poor, the lazy, and the destitute – which threatened bourgeois values, were segregated. However, the course of English developments did not follow this depiction. During this period, by and large, *non-institutionalised*, privatised means of dealing with all deviant groups prevailed. From 1660 onwards social life was still characterised by parochialism. Throughout the Middle Ages and beyond there was an absence of formal provision. It was not until after 1780, when the numbers of madhouses grew rapidly, that an era dedicated to the confinement lunacy began in England. There were 16 metropolitan licensed houses in 1774 – by 1819 there were 40. This expansion was also associated with a growth in average house size.

The last quarter of the eighteenth century and first quarter of the nineteenth century saw a dramatic move away from unregulated, *ad hoc* local arrangements to a system which was increasingly segregative, centralised and managed. Madhouses were not seen as panaceas; even then there was a public distaste for confining people. They remained diverse and small scale and were typical of eighteenth-century institutions in being characterised by heterogeneity. For example, prisons contained inmates of various criminal statuses, gender and age herded together, and the elderly and orphans could be found alongside the sick in infirmaries and hospitals. The establishment of public asylums changed all of this, replacing it with a panoptic rational centralised system of discipline specifically aimed at catering for the lunatic.

By the end of the eighteenth century, a number of institutions following the path of the growth of the voluntary hospital movement had emerged. Funded out of public donations, these have been viewed by Porter (1987) as the first wave of public asylums. These institutions had a broader-based clientele than the madhouses and were generally set up to cater for respectable local citizens and the 'deserving' poorer classes. Smaller establishments included the ward for incurable lunatics at Guy's Hospital, established in 1728. St Luke's Hospital, which opened in London in 1751, was a larger enterprise, as was a lunatic hospital established in Manchester in 1766. Similar organisations sprang up in other major cities in the second half of the century (York, Liverpool, Leicester and Exeter).

The significance of the emergence of these asylums lies not only in their contribution to the legitimisation of segregating the mad, but also in their associated therapeutic optimism. Two competing models emerged towards the end of the eighteenth and beginning of the nineteenth century. One was the idea of insanity as a medical matter. The other, a theory of moral insanity, viewed madness as intrinsically bound up with the social environment.

Medical versus Moral Insanity

Charitable funded facilities were often part of a hospital, attached to infirmaries or named 'lunatic hospitals'. Some were founded by eminent mad-doctors wishing to promote their medical sub-specialty. According to Scull (1979), St Luke's 'represented a major attempt to assert medical control over the problem of insanity' (p. 25). It banned casual sightseeing, the hallmark of Bedlam, incorporated 'asylum' (with its connotation of 'sanctuary') into its title, and indicated its commitment to medical science by accommodating medical students.

The development and acceptance of a medical model of insanity was characterised by a number of features. There was the construction of a theory, which defined madness as a medical category with a biological basis. The beginning of the nineteenth century saw a proliferation of medical categories with specified symptoms and aetiology. The causes of medical insanity were conceived to be inside the person; a result of physical imbalances and an eruption of nature. Spermatorrhoea (excessive loss of sperm) provides an example of a syndrome that received medical attention in the early nineteenth century. The disease was described by physicians as caused by:

> Constipation, worms, piles, gonorrhoea, heat, heavy bedclothes, highly seasoned food, alcohol, intense application of the mind and excessive indulgence in sexual intercourse usually of a promiscuous kind. The effects of spermatorrhoea are similar to those of masturbation. In general these are debilitating. In particular, there is an intimate connection between seminal loss and the condition of the brain. There is an inability to sustain mental and bodily fatigue; a heaviness in the head; giddiness; sleeplessness. Interestingly, the appetite increases, often becoming voracious. (Skultans, 1979, p. 72)

The establishment of hospitals for the insane marked out the treatment of madness as a separate medical specialism in the same way that voluntary hospitals did for other medical specialties during this period (Granshaw, 1989). Inside the asylum the medical model implied a certain set of relationships and organisational arrangements. The authority of the regime lay with the medical practitioner – patients were categorised by severity of illness and the curative force was by physical manipulation.

'Moral treatment' provided a different and competing model to all these early versions of the medicalisation of madness. Rather than a disease of the mind, insanity was viewed as a varying state where there were periods of lucidity in which the person was sensitive to the surrounding environment. Since a disordered mind was seen as being a function of a disordered environment, restoration to 'normality' required the provision of an orderly environment.

William Tuke, the first English protagonist of moral treatment, designed

the Quaker facility the York 'Retreat' to offer space where the patient
had the opportunity to re-learn a normal life. The regime at the Retreat was designed to keep the disordering influences of society out
and included a concern with the religion, social habits, lifestyle and
activities of the patient. Since it was assumed that moral change and
sanity emerged from social influences, mechanical restraints of all types
were eschewed. A model of 'normal' life was implicit to the organisation of patient activity. Staff were to act as role models representing
normality and interacting with patients to rejuvenate decency and normal social relationships through feelings of shame and guilt. Both of
these models, but particularly moral treatment, predicated as they were
on therapeutic optimism, fed a zeal for establishing a publicly funded
comprehensive asylum system. Asylums would restore the mad to health
at the same time as relieving the financial burden on the community.

The Growth in State Regulation and Provision and the New Poor Law

The insanity legislation of the first half of the nineteenth century was
part of increased state intervention in social problems more generally,
where legislation included the Poor Law Act of 1834, the Factory Acts
of 1833 and 1844, the Mines Act of 1842 and the Public Health Act
of 1848. The force of government policy on lunacy was concentrated
almost exclusively on its 'pauper' variant. Lunacy reform was linked
to changes in the wider Poor Law system brought about by the 1834
Poor Law Amendment Act. This in turn was linked to the poverty
caused by the vagaries of industrialisation and its associated social
exclusion.

The major social, economic and demographic upheaval which
industrialisation brought about had changed the nature of poverty. A
second wave of enclosures (making common land into private) created
a surge in the number of landless workers, rural unemployed and those
dependent on the vagaries of the wage labour market. This increased
the cost of poverty massively which the Old Poor Law was incapable
of subsidising. Moreover, the informal familial structures which the
Old Poor Law relief was designed to supplement were being eroded
by mass urbanisation.

Certain enlightenment ideas were also detectable in the type of reform that the 1834 Act represented. In his *An Essay on the Principle
of the Population*, first published in 1798, Thomas Malthus suggested

that poverty was inevitable in any society. Jeremy Bentham held the view that it was desirable to extend rationality and scientific principles to the social world with a view to obtaining a well-regulated and disciplined society and advocated the development of new types of social institution in which order could be sustained through discipline and surveillance. Bentham considered his design for an 'inspection house' to be suitable for a range of social institutions including schools, asylums, workhouses and prisons.

Whereas the 'Old' Elizabethan Poor Laws provided a system of locally funded outdoor relief with which to support the poor, the new Poor Laws brought about a shift in values and type of provision. The 'old' Poor Laws were predicated on entitlement, the New Poor Law stressed deterrence. The system of outdoor relief was replaced with institionalisation based on the principle of 'less eligibility' or 'workhouse test' – indoor relief had to be more distasteful than available work outside the workhouse.

Lunacy Legislation 1801–1845

Between 1801 and 1844 there were 71 Bills, reports of select committees and inquiries relating to lunacy. The main government legislation leading to the establishment of a full-blown pauper asylum system provided by local authorities in England and Wales included the following:

(1) The Select Committee of 1805 reporting in 1807 heard evidence about the appalling conditions in which many pauper and criminal lunatics were being kept by madhouse-keepers. The solution advocated was the building of large asylums – up to 300 beds to ensure economies of scale. The 1808 Act the following year authorised, although did not compel magistrates to erect publicly funded asylums in each county.

(2) The 1815–16 House of Commons Select Committee undertook a two-year inquiry into the conditions in which pauper lunatics were kept (including charity hospitals, the new 'county' asylums, private madhouses and workhouses). Much of the evidence was provided by the philanthropists who had developed an interest in lunacy reform. The shortcomings documented in the Committee's report included serious deficiencies: overcrowding; a lack of attendants; an inappropriate mixing of types of patient; a lack of medical input; the over-use of mechanical restraints; poor physical health of patients; unwarranted detention; and inadequate certification procedures and inspection of

private madhouses. Mistreatment was found to be prevalent in all types of institution. Yet, as Scull (1979) points out, 'both the Committee itself and those who disseminated its findings to a wider public interpreted these revelations as proof of the need for more institutions' (p. 77), albeit ones under direct public control with an improved system of inspection and supervision.

(3) The 1828 Madhouse Act repealed the 1774 Act and replaced it with a more rigorous system of licensing and visiting. The County Asylums Act passed in the same year required asylums to make returns of admissions and discharges to the Home Office and gave rights of visitation to the Secretary of State.

(4) The 1844 Report of the Metropolitan Commissioners in Lunacy was able to provide systematic data of lunatics in all types of institutions for the first time. It conceded that the existing asylum system was a failure. The building of asylums could not keep pace with demand, which quickly outstripped supply. The report for example showed that nearly half of all lunatics were being kept in workhouses and elsewhere. The fact that the number of admissions was not matched with discharges also indicated that the asylum had failed to realise its therapeutic promise in delivering cures for mental disorder. However, rather than abandoning this policy pathway, the government chose to reinforce the asylum system by the passing and implementing of the 1845 Lunacy Act. This act made the building of County Asylums compulsory and created a central regulatory body, the Lunacy Commission, which was authorised to carry out regular inspections of asylums. A system of medical records was also established. The Act also authorised the building of cheaper separate asylums specifically for chronic patients but local authorities did not act on this permission (Busfield, 1986).

Subsequent to this new legislation the numbers of asylums and their inmates grew quickly.

Stakeholders in Government Reform

The Campaign for Lunacy Reform was led by an influential lobby of aristocratic philanthropists (such as Lord Shaftsbury), successful entrepreneurs and Quakers and Evangelists. Over and above a belief that medicine could cure insanity, the campaign focused on three issues:

1. the lack of asylum provision – charitable funding was limited;
2. harsh treatment of inmates by profit-seeking madhouse-keepers;
3. the inappropriate placing of lunatics in workhouses.

The Campaign was opposed by a coalition of equally powerful interest groups, which acted as a brake on reform. The latter was largely responsible for the length of time taken for parliament to establish a comprehensive public asylum system. The anti-publicly funded asylum movement included: madhouse owners, who saw their business being threatened by state intervention; medical practitioners, who did not want outside interference in their work; rural aristocrats, who were generally opposed to increased state intervention in local matters; and local authorities uneasy about the demands that may be placed on them to spend money.

The Reformers

Although there is general agreement that philanthropic concern played a central part in bringing lunacy to the forefront of government thinking and action, commentators suggest a variety of underlying motives. Skultans (1979) considers that the philanthropists' campaigns were based on benevolence and humanitarianism. Scull provides a more critical account of the lunacy reformers, whom he viewed as being stimulated by the less admirable values of evangelicalism and Benthamism, which were imbued with dominant class interests. Evangelicalism he describes in the following terms:

> Evangelicalism was at its very core a conservative movement, concerned to shore up a disintegrating social structure and a paternalistic morality against the threats posed on the one hand by an undisciplined lower class rabble, and on the other by a purely materialistic entrepreneur class. (1979, p. 98)

According to Porter (1987) Georgian doctors had generally not been interested in legal reform or lunacy policy. However, their early Victorian counterparts were deeply immersed in the shaping and making of policy and the relationship between the state and mad-doctors was of mutual benefit. The attractiveness of a medical monopoly of madness for the state seemed to rest on medical claims, which coincided with the broad sweep of government thinking. Psychiatry could claim not only that there was a rising incidence of mental illness that had to be managed, but that investment in asylum building was warranted because of the promise of returning a large number of cures which would deliver orderly and economically active citizens back into society. Thus, psychiatry made asylum building an attractive option in the face

of reticence about the cost. In turn the acceptance of medical management by the state reaped huge rewards for the mad-doctors. The establishment of a comprehensive asylum system provided both a rationale
for the confinement of lunatics in one place and an *opportunity* for
the close scientific scrutiny of odd behaviour, delusions and delin-
quencies necessary for the development of a conceptual framework.

   The 1845 Lunatics Act sounded the death-knell of lay administrators
by awarding a monopoly of the running of institutions to medical practitioners. The term 'psychiatry' which was introduced into British
medicine for the first time in 1846 is evidence of the link between the
1845 Act and the emergence of a sub-specialty of medicine. Just over
a decade later (1858) the General Medical Act gave medical practitioners a monopoly of control over illness. The same year the editorial
of the *Journal of Mental Science* (now the *British Journal of Psychiatry*) pronounced that 'Insanity is purely a disease of the brain. The
physician is now the responsible guardian of the lunatic and must ever
remain so.' These two sentences capture a political project of organised medicine which was to last for over a hundred years: madness
was a biological disorder and only doctors could oversee its management.

Accounts for the Rise of the Asylum

It is likely that the lobbying activities of lunacy reformers and medical practitioners were only responsible in part for the genesis and growth
of mass confinement. The increase in lunatics was massive and far
outweighed the growth in population. In the half-a-century following
the introduction of the compulsory asylum system the population grew
by 80 per cent whilst the numbers of lunatics quadrupled (Scull, 1979).

   That the population of asylums grew enormously is undisputed.
However there is far less agreement over the reasons for their growth
and a number of competing explanations have been offered. Most accounts view aspects of industrialisation as a causal factor in the process. The main features of industrialisation can be summarised as follows:

- A rapid growth in population and geographical mobility
- Population and production mobility from rural to urban areas
- A shift away from agricultural to factory-based production
- A transformation of the social and political ordering of dominant
  ideas.

Whilst these features were clear, the interpretation of the influence has varied. Below are some competing explanations as to why mass segregation expanded so rapidly and in such volume.

1   A rise in rates of mental disorder

This was the theory most popular in arguments for the establishment of asylums, particularly those made by medical practitioners. Whilst it is a truism that in absolute terms the population experiencing psychological distress was likely to grow given the explosion in population accompanying industrialisation, the means of establishing relative rates of mental illness in the population had not developed in any meaningful way. One psychiatric theory which aims to compare schizophrenia with the pattern of etiology of other major physical diseases attributes the increase in beds to the emergence of an early onset type of schizophrenia which is linked to 'the mutation of an infectious agent' around 1800 (Hare, 1988).

2   Humanitarianism and benevolence

Another focus of analysis views the process as part and parcel of medical progress and an increasingly humane way of dealing with 'mentally ill' people. For example Jones (1960, p. 149) sees the implementation of the 1845 Act in a humanitarian light:

> Ashley and his colleagues had roused the conscience of mid-Victorian society, and had set a new standard of public morality by which the care of the helpless and degraded classes of the community was to be seen as a social responsibility.

This type of Whig or, from a feminist perspective, 'great man' version of history (usually written for and by the confident and successful) tends to emphasise the altruism and actions of key individuals and plays down the impact of social and economic factors.

3   Breakdown in familial and community support networks as a result of urbanisation

Others see the growth of the asylum system as an inevitable result of the rise of industrial society. According to Mechanic, segregative forms of social control arose as a response to the inability of family- and

community-based systems of support to contain mental illness in the
community. Mechanic (1969, p. 54) writes:

> Industrial and technological change . . . coupled with increasing ur-
> banisation brought decreasing tolerance for bizarre and disruptive
> behaviour and less ability to contain deviant behaviour within the
> existing social structure.

Mechanic emphasises the decreasing tolerance of society for deviant
behaviour as inevitably arising from the replacement of old paternal
relationships with a chaos caused by mass geographical mobility and
urban anonymity.

4   The capitalist economy

Scull challenges the industrialisation emphasis. He claims that there
was no clear-cut link between the growth of urban populations and the
rise of the asylum. In the first decades of the nineteenth century, when
pressure for the establishment of a compulsory asylum system was
well under way, only a third of the English population lived in large
cities. Moreover, when, in 1808, countries gained discretionary rights
to establish asylums for pauper lunatics, 'whether any given county
adopted this solution to the problem bore little or no relationship to
the degree of urbanisation of its population' (Scull, 1979).

   Scull suggests an alternative explanation for the rise of segregative
control for the mad which 'can much more plausibly be asserted to lie
in the effects of the advent of a mature capitalist market economy and
the associated ever more thoroughgoing commercialisation of existence' (Scull, 1979, p. 30). He goes on to argue that whilst industrialisation is viewed as having a limited geographical impact on urban
society, the thoroughgoing organisation of society along market principles which took place in the final quarter of the eighteenth century
and first quarter of the nineteenth, had far-reaching effects on both
traditional rural and urban social arrangements. In particular, there was
a shift from a master–servant relationship based on rank and order to
an employer–employee relationship with a corresponding social order
based on class. The paternal responsibilities characterising the master–
servant relationship had little place in the superordinate/subordinate
relationship which succeeded it. For Scull, institutions such as workhouses and asylums not only provided a solution to the problem of the
growth in the cost of poverty that arose as a result of a market econ-

omy system, but they also provided a disciplinary regime geared to the labour needs of a capitalist economy:

> The quasi-military authority structure which it (the asylum) could institute seemed ideally suited to the means of establishing 'proper' work habits among those elements of the work force who were apparently more resistant to the monotony, routine, and regularity of industrialized labour. (Scull, 1979, p. 35)

5 Changes in psychiatric knowledge

Rather than the 'real' rates of mental illness amongst the population increasing, the proliferation of 'new' psychiatric classifications may have been important in drawing people into the asylum system. Insanity became 'such an amorphous, all-embracing concept, that the range of behaviour it could be stretched to encompass was almost infinite' (Scull, 1979, p. 238). According to Scull, the mad-doctors' motivation for the expansion of insanity classification was their increasing professionalisation:

> since they had convinced themselves that asylums were benevolent and therapeutic institutions, and believed that laymen were incompetent to cope with, and liable to maltreat the mad, they were impelled to seek out still more cases, rather than to reject any who were proffered . . . By increasing the population which fell within their purview, the profession also became entitled to obtain increased resources to support their activities. (Scull, 1979, p. 238)

It is unlikely that the numbers of certified lunatics increased simply as a result of the widening definitions of insanity formulated by asylum doctors. Administrative and financial matters at a local level were also important.

6 Administrative changes in the operation of the Poor Law

In the second half of the nineteenth century administrative convenience and financial incentives at local authority level accentuated the upward trend in the growth of asylum numbers. By 1867 the government was forced to act over the problems which had arisen with the implementation of the 1834 Poor Law. Most of those presenting for indoor relief were the 'non-able-bodied' poor, the sick, infirm and elderly, and it had never been the intention of the Poor Law Commissioners that the principle of 'less eligibility' be applied to this group (Cochrane, 1988). Moreover, despite the intention of the Benthamite reformers, outdoor relief still predominated for able-bodied paupers. (According to the Report of the Royal Commission on the Poor Laws in 1909, in the period 1871–9 the 'outdoor poor' outnumbered those in workhouses by 4.5 to 1. In 1896–1905 this proportion reduced to 2.6 to 1.9.) During the latter half of the century, government attention focused on centering poor relief on the workhouse. Chronic lunatics in workhouses posed an impediment to such change. Many 'chronic lunatics' who remained incarcerated in workhouses did not fit the 'less eligibility' rule; also 'their detention in workhouses was objectionable on humanitarian grounds, and they were difficult to manage in workhouse wards' (Cochrane, 1988, p. 250). The aim of the 1867 Metropolitan Poor Law Act was to separate out chronic lunatics and those with life-threatening infectious diseases. In London there were strong financial incentives for the metropolitan unions to rid their workhouses of pauper lunatics. Additionally, the extra cost of maintaining pauper lunatics in county asylums was offered to local unions. In London the metropolitan unions could save up to 60 per cent of the cost of transferring inmates from the workhouse to a lunatic asylum.

The Triumph of Custodialism

The realities of the pauper asylum system bore little relation to the aspirations of the reformers. Although some asylums tried to copy the moral treatment regime this was quickly abandoned as were all other therapeutic regimes. Like the workhouses, asylums became large regimented institutions of last resort, which if anything were more stigmatising. Although they were run by medical men, they failed to deliver the cures that a medical approach to insanity had promised.

According to Busfield (1986) a number of factors contributed to the custodial nature of the asylums. Firstly, certification was a legal requirement for all inmates of public asylums, which acted as a deterrent to attracting cases likely to be 'curable' in that it encouraged early admission and prevented discharge . Secondly, the physical design and running of the buildings encouraged custodialism. Expensive, ostentatious asylum facades disguised a preoccupation with security (high perimeter walls and strictly controlled access) and the gloomy and drab prison-like interiors. Security concerns also came to predominate in the staff culture – 'the lack of furniture and of knives and forks in the male refractory wards was explained by attendants of the groups that "the men were all of them too dangerous to be trusted"' (Busfield, 1986, pp. 258–9). Thirdly, there was the size of the asylum. The earliest asylums had been built for less than 100 persons. By the end of the nineteenth century the average asylum contained 1,000 inmates with some taking up to 2,000. Fourthly, the management of inmates was based on the norms of the Poor Law. Control was exercised through regimentation, routine and engendering passivity and dependence.

Finally, there was little in the way of a therapeutic regime in the asylums. Mechanical restraint was used sparingly by British psychiatry in comparison with both Europe and America. The use of physical restraint by attendants, and seclusion in preference to the use of mechanical restraint, were encouraged by the Poor Law Commission. But even this became a lessening concern toward the end of the century. Younger doctors took over from the older asylum attendants, state regulation became a fact of life, and therapeutic pessimism gained ascendance. Asylum administration, predicated as it was on the norms of Poor Law institutions, militated against the introduction of a therapeutic regime. Those who were usefully employed received preferential treatment, being allowed occasional entertainments, visits to the local town and greater physical comforts than those who were unable to contribute in this way. The less physically and mentally able were confined to 'refractory wards', where restraint in padded cells and use of nocturnal sedatives were used. Some asylums used belts, straps and locked gloves to constrain patients and at the end of the century some returned to using mechanical devices (Tomes, 1988).

Although the asylums were run by medical men, the superintendents of public asylums and their medical assistants assumed mainly an administrative role, concerning themselves with the day-to-day running of the asylum and carrying out statutory duties such as keeping registers and writing up case notes. Some inmates were prescribed purgatives and sedatives. Hydrotherapy was popular in some asylums. The diet of inmates was also subject to medical scrutiny. However, overall there was little attempt at instilling a therapeutic regimen. The lack of treatment input was compounded by the nature of staffing at ward level. Low staffing levels made individual attention difficult and low wages and harsh conditions meant that the quality of staff was poor. Apart from an administrative imperative (e.g. initial patient assessments for the writing of case records), medical activities encouraged by the Lunacy Commission centred on the development of medical knowledge. Post-mortem examination of brains was afforded particular attention. The rationale for performing autopsies was in order to advance:

> the knowledge of the pathology and treatment of the various forms of insanity . . . and also in showing that insanity is not solely a disease of the mind, but is frequently associated with bodily lesions, and within the reach of medical treatment. (Hunter and MacAlpine, 1964, p. 254)

The culmination of custodialism in the latter part of the nineteenth century, which continued into the first decades of the twentieth, found expression in the 1890 Lunacy Act. Although critics of the asylums argued for trying to make them more therapeutic and less custodial, by allowing admission without certification, early intervention and the boarding-out of the more chronic cases, they lost the argument. The 1890 Act is regarded as the triumph of a legalistic approach. Concentrating as it did on wrongful certification and detention, it prioritised and protected the civil rights of those *outside* of the asylum. Legislation concerning the voluntary admission to hospital and a focus on treatment and therapy had to wait until well into the twentieth century. But, as we shall see in the next chapter, it is a moot point whether or not these changes which placed power and responsibility more firmly in the hands of the medical profession represented a more enlightened approach.

Whilst some commentators have talked of an oscillation between medical and legal reform (Bean, 1986), another reading of the history of asylums suggests a symbiosis of state (legislative and judicial) and medical interests. Within this symbiosis the legal profession has never achieved the same degree of recognition and power afforded by government to the psychiatric profession. Ultimately, so-called 'legalism' has been administered by and large by the medical profession.

Gender and the Asylum

Most of the above has examined the reasons given by historians for the rise of the asylum. Before leaving this chapter, the question of gender will be addressed. Some feminist researchers have emphasised the patriarchal character of psychiatry. Showalter's *Female Malady* (1985) is frequently cited in this field of inquiry. She argues that during the nineteenth century women were over-represented in the asylum system and that madness was mainly a female condition. Moreover, she claims that whilst furious male madness was the dominant cultural motif in the eighteenth century, in the Victorian period madness was feminised in artistic representations. This view has been challenged substantially by Busfield (1994), who argues, using official records from the time, that admission rates were similar for men and women to the asylum system but that because of differences in life expectancy more female lunatics accumulated. Women were discharged more frequently than men and the latter were more likely to die in the asylum than were women. To summarise Bustfield's argument, which is at odds with that of Showalter's, in epidemiological terms the incidence for madness for men and women was similar but the prevalence was greater for the latter.

Busfield also disputes Showalter's emphasis on the cultural representations of madness being slanted towards female images. Showalter emphasises images such as suicidal Ophelia, crazy Jane or Kate and the violent Lucia in Victorian art. Busfield does not deny that these images were present but she also argues that there were also three common cultural representations of male madness (the mad genius, the criminal lunatic and masturbatory insanity). For Busfield, psychiatry was gendered but it contained a complex admixture of attributions of both female and male irrationality. What supports her argument is the emphasis within Victorian psychiatry on the use of both restraint and male asylum attendants. These suggest that violent and disruptive behaviour were the organisational priorities in asylum work. The issue of gendered mental health work will be considered again in the next chapter in relation to the changes involved in outpatient work.

Conclusion

The Victorian period was marked by the robust rise of psychiatry and a routinisation of segregation. However, despite these setting the scene for most of the mental health policy of the early twentieth century, matters were to become more complex. As we explore in the next chapter, mad doctors had to expand their expertise beyond the management of pauper lunacy, and the asylum was to provoke an increasing swell of opposition.

Contemporary mental health policy also owes much to this Victorian legacy. The asylum system provided an all-embracing and systematic way of dealing with emotional deviance. The 'mentally ill' remained out of sight and therefore out of mind of the general public. There was an efficiently administered and run system, with clear-cut authority emanating from the medical profession. The recent removal of this 'total' solution has had major implications for the way in which current policy and services have been configurated. As we shall examine in later chapters, the asylum system was gradually transformed during the twentieth century into a complex, diverse and fragmented system. This has also entailed changes in the roles, responsibilities and sitings of intervention of psychiatric personnel, and a change in how mental health problems are described and conceptualised.

4

The Great War and After

Introduction

This chapter will examine a period stretching from the outbreak of the First World War in 1914 to the election of Margaret Thatcher in 1979. This span of 65 years witnessed a series of policy shifts which involved controversies surrounding the role of the mental hospital, psychiatric knowledge and the citizenship, or lack of it, of psychiatric patients. For convenience of discussion these debates will be reviewed under seven sub-headings which help to punctuate the period under consideration:

- Shellshock and industrial fatigue: mad-doctors found wanting
- The 1920s: the legacy of the war years
- The 1930s: business as usual in the asylums
- The 1940s: warfare and the seeds of the NHS
- The 1950s: the return of peace and bio-determinism
- The 1960s: the crisis of the institution
- The 1970s: the fiscal crisis of the state

Shellshock and Industrial Fatigue: Mad-Doctors Found Wanting

The previous chapter explored two features which characterised Victorian psychiatry – the role of the asylum in containing pauper lunatics and the biological emphasis within psychiatry. The former emerged as one institutional response to the burden and disruption posed by one group of the underclass in civil society under British capitalism. Closely linked to it was the second feature which was part of a wider eugenic trend within Western natural science. The inmates of asylums were assumed to be mad because of faulty brains which were in turn a product of a tainted or flawed gene pool. This interplay between the incarceration role of the asylum and the bio-deterministic knowledge base of psychiatry was well suited for the regulation of a peacetime population.

However, the First World War was to pose a different set of problems for government in relation to mental abnormality. At home a predominantly female work force in the munitions factories was suffering the physical and mental consequences of stress. Over the English Channel soldiers were breaking down under the peculiar stresses of a war of unprecedented attrition and futile slaughter. Let us now look at how government responded to the two groups and how this changed the pattern of mental health services from its singular focus on the Victorian asylum.

Industrial fatigue

The 1911 National Insurance Act was the first piece of legislation to provide for non-fee-paying patients. However, this was only for working men. With the outbreak of war in 1914 industrial output was at the expense of female labour. Moreover, the latter did not merely replace men in the factories, they literally doubled their effort. In 1913 men worked between 48 and 55 hours per week in factories. By 1916 women were working 90 hours on average, with some exceeding 100 hours per week (Hearnshaw, 1964). Such was the concern about the physical and psychosomatic consequences of these conditions, which included anxiety reactions, miscarriages and exhaustion, that in 1915 Lloyd George set up the Health of Munitions Workers Committee (which was to become the Industrial Fatigue Board before becoming part of the Medical Research Council in 1929).

Other indications that government after 1911 was taking the health and welfare of women and children (i.e. not just working men) seriously was that by the war's end the Maternal and Child Welfare Act (1918) was passed. This required local authorities to set up committees to review antenatal and child medical services. As Busfield (1986) notes, at least some of the pressure for this focus on women during the war was the concern about the loss of male infants. The general point to note here, though, is that whereas in the pre-war period the focus was on purported genetic inferiority and its containment in institutions, government concern was now extending to stress conditions which were accepted to be environmental and whose victims were deemed to be honourable and genetically healthy (not 'degenerate'). This was one source of crisis for services based upon the bio-deterministic ideas and institutional containment. But the more salient pressure came from the mental problems of male combatants.

Shellshock

This point about the crisis for Victorian psychiatric theory and practice created by shellshock is summarised well here by Stone (1985) who documents the topic in detail:

> The monolithic theory of hereditary degeneration upon which Victorian psychiatry had based its social and scientific vision was significantly dented as young men of respectable and proven character were reduced to mental wrecks within a few months in the trenches ... Not only had shellshock effectively blurred the distinction between the 'neuroses' and 'insanity', but many chronically 'war-strained' ex-service men were, by the early 1920s, being transferred to asylums as inpatients.

The claim that these soldiers ('England's finest blood') were degenerate – the simplistic theory of Victorian eugenics to explain all manner of deviance – was logically impossible and tantamount to treason. This tension between explanatory notions of degeneracy and environmental stress became more evident as it was recognised that upper-middle-class officers were actually breaking down at higher rates than their subordinate ranks. As early as December 1914 reports from France indicated that 7–10 per cent of officers and 3–4 per cent of other ranks were suffering breakdowns. Consequently, as with the industrial fatigue problem at home, environmental theories were to be offered a place in the range of psychiatric theories. In the case of shellshock this was to allow the emergence of Freudian-derived psychotherapy.

The scale of the shellshock problem is indicated by the medical records of the time, with 80,000 cases passing through army hospitals during the war and 30,000 being placed in psychiatric institutions. However, as Stone (1985) notes, this may be an underestimate given that many cases were given less stigmatising labels such as 'Disordered Action of the Heart'. Also, the distinction between 'normal' mental states and 'shellshock', under conditions of the daily filth and carnage of the trenches, could be arbitrarily determined by the extent to which local officers expected all under their command to 'tough it out'. Thus the more tough-minded officers would refer out less cases than more tender-minded colleagues.

If we consider the combined effect of industrial fatigue at home and shellshock on mainland Europe we see four features emerging which were to change irrevocably the face of twentieth-century psychiatric services:

1. Neurosis and not just psychosis was to become a focus of professional interest.
2. Environmental theories were to become a challenge to the bio-deterministic legacy of the Victorian period.
3. Services were to be organised on an outpatient as well as inpatient basis.
4. The gendered character of mental health shifted away for a while from that of asylum routines (see the discussion near the end of Chapter 3). The psychosomatic reactions of female munitions workers and the neurotic reactions of male combatants, rather than madness in either sex, became a focus for experts working outside of the walls of the asylums.

The 1920s: The Legacy of the War Years

A number of events shortly after the Great War substantiate the conclusions drawn above. Changing professional interests in outpatient psychotherapy with neurotic patients was evident in the new legitimacy accorded to Freudianism. The first section of the British Psychological Society (the Medical Section) was set up in 1919 by shellshock doctors returning from the war. In the same year the British Psychoanalytical Society was formed. Prior to the war Freudian ideas had been rejected by the bulk of the British medical profession. In 1920, again with a Freudian character, the Tavistock Clinic was founded with its first honorary vice presidents being Admiral Beatty and Field Marshal Haig.

The Ministry of Pensions set up a hundred outpatient treatment centres for shellshock cases returning from the war, and by the end of the war inpatient facilities such as the asylum at Maghull near Liverpool (now Ashworth south) were being used as intensive training centres for medical psychotherapists to practise on an outpatient basis. In the 1920s shellshock became a focus for both new forms of treatment approaches and a social administrative problem of compensation. As Stone (1985) notes, there were 100,000 such cases returning from the war, and so psychiatric disability, other than the lunacy identified by Victorian mad-doctors, had a double cost implication – from outpatient treatment facilities and from compensation claims.

This picture, with its emphasis on environmental causes of mental abnormality, meant that the legitimacy of asylum doctors in the eyes of both government and the public had been undermined in the war years. When, in 1924, the Royal Commission on Lunacy and Mental Disorder was set up not a single asylum doctor was invited as a member.

According to Busfield (1986) the stimulus for this commission, chaired by Macmillan, was public concern about wrongful detention (not primarily at the time about voluntary and early treatment, the motifs of later legislation). After the war, Lomax had exposed problems about wrongful detention when writing about Prestwich asylum (Lomax, 1921). This prompted the Minister of Health to set up an inquiry into these problems in public asylums. The outcome of its deliberation did not quell public anxiety and the larger brief of a Royal Commission was demanded. Of course this interpretation has to be put into the wider context of a post-war era when public sensitivity about mental distress may well have been greater than in the pre-war period. After all, with all cases being certified under the 1890 Act, wrongful detention must have been rife at the turn of the century. The association between mental abnormality and a narrow band of 'riff raff' from what Marx called the 'lumpenproletariat' – pauper lunatics – had now broken down. People with severe mental distress were visible from all class backgrounds in the wake of the war. Their treatment in the community in outpatient settings made this visibility greater. The expansion of the ambit of professional acivity from pauper lunatics to include other social classes and forms of mental problem was both reflected in and shaped policy developments after the war. Accordingly, compassion about mental distress and concerns about softening the segregative emphasis of the 1890 legislation were prevalent.

In the context of this *Zeitgeist*, the Macmillan Commission extended (or arguably ignored) the narrow brief it was given about wrongful detention. Bean (1980, p. 23) puts it succinctly here:

> It interpreted the criticisms of existing legislation as demands for some measure of change, not as demands for additional legal safeguards. The Commission wanted what it called 'the enlightened approach'. This meant a move towards greater medicalization, and as such failed to meet many of the more pungent criticisms of the existing legislation.

The Commission reported in 1926 (HMSO, 1926) and its opening statement contained the following four emphases which demonstrate that
its prime concerns were more theoretical than legalistic:

1. Mental and physical illness should now be seen as ovelapping not
   as distinct.
2. Mental illness typically has physical concomitants (even though they
   are not always readily discernible).
3. Physical illness typically had mental concomitants.
4. There are many cases in which it is difficult to decide whether
   physical or mental symptoms and causes predominate.

Thus, although asylum doctors were not invited on to the Commission,
the outcome of its deliberations was remarkably consistent with the
medical emphasis of Victoria psychiatry. Later in the report other assumptions were made, which mixed these musings about mental illness with certain programmatic suggestions:

- Compulsory detention should be governed by the main goal of protecting, caring for and curing the patient.
- The past was concerned with detention, the future should be concerned with prevention and treatment.
- Although physical and mental illnesses had overlapping features, mental
  illness did at times need to be treated forcibly. But compulsion should
  now be about treatment not mere detention.

These assumptions of course led to an unresolved contradiction for
the Macmillan Commission's position, and one still bedevilling modern attempts to make therapeutic law. On the one hand, there was an
emphasis on the need for benign care, curative intent and consideration for the individual sufferer's needs. On the other hand, the emphasis on the need for the use of force in the case of mental illness actually
requires the deprivation of liberty without trial – the removal of a
fundamental civil right. The medicalisation emphasis of the 1930 Mental
Treatment Act, in the wake of the 1926 Commission's report, thus
incorporated such a contradiction. This legislation also marked a step-
ping-stone between the judicial emphasis of 1890 and the move away
from the use of courts and towards even greater medical control under
the 1959 legislation (see later). The 1930 Act, in accord with the
Macmillan recommendations, extended the voluntary boarder system
of the 1890 Act.

By 1930 the 1845 legislation's strictures about mandatory public asylums had installed a nationwide network of grand and extensive buildings near every major population point. England and Wales had 98 asylums which contained 120,000 patients (Jones, 1960). Only one new mental hospital was built in the inter-war period, at Runwell, Essex, but the Bethleham was re-built for the fourth time (Webster, 1988). Would the post-war debates about mental health policy dent the practices in, or power of, this well-established Victorian asylum system?

The 1930s: Business as Usual in the Asylums

The 1930 Act on the one hand signalled the end of a narrow segregation emphasis within British mental health policy but on the other reinforced the medicalisation of mental abnormality. For this reason, it is little surprising that it did not in fact lead to a substantial alternation in asylum practices. A number of supportive findings and recommendations from the 1926 Commission's report worked in the interests of doctors. The prevention and treatment emphasis has been mentioned, but in addition there was the recommendation that doctors should be protected from being sued by patients or relatives (unless they were shown to be acting in bad faith). Overall the doctors' hand was substantially strengthened by the 1930 Act derived from these features of the Macmillan report, as well as the finding that asylum life was not as black as that painted by Lomax and others. The 1926 Commission had found no evidence of bad practice in their 25 asylum visits (23 of which were unannounced). On the contrary, staff were complimented for their standards of care (Ramon, 1985).

Whilst most of the 1926 recommendations were converted into the 1930 Act the ones which were *not* influential also reveal the intended or unintended support from parliament for continued professional and asylum dominance in service organisation. For instance, Macmillan wanted information about legal rights for patients and relatives to be posted on hospital wards but this was omitted from the 1930 Act. Likewise, the emphasis in 1926 on outpatients clinics and observation beds in general hospitals (i.e. not asylums) was weakened and after-care given over as a discretionary or 'permissive' duty for local authorities, with no central state finance being allocated for the purpose.

Thus, the first real opportunity to give formal state legitimacy to a policy of community- rather than hospital-based mental health services was lost with the passing of the 1930 Act. In 1929 the minority Labour government drafting the Act was in no position to guarantee resources for any new project. In the debate about the bill, commmunity-based hostels were suggested twice by MPs but not incorporated into the Act.

Overall, the endorsement of most of the 1926 recommendations and the telling selective omissions led to the Mental Treatment Act emphasising asylum-centred services in the 1930s. Moreover, the original public sensitivities about wrongful detention in the early 1920s could not have been assuaged by the 1930 legislation. Whilst the 1890 Act was overly and overtly legalistic – 'nothing was left to chance' (Jones, 1960) – the greater medical emphasis of the 1930 Act meant that legal protection was weakened for patients and forced treatment become a mystification of, or rationalisation for, detention without trial. The legislators' trust in a medical-therapeutic ethos in mental health work bolstered professional power at the expense of the rights of patients.

It might have been predicted in the immediate aftermath of 1918 that psychological (especially psychoanalytical) models would come to displace the somatic emphasis within psychiatric theory and practice. But by 1930 the shellshock problem was dissipating (at least as an administrative issue, if not for the afflicted war veterans). What emerged instead was a split between a weak psychotherapeutically-orientated outpatient clinic development and a strong retention of hospital-based psychiatry. It would seem that the social administrative problem focused on by the war (stress neurosis) was not the same as that facing public and government in civil society in peacetime (madness).

This was to set a pattern for the whole of the twentieth century. The Great War was associated with the introduction of talking-treatments and an emphasis on stress reactions, a theme to return after 1939. The inter-war periods, though, re-established the central role of the containment of lunacy, but now clothed in the language of the treatment of illness. What these competing trends (somatic and psychological) had in common was that they were therapeutic – the discourse of organised and professionalised medicine. The problem of Victorian eugenic psychiatry was now resolved by the formula of eclecticism in medical theory and practice – environmentalism as well as genetic explanations were now on offer. Thus the crisis created by the First World War about the ligitimacy of psychiatry had subsided.

In the inter-war period, for better or worse, the State was shifting its trust from judicial to medical regulation of mental abnormality in society. In fact, there were few empirical grounds for having confidence in the shift's beneficial value for those afflicted by mental distress. The hospitals of the 1930s were really little different from the

Victorian asylums. They were merely the same buildings but with a new treatment rhetoric. In the early 1930s treatments were crude and somatic – chloral hydrate, cold baths, laxatives and paraldehyde. Somatic interventions had clear advantages for staff, in terms of producing a sedated and controlled inpatient population. But there was no evidence that they led to permanent cure. The one exception in this regard was the treatment of syphilitic psychosis ('General Paralysis of the Insane') and even the prevalence and salience of this has been contested as being inflated (Prior, 1993).

The death rate in hospitals hardly inspired confidence either. Ramon (1985) reports that in the 1920s the number dying per year, around 9,000, was virtually the same as those being discharged, around 10,000. This pattern of high death rates in hospital continued in the 1930s, and beyond, indicating that the physical health of inpatients was very poor despite them living in a medical regime.

Other contributory factors to the mortality rate may have been the iatrogenic deaths from the new somatic treatments (insulin coma, psychosurgery and unmodified ECT) which were intoduced during the mid-1930s, and the wholsale removal of tonsils and teeth (Clare, 1976). Any treatment involving coma or general anaesthesia had and has a predictable mortality rate. In the case of unmodified ECT (electroconvulsive therapy), the absence of anaesthesia or muscle relaxants rendered the procedure even more dangerous to its recipients. As for hopes about a more benign and less restraining regime, in the mid-1930s around 90 per cent of patients were still detained in hospital compulsorily, this despite the new emphasis on the voluntary patient.

The question begged, then, is that if the 1930 legislation, and service organisation in its wake, engendered little inprovement for patients on the plight of Victorian lunatics, why did politicians hand over greater powers for the management of mental abnormality to hospital-based doctors? A number of factors can be suggested to account for this, many of which still apply today.

First, mental patients had no organised lobby and so interest in and accurate knowledge about this group was weak among parliamentarians. In the debates preceding the 1930 Act the views of patients were hardly mentioned.

Second, MPs would gain few votes by taking an interest in the topic of mental illness and even fewer if they supported patients' rights at the expense of increasing public fears and prejudices about madness.

Third, where interest was taken by MPs some of these were doctors and so were directly representing a medical interest. However, this was only a *post hoc* opportunity for influence on the 1926 Commission's report.

Fourth, the perplexity surrounding irrationality and its causes meant that on the one hand MPs were unclear, as was everyone else, about what to make of mental abnormality and, on the other, this ignorance induced a need to look somewhere for authoritative answers. Medicine obliged, given that it had developed a tradition going back to the mid nineteenth century of making confident, if dubious, claims about both the etiology and cure of mental illness (Scull, 1979). It provided answers, even if they were of questionable validity. This warded off the risk of a policy vacuum – a dread of politicians (see Ramon, 1985, p. 125).

Putting these factors together, it is likely that the origins of this inter-war policy formation are to be found in confusion, ignorance and unintended consequences from legislators, not in a medical conspiracy. After all, asylum doctors were out of favour and did not sit on the Macmillan Commission. Medical interests were certainly favoured in this period and doctors were not coy in offering assurances to politicians about their curative skills and capabilities; but they are probably best seen as beneficiaries of political confusion rather than as successful conspirators.

The 1940s: The Return of War and the Seeds of the NHS

Despite the return to hospital-based somatic psychiatry in the inter-war period, when hostilities with Nazi Germany looked inevitable, the authority of asylum doctors was once more rejected by central government. In 1938 the psychoanalyst and Director of the (outpatient) Tavistock Clinic, J.R. Rees, was appointed as Consulting Psychiatrist to the army along with two Clinic colleagues (Hargreaves and Wilson). In 1939 Rees was elevated to the rank of brigadier and made head of the Army psychiatric services.

Another indication that psychological rather than somatic methods were in favour under war conditions was the introduction of objectivist differential psychology in the tradition of Galton. Within this tradition, H.J. Eysenck, the incipient founder of post-war British clinical psychology, was appointed as a psychologist working with armed service patients at Mill Hill in 1942 (Pilgrim and Treacher, 1992). During the war years psychological methods of both currents (differential and psychodynamic psychology) were applied to armed service problems of selection, training, morale and rehabilitation from stress reactions

(Privy Council Office, 1947; Vernon and Parry, 1949; Morris, 1949). In the latter regard, at the outbreak of war, the Ministry of Defence was aware of the dangers of a repetition of the shellshock problem of the previous European conflict.

The pressures and demands of warfare stimulated a rush of quickly tried innovations from these psychologically orientated workers. As well as Eysenck developing the beginnings of psychometrics in clinical settings, small group psychotherapy and therapeutic community approaches were introduced (Main, 1957; Jones, 1952; Bion, 1958) which were to extend the range of therapeutic technologies available for both inpatient and outpatient work in later years.

This resurgence of psychological approaches to psychiatric work has to be placed in the context of the structural changes in health care organisation which the war facilitated. In 1929 the Local Government Act marked the end of the Poor Law. The workhouses and infirmaries were placed under the administration of public assistance committees. These were expected to secure accommodation for sick people, which facilitated the (uneven) development of local authority hospitals. These hospitals came under the jurisdiction, like other public health facilities, of the local medical officers of health. Thus there were the beginnings of public hospitals prior to 1939. Of course the asylums had been a special case in this regard since 1845.

The war itself encouraged a further nove towards a prototype of the NHS. The EMS (Emergency Medical Service) was set up, which co-ordinated the work of public and voluntary hospitals and had a regional strcuture. This also exposed the uneven standards of care, particularly in the smaller local hospitals. This range of quality was documented by a set of regional surveys of the nation's hospitals conducted by a voluntary body, the Nuffield Provincial Hospital Trust in conjuction with the Ministry of Health. Because of the existing regulations surrounding asylums (and mental deficiency hospitals), these were not surveyed by the Trust.

The Board of Control was conscious of shortcomings of the existing mental health services during the 1940s but saw little point in surveying and reviewing their organisation in the absence of reforms of the 1930 Act. According to the chair of the Board this would require a review on the scale of a Royal Commission, so a case was made for leaving the old asylums out of any new plans for a national hospital service (Webster, 1988, p. 327). However, in 1943 the Board conceded the need for a closer linkage with general hospitals, and mental health services were at the last minute included in the 1944 White Paper on health.

Analysts of this period (Ham, 1985; Webster, 1988) point to a confluence of mounting pressures for a publicly available, centrally administered and centrally financed medical service. (From its inception the NHS has been a misnomer. The main concerns of planners were about illness, hospitals and medicine rather than health.) A number of reports about hospital organisation prior to the formation of EMS and the Nuffield surveys had indicated concern about organisational incoherence and inefficiency, inadequate and inconsistent funding and variable standards (Dawson Committee, 1919; Royal Commission on National Health Insurance, 1926; Sankey Committee on Voluntary Hospitals, 1937; and the British Medical Association, 1930 and 1938). However, the BMA wanted a co-ordinated national service but based on an extension of the 1911 legislation on National Insurance rather than on general taxation.

Thus, although the British National Health Service is often cited as the main achievement of democratic socialism in 1948 (the 'jewel in the crown' of the post-war welfare state) it would seem that some version of an NHS was inevitable with these prefiguring reports and trends. This inevitability was reinforced by events in the war. In 1941 the coalition government had indicated the intention of setting up a national hospital service with the arrival of peace. In 1942 the Beveridge report on Social Insurance and Allied services included the recommendation of the formation of a national health service.

Notwithstanding the reluctance of the Board of Control about reorganising mental illness hospitals in line with the new NHS structure, after 1948 these hospitals were brought into line. However, in England and Wales this did not lead to a unified local administration of mental health services. Administration was divided between hospital authorities and local health authorities. In Scotland the old voluntary Royal Mental Asylums were brought under the control of Regional Health Boards. Generally local authorities would delegate control to autonomous visiting committees linked to particular hospitals.

The 1950s: Another Royal Commission

Throughout the first half of the twentieth century the number of beds in large institutions continued to rise, and peaked at around 150,000 in 1954, after which the numbers started on a downward spiral so that by

1992 this figure was reduced to 50,000. It is a common error to associate the 1950s with the so-called 'pharmacological revolution'. This account given by some social policy analysts (e.g. Jones, 1988; Martin, 1985) suggests that the beginnings of post-war de-institutionalisation took place because of the technical breakthrough of neuroleptic medication. The myth is also repeated in the report of the House of Commons Social Services Committee in 1985 (see Goodwin, 1992, p. 17).

There is no evidence for this causal link. Neuroleptics were introduced in 1954 but the patterns surrounding discharge and inpatient levels had already been set in prior years. Goodwin (1992) and Scull (1977) review the evidence about the impact of neuroleptics and conclude that although the drugs can control florid symptoms in some psychotic patients, they cannot explain changes in discharge policies implicating wider ranges of psychiatric patients with different symptomatology and diagnoses, who were not in receipt of neuroleptics. Nor can they explain why the de-institutionalisation took place of other groups (elderly and mentally handicapped patients). At that time these were not seen as prime candidates for neuroleptic treatment although later psychiatrists developed an enthusiasm for using the drugs on them. Also, whilst bed numbers were dropping in British hospitals before 1954 and continued after, in some other European countries bed numbers actually *increased* after the drugs were introduced.

If the neuroleptics did not actually stimulate deinstitutionalisation and the 'pharmacological revolution' was a myth, why did British asylums start to run down by the end of the 1950s? One explanation given within a Marxian framework is that the cost of institutional care became too great for a publicly funded welfare system to accommodate within a capitalist economy. This 'fiscal crisis of the state' explanation (Scull, 1977) does not fit the 1950s because such an economic crisis was not salient at that point of post-war reconstruction. Spending on hospital services actually increased during this period. Also this is a crude economistic explanation, which is too global. It cannot account for cross-national differences within international capitalism, nor for the differential policies for groups within nations.

By 1956, two years after the introduction of neuroleptics and at a point when Scull claimed fiscal constraints applied, there were 2,000 more beds in use than in 1952 and 1,000 more psychiatric nurses and 77 more consultant psychiatrists employed. However, then, and even a year earlier, there were signs that the government was recognising the problem of basing a mental health policy solely on traditional hospital-based psychiatry (Ministry of Health, 1955, 1956). As Goodwin (1992) points out, the middle of the decade was rife with conflicting messages from government. Hospitals were both supported and undermined at the same time.

In anticipation of elements of the 1957 Royal Commission and of the 1962 Hospital Plan, in 1956 the Chief Medical Officer argued that the future of services should emphasise community siting, an expansion of general hospital work and an upgrading of existing mental hospital facilities. It was not likely that there would be such an expansion on all three fronts – until then only the mental hospitals were resourced in the main. But what is significant is that the three elements were being mooted at all. They reflect changes in ideological forces not economic factors. Why were community care and general hospitals returning from the late 1920s as features of a debate about mental health? They surely must suggest that doubts were evident about a monolithic mental health policy being centred on the old asylum system. In other words, whatever fiscal concerns there were about the management of non-productive deviance by running down institutions, there were also pressures, and sincere aspirations, to improve the care of people with mental health difficulties. Wider cultural factors also contributed to the sounding of the death-knell of the old mental illness hospitals. After the Second World War, the image of the Nazi concentration camp haunted Western Europe.

In this context of mid-1950s contradictions, the Percy Commission was launched. This Royal Commission began in 1954 and reported in 1957. The tension, dating back to the nineteenth century, between legal and medical power was evident in its deliberations. The central issue here was the residue of certification from the 1890 Lunacy Act in the extant 1930 Mental Treatment Act. Legalists like the Magistrates Association and the Justices Clerks Association emphasised to the Commission that certification should remain and that the non-medical court forum was still appropriate to make judgments about sanity and insanity. This position was also supported by the National Association of Local Government Health and Welfare officers. However, whilst the Commission did not reject the need for compulsion, it went further than the 1930 Act in recommending that judgments about it should be left to clinical professionals. This excluded the final check on medical power by the courts, at least as far as civil or non-offender patients were concerned.

As with the 1926 Commission and the 1983 Mental Health Act, the 1957 Report accepted very uncritically the formula of medicalising complex dilemmas about responding to madness and respecting civil liberties. This formula accepted that:

1. Cases of mental illness were validly and reliably identified by psychiatrists.
2. The identification of mental illness automatically implied a *need* for treatment.
3. The obligation to treat was so compelling that individual loss of liberty was warranted.
4. Psychiatric treatment was effective.
5. The integrity of medical practitioners was beyond doubt.

As Bean (1980, p. 19) notes, the Commission operated a Benthamite utilitarianism in this regard: a tradeoff between the assumed benefits of treatment against a necessary loss of liberty. This formula also marked a shift in discourse about freedom. The older legally defined form referred to the freedom of citizens from unlawful restraint. The new medical discourse entailed the lawful freedom of professionals to treat disease – even if this required the use of force against patients. Albeit using a tortuous logic, the use of force could be increasingly justified by doctors and their supporters as a means of ensuring the right of all psychiatric patients to be treated, and as facilitating the freedom of patients as citizens once their illness was cured or their self-injurious actions restrained.

One of the reasons why psychiatric legislation remains so controversial is that all five of the assumptions above are contestable and the shift from patient liberty to the medical right to treat remains disconcerting to many. However, the post-war legislation enacted in 1959 and 1983 by Conservative governments, but not challenged substantively by their parliamentary opponents, suggests that therapeutic law, with all its dubious premises, is accepted by politicians in principle.

Apart from a treatment emphasis, the 1957 Commission also had a wider programmatic focus, as this paragraph from the Report indicates:

There is increasing medical emphasis on forms of treatment and training and social services which can be given without bringing patients into hospital as inpatients, or which make it possible to discharge them from hospital sooner than was usual in the past. It is now generally considered in the best interests of the patients who are fit to live in the community that they should not be in large mental institutions such as the present mental and mental deficiency hospitals. Nor is it the proper function of the hospital authority to provide residential accommodation for patients who do not require hospital or specialist services. . . The local authority should be responsible for preventative services and for all types of community care for

patients who do not require in-patient hospital services or who have
had a period of treatment or training in hospital and are ready to
return to the community.

The 1957 Report led on to legislation passed in 1959 which:

• emphasised medical treatment
• weakened remaining legal checks on medical discretion
• but also began to point to the demise of the Victorian asylum.

The 1960s: A New Hospital Plan

It is not clear, even with this distance of time, whether the 1959 Mental Health Act was to be a salient factor in explaining one motif of the
1960s and 1970s – a series of hospital scandals. Possibly it was a
background factor. The state had effectively handed over the management of mental abnormality lock, stock and barrel to a medically managed regime and had washed its hands of any independent responsibility
for the fate of individual patients. These scandals, which will be touched
on again below, occurred in long-stay and old asylums. The latter were
the scornful target of Enoch Powell the Minister of Health, who in
1962 announced his Hospital Plan, which was to have as much of an
influence on psychiatric services as the 1959 Act.

    Powell laid out his ideas for the Plan in the previous year at the
Annual Conference of the National Association of Mental Health (now
MIND). He viewed the Victorian asylums as outdated for the functions of modern psychiatric treatment and described them thus: 'There
they stand, isolated, majestic, imperious, brooded over by the giant
water tower and chimney combined, rising unmistakable and daunting
out of the countryside.' However, once again the assumption held was
that psychiatric treatment was effective – a sentiment repeatedly expressed by politicians sporadically since the beginning of the twentieth century. The intention was to phase out the old asylums and so
only minimal finance was given for their upgrading (the third element
proposed in 1956 by the Chief Medical Officer). Asylum beds were
running down and projected to be halved by the mid-1970s. A second
major feature of the Plan was the combined use of community facilities and general hospital wards. The 1959 Act had a new clause which
permitted patients to be admitted to any hospital facility, not just a
mental hospital. This opened up the possibility of acute psychiatric

admissions being diverted to general hospital units. A pincer policy of new acute units in general hospitals plus decanting chronic patients into community residential facilities would eventually make the old asylums empty and thus redundant.

Scull's (1977) cost-cutting thesis is persuasive in relation to this episode of policy formation. Powell and his Conservative government were keen to minimise public expenditure, and the run-down of the old expensive hospitals was a good opportunity to make fiscal savings. The need for run-down would increase over time with the progressive reduction in the cost-effectiveness of the asylums as patient numbers declined, since core maintenance costs would be the same independent of bed occupancy. Suspicion about Powell's commitment to a positive vision of a post-asylum world was reinforced by his emphasis on the short-term role of the district general hospital (DGH) units but with little flesh for the bones of his predicted community facilities. Indeed, when eventually he produced in 1963 his follow-up plan *(Health and Welfare: The Development of Community Care)* this lacked the clarity and detail of the Hospital Plan. While most remember Powell for his Hospital Plan the follow-up document on community care is scarcely recalled.

If the 1959 Act had given the green light to medical power in the area of decision-making about patients, the 1962 Hospital Plan offered a different type of signal for psychiatry to increase its role in DGH units. These provided the perfect organisational opportunity to abandon the Dickensian image of psychiatry and move into the same organisational framework as other medical specialities. Psychiatry was, and arguably still is, the lowest-status medical branch. What ensued was a transfer of asylum theory and practice to DGH units and no new evidence of staff involvement with the communities of the patients they admitted (Baruch and Treacher, 1978).

What Powell's uneven policy prompt seemed to do was encourage a process of re-institutionalisation, from old to new hospitals, not community care. Whilst the rhetoric of community care was strongly present after 1962, no asylum was closed for many years. Hospital admissions increased during this period even though total inpatient numbers continued to reduce. The policy momentum for hospital run-down really only gathered pace in the subsequent decade.

The 1970s: The End of the Victorian Asylum?

The Victorian asylums were in crisis by 1970. A number of factors contributed to this. Inpatient numbers continued to drop. Central government was reluctant to finance large expensive hospitals which were due to be phased out. Psychiatrists were starting to enjoy the status advantages of new facilities in DGH units. Social critics and dissident clinicians, together dubbed 'anti-psychiatry' (Goffman, 1961; Laing, 1967; Szasz, 1963; Cooper, 1968), were attacking the dehumanisation of institutional psychiatry. Even social psychiatrists, who, in principle, accepted the legitimacy of psychiatric theory and practice, pointed to the anti-therapeutic impact of institutional life (Wing and Freudenberg 1961; Brown and Wing, 1962). To compound this picture, the worst fears of these critics were being demonstrated by official inquiries into neglect and mistreatment in disparate hospitals.

Martin (1985) documents this series of hospital scandals. The fact that they occurred in both mental handicap and mental illness hospitals suggests that the responsible factors for a failure of care were organisational and not linked to patient variables. The main source of personal degradation for patients was simply institutional life itself. At this point the organisational *raison d'être* of the old hospitals is worth restating – they existed to segregate burdensome or threatening deviance.

The sensitivities of inmates were always a secondary (and sometimes merely rhetorical) consideration. The complacency of policy-makers at this time about what was going on in the asylums is indicated by the cessation of the monitoring of activity in mental illness hospitals between 1959 and 1965. Data collection recommenced just before the public exposure of the string of hospital scandals (Davidge *et al.*, 1993).

It is not surprising, then, that large hospitals led to what Martin describes as 'the corruption of care'. Places ostensibly designed to care for people ended up betraying and mistreating them. The scandal hospitals, Martin reviews, demonstrate this phenomenon repeatedly. The common features of the places explain this outcome – they were closed systems unchecked by external corrective feedback. Life in the old 'bins' was isolated in the following ways:

1. Geographical – the hospitals were away from main populations.
2. Ward – individual wards became separate 'feifdoms'.
3. Personal – staff alone or in very small numbers would be left in charge of difficult-to-manage or unrewarding patients.
4. Consultant – responsible medical staff would visit infrequently.

5. Intellectual – staff would be out of touch with innovations elsewhere and cut off from new training.
6. Privacy – this was a prerequisite for abuse; patients visited regularly by relatives were rarely the focus of the inquiries.

The response of the government to this crisis in the old hospitals system was to establish visiting teams from the Hospitals (now 'Health') Advisory Service (HAS) which was created in 1969. Members of visiting teams were drawn from a multi-disciplinary mental health background and therefore had been, or were, involved in directly providing services themselves. Reports of these visits acted in a limited way to bring about improvements in the quality of care by highlighting resourcing and staffing problems and exposing institutionalised staff to scrutiny informed by a broader set of norms. Staff and management were forced to account for practices and conditions within the hospitals in which they worked. The HAS teams, however, suffered from the same deficiencies as previous inspectorates. They were unable to enforce any change and were limited to making recommendations with no direct access to resources. Nonetheless, it is likely that the existence of the reports of these visits, which highlighted poor physical amenities and staff practices, contributed to the view that the old asylums had outlived their utility and needed to be replaced as a matter of urgency.

The HAS reports certainly carried some weight in drawing the attention of government departments to the problems of organising and managing mental illness hospitals. The Nodder Report (DHSS, 1980b) was the outcome of the considerations of a DHSS-initiated working group, set up in order to examine these highlighted problems. The working group recommended the establishment of clearly defined management structures for mental health services, including the creation of district psychiatric services management teams and hospital management teams to provide leadership in the development of local services. The report also emphasised the need for clear objectives, standards and targets to be set, against which progress could be measured. Annual progress reports were another recommendation. Nodder underlined the importance of joint planning with local authorities and, in a departure from previous policy statements, stressed the desirability of the involvement of community-based groups and organisations, such as the Community Health Councils and voluntary organisations.

This may explain why there was a post-war sensitivity to the degradation risked in closed institutions. Given the other professional, policy and economic factors stacked against the old hospitals, their days were clearly numbered. However, whilst it was one thing in political and professional circles to condemn the degradation of the old hospitals, it was another thing to be able to claim that their closure automatically marked progress. Three difficulties were already apparent in this regard, which remain important agendas today and will be explored in later chapters: clinical professionals showed no sign of embracing community-sited interventions; a gross imbalance of resourcing had emerged between hospital and community facilities; and there were fiscal pressures on the British government to reduce even further its commitment to public spending. Labour politicians of the 1970s were clearly uncomfortable, but also impotent, about this hospital-centred legacy. Busfield (1986, p. 348) here quotes the 1975 White Paper *Better Services for the Mentally Ill* issued by Barbara Castle, the Minister for Social Services in the Labour government:

> although it is sixteen years since the Mental Health Act of 1959 gave legislative recognition to the importance of community care, supportive services in a non-medical, non-hospital setting are still a comparative rarity. In 1973–4 nearly £300 million was spent on hospital services for the mentally ill; by comparison just over £15 million was spent on personal social services of which some £6.5 was on day and residential facilities. In March 1974, 31 local authorities, as then constituted, had no residential accommodation for the mentally ill, and 63 no day facilities.

Such a gross imbalance between health and social services shows the problems which existed about constructing a genuine policy of community care – even if it were sincerely desired by politicians. This difficulty was compounded by the difficulties affecting Western capitalism in the wake of the oil crisis. (In 1973 OPEC increased the price of oil fivefold.) Britain, under a Labour government, was obliged to go to the International Monetary Fund and ask for help with its fiscal problems. The IMF indeed offered a rescue package but with certain strings attached. One of these was a commitment to reduce public spending. Although the monetarist policies of the Thatcher years after 1979 might imply that public sector cuts were instigated by 1980s Tory ideology, in fact it was a Labour government of the 1970s which was obliged to impose the first major NHS cuts.

It is in this decade, not the 1950s, that Scull's cost-cutting thesis, to explain a policy of hospital run-down, finds its full time. Even then it gives undue emphasis to the single factor of economics. Within the economic constraints of the time, pressures and aspirations were still evident about improving services. Hostility towards the old hospitals in many quarters was real, as were aspirations to give 'the mentally ill' a better deal. Nonetheless, if we put together the bias towards the funding of hospitals at the expense of community facilities alongside the wider constraint on public spending, then community care was a vulnerable policy. Whilst the prospect of closing the old asylum and re-siting acute psychiatric care in new DGH units was good, the prospect of a well-resourced community service for the person with long-term mental health problems was not.

Gendered Mental Health Work Revisited

At the end of Chapter 3 we noted the discrepancy between Showalter (1985) and Busfield (1994) about gender and the asylum. At the beginning of this chapter we also noted that the Great War brought with it new forms of gendered concern – the psychosomatic toll of female workers and the shellshock suffered by returning male soldiers. By the final quarter of the twentieth century, women were consistently over-represented in psychiatric statistics. However, as with Busfield's caution about the gendered nature of Victorian psychiatry being complex and implicating men as well as women patients, so too with more recent times. Elsewhere (Pilgrim and Rogers, 1993a, ch. 2) we have argued that the over-representation of women in the mental health system is largely accounted for by the expansion during this century in the ambit of mental health work to include outpatient and primary care interventions. This has been associated with the greater diagnosis of neurotic conditions, especially depression, in women, only part of which is referred on to inpatient facilities. When we look at the diagnosis of schizophrenia in inpatient settings gender differences are not apparent but women are over-represented there because of higher rates of depression. As with Busfield's point about asylum statistics, another continuing factor which sustains gender differences is the greater average life expectancy of women. This has meant that mental health problems in old age during this century (including depression and dementia) have been more prevalent in women.

An implication of these gender differences is that whilst men remain under-represented, overall, in psychiatric statistics, they are *over-represented* in certain settings like secure provision, which entail more coercive regimes. Moreover, whilst from the mid-1960s to the present day the trend has been for a greater throughput of both male and female patients to open psychiatric facilities (i.e. an increase in the frequency of admission and discharge), the increase in female admissions has been less than for men. This has led to a trend in which the over-representation of women in psychiatric settings is declining. For example, in 1980 the ratio of female to male admissions was 1.4 to 1. By 1986 this had dropped to 1.28 to 1 and 1.25 to 1 by 1989 (DH, 1989; 1992).

However, in contrast to this shift in hospital admissions towards men, the higher prevalence of female mental health problems in the community, in the context of poorly developed community care, has meant that services have not been developed to meet women's needs, especially in relation to the stresses involved in the caring role (Cobb and Wallcraft, 1989). Indeed, community care may be construed as a double disadvantage for women. They have had poorly developed dedicated services *and* they now carry the main burden of unpaid care for others. We will return to the question of gender again, but in relation to the mental health workforce, in Chapter 6. We will explore more about recent developments in mental health services in the next chapter.

Conclusion

By the late 1970s the new service pattern becoming discernible was one of revolving-door patients going in and out of acute psychiatric units but being backed up by sparse and unevenly distributed social service facilities. The DGH unit was to mark a successful outcome of the Powell project of 1962. However, an important caveat to this conclusion is that the new units became increasingly stretched over time, as bed numbers in the old hospitals dropped and community facilities did not keep pace with these changes. Powell's weaker plan in 1963, when inherited by a Labour government in financial crisis, meant that services in the 1980s bore the imprint of hospital-centred practice, clothed in an ill-fitting community care theory. We will now turn to developments after 1979 to examine the fate of these services.

5

After 1979

Introduction

At the time of writing, the United Kingdom has experienced an unbroken period of single party rule since 1979. Successive Conservative administrations since then have radically pruned and restructured
the public sector. Before 1979 there was a welfare state; now there is
a 'mixed economy of welfare', which contains an engineered blend of
public, private and voluntary services. However, during the 1970s a
Labour administration had struggled with debt problems amplified by
the OPEC oil crisis in 1973 and had to approach the International
Monetary Fund for a loan. A condition of this arrangement was that
public spending had to be brought under control. And so a Labour
government began a period of welfare cuts even before Thatcher came
to power in 1979. Offe (1984) has noted that the crisis of the British
welfare state can be viewed as endemic to any capitalist country which
attempts to solve its social problems by the use of public finance.

These financial considerations put pressure on expensive institutions
like the Victorian asylum system, but the latter had in any case been
losing their credibility since the mid-1960s. Thus the run-down of the
old asylums gained momentum for both economic and ideological reasons.
Indeed, whilst economic factors were influential, it is worth noting
that asylum run-down, and the absence of new large institutions being
commissioned, had become a global trend, independent of particular
nation-state economic conditions. Sometimes a reaction against the large
hospital and for new community developments was stronger in some
capitalist countries during the 1960s and 1970s (e.g. the US and Italy)
than in others (e.g. Spain and Japan). What was clear though was that
the overall trend was one of what has been variously called the 'de-
segregation', 'de-institutionalisation' or 'decarceration' of those diagnosed as being mentally ill.

Britain during the 1980s followed this global trend but pursued de-segregation within a wider framework of Conservative social policy. Essentially the latter abandoned versions of Keynesian compromise in fiscal policies and opted increasingly for a mixture of privatisation and marketisation. That is, what were previously publicly provided services were now put out to tender and contracted in. At first, large public bureaucracies, like the NHS, were only tinkered with – for example, the privatisation of hospital cleaning services. Marketisation was the other government strategy applied later in the 1980s – the application of an internal market (or 'quasi-markets') to the NHS.

What privatisation and marketisation had in common was the ideological assumption that market mechanisms would provide the most cost-effective or efficient method for limiting the fiscal burdens that a capitalist economy both created and had to tolerate. These burdens result from non-productivity, i.e. those groups of people existing outside the productive process. These include children, old people, those mentally or physically inefficient for work purposes, the short-term sick and the long-term disabled, and those who are able but simply not required. It is little surprising, therefore, that these groups became particular targets for government reform during the 1980s.

A third thread (in addition to privatisation and marketisation) which can be identified as running through government policy in the 1980s was managerialism. The strong presence of this trend (the NHS is now managed not merely administered) itself marks a contradiction. The main ideological thrust of Thatcherism was a claim of 'rolling back the state' and letting a combination of market forces and individual choices and initiatives (like charitable actions) determine the outcome and organisation of civil life. Thus, managerialism was not a necessary consequence of monetarism. Indeed, it indicated a bureaucratic, not a market, strategy to improve efficiency in the public sector.

Managerialism has reflected a political compromise for Conservative governments fearful of the electoral consequences of full-blooded privatisation of the NHS. If an internal market could be effected and managers installed, as in private companies, then the public sector could be run as a business. Making managers into purchasers of services pushed this logic even further. Compared to the more radical New Right thinkers in the US (e.g. Spicker, 1993), Thatcher offered a substantial compromise with welfare. The former have sought to expunge 'welfare paternalism' from their society. Thatcher was a politician not an armchair ideologue and so she had to confirm in practice what neo-Marxian analysts had already predicted – that capitalism could not live comfortably with the welfare state but ultimately it could not live without it either.

Mental Health Services in the 1980s

The sketch of wider changes in the British welfare state provides many hints to the fate of mental health services in the 1980s. However, some of these changes cannot simply be reduced directly to the triple impact of privatisation, marketisation and managerialism and one of its main consequences, consumerism. In addition to the these factors, there were policy processes which had been set in motion earlier. For example, in the last chapter the consensus about de-institutionalisation can be noted. With the crisis about the old asylums in mind, let us now consider changes in mental health policy in the 1980s under a series of headings which respond to the following four questions:

- Why were the old hospitals vulnerable to closure?
- Why, though, did a reliance on inpatient work continue?
- What was the impact of a restructured welfare state?
- What was the impact of legislative changes in the 1980s?

The rest of this chapter will deal with these questions.

1   Explanations for Hospital Run-Down

Explanations for the trend of large hospital run-down and closure have been summarised well by Busfield (1986). She points to three main models:

- The pharmacological revolution
- Economic determinism
- A shift to acute problems

We will augment this comparison of three models with a fourth:

- A shift in psychiatric discourse

Figure 5.1 sketches the assumptions of the model which suggests that hospital run-down occurred because of the successful use by

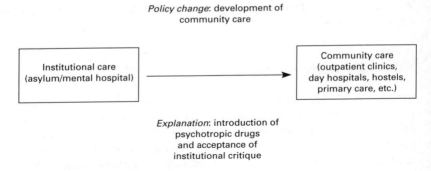

FIGURE 5.1   *The pharmacological revolution*

Source: Busfield 1986.

psychiatrists of major tranquillisers from the late 1950s onwards.

This model is problematic for a number of reasons. A drop in numbers in psychiatric hospitals in Britain actually began *before* the introduction of the drugs. Additionally hospital run-down emerged as a policy for a wide range of patient groups who did not receive the drugs (e.g. people with learning difficulties, elderly people). Also, the rate of hospital run-down did not accelerate after the drugs' introduction.

A final problem with the pharmacological explanation is that drugs are not always effective and discharged groups of psychiatric patients include those who are resistant to their symptom reduction impact. We can only speculate that such a weak explanatory model emerged and was maintained because it suited the interests of the psychiatric profession to emphasise the purported 'revolutionary' impact of major tranquillisers.

Figure 5.2 emphasises economic rather than pharmacological determinism. It has been mainly advocated by Scull (1977) who argues that after the Second World War governments increasingly struggled to contain the fiscal pressures of the welfare state.

Given that institutional care or segregative control was expensive, the large hospitals could be eliminated to save money. Scull's model is not only economistic in its explanation but cynical and depressing in its political conclusion. He contends that the horrors of the asylum have simply been replaced by ones of a different type, placing patients between a rock and a hard place:

less and less well with the old large institution. We have argued elsewhere (Pilgrim and Rogers, 1994) that these newer sociological accounts, which shift our attention away from government policy and
towards a new psychiatric eclecticism, have been useful. They are not
limited to the biological and hospital focus of, say, Scull's work. However,
as we argue recurrently in this book, services may not be limited to
this focus but they are *dominated* by it.

Both Busfield's model and that described by Rose and by Prior indicate an important differentiation of policy in the 1980s – a separation of acute and chronic services. Ramon (1985) pointed out that at
the time of writing there had not been the full closure of a single
Victorian asylum in Britain. However, because, in the period after that,
old hospitals were indeed run down and closed, the configuration of
mental health services included:

1. The remaining unclosed large hospitals, which were often in poor
   repair and containing anxious or demoralised staff (who were themselves often institutionalised).
2. Newer acute inpatient services, which varied from purpose-built units
   in new general hospitals to wards of older general hospitals designated for psychiatric purposes.
3. A mixture of community residential facilities (hostels, group homes,
   private bedsits and other tenancies, nursing homes).
4. Community mental health centres and day centres run by both the
   NHS and social service departments.
5. Regional secure units.
6. The special hospitals.

Such a mixed picture of provision demonstrates that the term 'de-
institutionalisation' fails to accurately capture what was (and still is)
happening. Services were still dominated by forms of hospital organisation and so it is more appropriate to think of a process of *re-institutionalisation*, rather than full-scale and proper de-institutionalisation.

2 The Inertia of Hospital Dominance

On the face of things the last decade has witnessed a decline in the
pre-eminent position of the hospital in Britain, as in most other countries. Thirty-five 'water tower' hospitals closed between 1980 and 1990.
Additionally, the number of patients in large hospitals also halved from

an average of 468 patients per hospital in 1986 to 223 per hospital in 1993 (Davidge *et al.*, 1993). However, most of this activity has oc- curred since the 1990s – over half of these hospital closures occurred in the four years prior to 1993.

Notwithstanding the diversification of provision away from large NHS hospitals to a wider range of provision, including local auth- orities, and the voluntary and private sectors, the shift of emphasis in psychiatric services was not predominantly from the old asylums to community facilities but from old to new hospitals. This is not say that community facilities failed to expand during the 1980s – it is simplistic to argue (as some critics did at the time) that community care was non-existent. It is, however, fair comment that the vision of community care, implied in the 1930 Mental Treatment Act and advo- cated by the Royal Commission of 1957 and in the Powell legislation in 1963, was still clouded throughout the 1980s by the inertia of hos- pital dominance. The closure plans for the remaining 89 hospitals open in 1993 shows the reluctance to make a clean break with the old hos- pital sites even with the accelerated rate of run-down evident at the beginning of the 1990s. A recent survey (Davidge *et al.*, 1993) indi- cated that in less than a quarter are there plans for the closure and disposal of the whole hospital site. The intention, in over half of the cases, is to close the main building but retain some for mental health units on site.

It will be remembered from the last chapter that the Hospital Plan of 1962 had more of an impact than the Community Care Plan a year later. It was clear from the early 1960s onwards that planners and medical lobbyists in each locality were inclined to reform and adapt *hospital* facilities rather than innovate around community support services for home-based patients.

Hospital dominance was also evident in the way in which day care was offered to patients. For example, only 9,000 new day places be- came available between 1975 and 1985 and these were mainly on hos- pital sites (Audit Commission, 1986). By the late 1980s, 85 per cent of government funding of mental health facilities was spent on hos- pital services (Sayce, 1989). By 1987 there were 49 CMHCs (Com- munity Mental Health Centres) in existence with 44 planned. Whilst the stock of CMHCs expanded rapidly, because they started from a low base their absolute numbers and levels of funding remained small compared to psychiatric inpatient facilities by the late 1980s.

Tomlinson (1991) describes how the sources of this hospital focus, rather than community focus, were formalised by the DHSS in 1968 by them commissioning a development project in Worcester to demonstrate how a large asylum could be replaced systematically by other facilities. Powick Asylum was to be phased out and replaced by district general hospital (DGH) and hostel facilities at Worcester and Kidderminster, with day facilities in Malvern and Evesham.

The Powick run-down programme encountered problems that were to reappear recurrently during the late 1980s in other places: the tendency to leave the most difficult chronic patients until last as a discharge priority; staff morale problems in a declining institution; and the deterioration in the fabric of buildings that were to be shut. Powick closed eventually in 1989. A positive finding from research on the Worcester project was that the day facilities opened to support the closure programme were endorsed by service users in boosting confidence and warding off loneliness. Later research on users' views of services also suggested that non-hospital services are highly valued (Rogers *et al.*, 1993).

The assumptions behind the Worcester development project reflected deep-seated difficulties about local and national politicians being able to think beyond the bricks and mortar of hospitals. The fact that there was such a strong rhetoric from Labour and Conservative government sources over a twenty-year period about community care only highlights this picture. The selective attention to the legislation in the early 1960s (spotlighting the DGH and marginalising the need for non-hospital facilities) was evident in the mindset of planners in both the 1970s and 1980s. Part of this was probably a function of the political reliance on professional advice. As key stakeholders psychiatrists are not only clinicians who lobby government via their Royal College (which was set up in 1971), they also dominate the civil service roles in the DoH which develop mental health policy and advise ministers.

Another factor which may have induced inertia about hospital dominance is the caution and conservatism from British politicians about the containment of deviance. The appeal of segregation to politicians is obvious – people who are disruptive, difficult or frightening can be dealt with in hospitals. The regime separates these people from those around them who are discomforted by their presence. The non-mad are in the majority and the majority cast votes in elections. The circle that politicians have to try and square is that segregation is both wanted and distrusted by the general public. Madness in the street and the home can be swept into hospital but what if this strategy is both ineffective and offensive in its response? It is not an uncommon experience for ordinary citizens to want madness removed from their presence whilst fearing for their own arbitrary incarceration. The 1983 Mental Act, to be discussed below, responded to this contradictory demand.

3   Health and Social Services in Turbulence

Whilst the bias towards hospital services can be seen as a function of cultural inertia in Britain during the 1970s and 1980s, a wider concerted restructuring was to some extent to override these forces from the past. In doing so a number of contradictions were set up and problems posed for a variety of stakeholders. Politicians had to face awkward questions about the non-medical functions which the old hospitals had served, such as social control and that of *accommodating* one group of people outside of the productive process. By unleashing consumerism, via marketisation, the government offered hope to people whose views were previously ignored by service providers – psychiatric patients.

Psychiatrists and other mental health professionals were to find themselves victims of a wider attack by government on professionals. This genuinely new event was ushered in by Thatcher. Professional elites, like doctors and lawyers, are traditionally conservative groups (with a small and large 'c'). And yet throughout the 1980s the Conservative government systematically challenged or attacked the power of these elites. This was an ideological symptom of undermining the power of welfare 'bureau professionals' but it also reflected a more general attack on the authority of professionals. This authority had previously signified a form of power which was autonomous from the state. Despite the rhetoric of 'rolling back the state', Thatcherism was set upon reining in and controlling forms of authority which had been outside of central government.

During this period local government was similarly undermined and dominated from the centre. Strict limits on local spending were instituted and the traditional powers of local education and health authorities reduced. By the end of the decade the 1990 NHS and Community Care Act (see below) was to impose what was labelled as a 'poisoned chalice'. Local authorities were to be made responsible for community care but were not given autonomous powers or guaranteed finance for the task. In addition, throughout the 1980s, public services were converted systematically into business-type organisations.

A centrally driven and controlled policy of managerialism was a self-fulfilling prophecy from government in the early 1980s. If a business-man is given the task of reviewing the efficiency of public organisa-tions he will inevitably offer business solutions in response. Such was the case with the first Griffiths Report.

4   A New Legislative Framework

After 1979 there were two major pieces of legislation relevant to the focus of this book. The first of these was the 1983 Mental Health Act, and the second the 1990 NHS and Community Care Act. In the case of the 1983 Act, this has to be seen as part of a review process, which preceded the wider welfare restructuring imposed by Thatcherism. Con-sequently, it was part of a pattern recurring in Britain every twenty or thirty years this century – the Acts of 1930 and 1959 and their prior Royal Commissions. Such reviews have considered very similar issues:

- How is mental disorder to be defined?
- Who should have the power and responsibility to respond to mental disorder?
- What should be the balance between the right to be left alone and the right to be treated, especially when the latter is recognised by others by not by the mentally disordered themselves?
- Which aspects of citizenship should be legally protected for men-tally disordered people?
- Under what circumstances should a person be removed forcibly to a psychiatric facility and what rules should govern their detention and discharge?

Given the recurrent nature of these types of questions, which were considered in the review leading up to the 1983 legislation, the Act was a separate development from the wider social and health policy changes that were being effected after 1979. The impact of the Act was small in comparison with these other events. An extract from the Parliamentary Debate prior to the introduction of the Act summarises the purpose of the act:

that except in particular circumstances people should not be admitted to detention for treatment in hospital if their condition is not treatable; the provision of much more frequent access to mental health review tribunals; the more stringent regulations of the use of treatment without the consent of the patient; the institution of a special health authority, with particular responsibility to oversee the powers to detain and treat patients under the Act; the institution of interim hospital orders, the power to remand to hospital for assessment; and I think the limitations of the powers of a guardian to apply only to people over 16 years of age. (Lord Elton, *Parliamentary Debates*, 1.12.81: 935).

The Act did not endeavor to introduce new principles but to alter those of the 1959 Act and to improve administration (Bean, 1986). Its main achievement seems to be the formal codification of existing professional roles and practice in relation to the compulsory detention of patients (e.g. the requirement for social workers to interview in a suitable manner). It had little or no direct relevance for informally detained patients but it did introduce some new protections for those detained forcibly ('formal patients'). This included the right to lay or legal advocacy at Mental Health Review Tribunals, which could be applied for under the legal aid scheme, and the delegation of powers of discharge for patients who, under the 1959 legislation, could only be released by the Home Secretary.

Voting rights were introduced for informal patients only. Even these were nearly absent from the legislation. A Labour amendment was put forward for the preceding 1982 Mental Health (Amendment) Act 1982 to ensure the voting rights of all patients. Some Conservative MPs with mental hospitals in their constituencies wanted no voting rights for patients at all, but the government conceded a compromise, which remained highly discriminatory. Detained patients are not allowed a vote and informal patients can only vote if they complete an application without assistance. This subjects them to a literacy test which non-patients do not have to encounter at an election. In other respects the Act introduced new restrictions on patients' liberties. For example, under Section 5, registered mental nurses were given 'holding' powers to forcibly detain 'informal' patients in lieu of an assessment for compulsory admission.

The essential weakness of the 1983 Act was that it was overly concerned with individual rights. It had no direct implications for service organisation and the collective rights of patients. However, these very weaknesses meant that *the failure* of some aspects of the Act highlighted expectations of good care. For example, Section 117 for the first time raised the question about the duty of aftercare for discharged patients. Because this Section exists, it has allowed critics of inadequate services to draw attention to failed expectations about community care. A second unintended consequence for services has been the weakness of the Mental Health Act Commission (MHAC), the main structural innovation of the 1983 Act, in preventing the emergence of scandals and ridding the mental health system of bad practice.

The MHAC is a special (regionalised) health authority, which has a duty to check on the proper application of formal sections (detained patients). This watchdog role is limited to investigating individual complaints and so offers no solution to systemic difficulties. The first ten years of the MHAC has witnessed a public acknowledgment of its failure to deal with neglect and brutality, whilst, arguably, raising the expectation that civil liberties were now to be protected by such a statutory body. The most pointed example of MHAC failure was offered by the Blom-Cooper team investigating complaints of mistreatment at Ashworth Hospitals (DH, 1992). The three-person team included both the Chair and the Vice Chair of the national MHAC and they conceded that the Commission had failed where investigative journalists (the *Cutting Edge* programme on Channel 4) had succeeded in exposing bad practice. Nothing had changed since 1980, when another TV documentary had exposed brutality at Rampton Special Hospital. It seemed that with or without an MHAC, mistreatment was happening in closed isolated hospitals and a watchdog could not even be relied on to detect such events.

When introducing an early analysis of the 1983 legislation, Bean described the new Mental Health Act as:

> part of a change worldwide which seeks to reduce the paternalism of an earlier age, to identify the rights of the individual patient, and to reduce (albeit marginally) the power and prestige of the psychiatric experts. Of course not everyone would welcome such changes but, in my view, they represent something of an advance, if only because the legislation produces doubts where once there was certainty, and shows that there are other ways forward even if those ways sometimes appear unclear. (Bean, 1986, p. 14)

However, looking back from today's perspective, we would conclude that the 1983 Act has been flimsy in its impact on service improvements. Evidence of the mistreatment of patients at the hands of psychiatric professionals has continued, and the legalistic and individualistic nature of the Act has been inadequate in the face of wider structural changes in health and social services. It has not reduced the rate of compulsory admissions, and it has raised, but not provided the means to meet, expectations of better treatment and improved patient rights (Rogers and Pilgrim, 1989). As a piece of legislation it also appears to have lost its relevance far sooner than previous mental health legislation. It concentration on compulsorily detained patients in hospital, at a time of the rapid hospital closure programme, has meant that little more than a decade after its introduction the government has been forced to consider new legislative measures. The latter ('supervised discharge') will be used to manage and treat patients in a community context.

The weak impact of the 1983 legislation can be contrasted with the 1990 NHS and Community Care Act. This was a crucial piece of legislation in a number of ways. First, it established a framework of service organisation for the four constituent countries of the UK – previously England and Wales had separate legislation from Scotland and Northern Ireland. Second, it explicitly drew together duties across health and social service boundaries. Third, it was a catchall piece of legislation which set out duties for several client groups. Prior mental health legislation in both 1959 and 1983 was out of sync with wider health reforms (like the 1948 NHS Act). Thus, mental health law in Britain has been grafted on as an addendum to other relevant legislation, which has weakened both its remit and impact. (Rogers and Pilgrim, 1986).

The building blocks of the community care component of the 1990 Act originated in the review in 1988, *Community Care: An Agenda for Action* (HMSO, 1988). The Griffiths Report provided an official endorsement of the notion that community care should be directed towards obtaining the best quality of life possible for people leaving hospital. The report outlined the principles needed to assure the success of the policy in the future by securing the following:

1. appropriate services provided in good time to people who require them the most;
2. the principle that people receiving help will have greater choice and say in what is done to assist them;
3. help should be directed at allowing people to stay in their own homes for as long as possible, with nursing home and hospital care being reserved for those whose needs cannot be met in any other way.

The Griffiths vision was embodied in the 1989 White Paper *Caring for People* (HMSO, 1989), and, with the exception of the recommendation that a minister should be designated with special responsibility for community care, subsequently translated into the 1990 Act.

The new Act involved:

- Local authorities taking the lead in community care.
- A duty of individual needs assessment and care management to deliver packages of care which would enable people to live at home.
- Community Care Plans being drawn up in consultation with local people, either separately or in conjunction with health authorities.
- 'Arm's length' inspection units being set up to regulate standards in the 'independent' care sector and more effective complaints procedures in social services.
- The separation of commissioning (purchasing or contracting) and providing functions (although unlike the case in the NHS this is not obligatory).
- The retention of responsibility of community health services by the NHS.

Until May 1994, the last point meant that community mental health service planning was the responsibility of Regional Health Authorities. Since then, this power has been devolved to local commissioners of services for NHS authorities or Trusts. Regional Health Authorities are to be replaced in 1996 by regional outposts of the NHS Management Executive. It is likely that the role of these will be limited to monitoring services and facilitating service development.

The financial arrangements underpinning these policy changes indicate the ideological preferences of the enacting government: local-led authorities are not given the bulk of the budgets for mental health services, which remain in the NHS, but they are given the responsibility for co-ordinating community care. Thus local authorities, not central government, are now made responsible for untoward events, or when services are inadequate, but they are not the main budget holders. Blame but not power and resources has been allotted to them by central government. Moreover, the Act has been used to further privatisation. Resource transfers are directed by the Act. The first instalment in 1993 of £539 million was made from the social security budget. However, 85 per cent of this must be spent in the private or voluntary sector (together called the 'independent' sector).

Despite the radical implications of this new legislation, the debate about its impact has been rather lopsided. The NHS part has been the focus of considerable controversy, whereas the community care tag has attracted less interest. Carpenter (1994a) suggests that public and academic interest has been lukewarm because:

The NHS reforms are seen by politicians, public and the media alike as something that will happen to 'us'. Will I have to travel to a distant hospital for treatment? Will my doctor be forbidden from prescribing a drug I need because of its expense? By contrast, community care is something which happens to 'the other' who might be pictured favourably as a deserving elderly or disabled person, or less favourably as a socially disruptive or even dangerous mental service user. Either way, it is only regarded as important to the extent that it might impinge on 'us' as either threat or burdens. Thus community care has not been given the priority it merits, because it is seen as an issue affecting others who are less socially and economically important, and who are not politically well placed to challenge this ascription. (Carpenter, 1994a, p. 20)

Carpenter goes on to identify a series of potential problems with the legislation which, at the time of writing, are beginning to emerge:

(1) The transfer of funding from social security to community care local budgets is cash limited. Local authorities cannot necessarily respond positively to needs once they are assessed.

(2) A shift from hospital to community and from expensive to cheap or unpaid care labour represents a form of 'dumping', disguised as demedicalisation and empowerment.

(3) There is limited emphasis on rights for community care clients. For example community care is not identified as a right in the Citizen's Charter. This position has recently changed. In the summer of 1994 the Secretary of State for Health announced the intention to develop 'community care charters', along the lines of the Citizen's Charter. However, it has been pointed out that there is no mention of mental health services or a charter for people experiencing mental health problems (Clements, 1994).

(4) There may be difficulties in shifting beyond a rhetoric of user involvement and empowerment.

(5) Separate rather than seamless services are caused by splits and fragmentation of agencies: health/local authority/social security. This has had the effect of making rehabilitation more difficult as the successful settlement of people in the community is only achieved by the health care system approaching other systems in order to accomplish the designated central government task of hospital closure (Bean and Mounser, 1993).

(6) Managerialism may have a limited impact in promoting cost-effectiveness when faced with inaction on other fronts which affect

mental health – unemployment, poor housing, homelessness and discrimination. These imply a wider social policy framework to improve the quality of life and citizenship of community care clients, rather than merely increasing the efficiency and quantity of current (largely secondary and tertiary) services.

(7) A limited vision of care in the legislation in the dichotomising of the consumers and providers of care may be more (although not wholly) appropriate with reference to caring for people in the community with severe physical disabilities. However, this market assumption pre-empts a wider and more pluralistic possibility which recognises that service users may also be producers of care and the blurring that characterises the roles of carers and users in the area of mental health. Emotional support provided by informal carers, who are predominantly women, can be viewed as part of what has been termed the 'invisible welfare state' (Cobb and Wallcraft, 1989). Conversely, care givers may also require the support of mental health services. It has been estimated that up to one-third of relatives of people with mental health problems will themselves require mental health services at some stage and be dependent on 'patients' wages for sustaining a reasonable standard of living (Thornicroft *et al.* 1992).

The 1980s: An Overview

The 1980s demonstrates a complex picture associated with an inertia about shifting from hospital-dominated to community-based support for people with mental health problems. When reflecting on this inertia, Beardshaw and Morgan (1990) identified five main difficulties:

(1) Inter-agency collaboration is complex and often inefficient. Different parts of the system (NHS, social services, voluntary and private sectors) have different ideologies and priorities. The aims of, say, in-patient providers will be different from those seeking to emphasise community mental health facilities. The translation of the ideals of documents such as the Griffiths Report often fall short because, as Bean and Mounser (1993) point out, insufficient attention is given to the way in which the disparate systems providing aspects of community care operate in reality:

Too often the various systems such as the benefits system, or the housing system, or the employment system, or the education system, work in isolation, follow their own codes and regulations, are in practice inflexible and work mutually to exclude each other. (p. 25)

(2) Mechanisms for effecting the shift of finance from hospital to community care are inadequate. Monies have been lost following hospital closure for mental health facilities. If local authorities spend too much on building up community facilities they can be penalised by central government. Bridging funds for the transition between large hospital provision and alternatives have not been made available.

(3) The funding of private home placements by social security funds has created a perverse incentive to generate mini-institutions in the community (rather than a range of ordinary living options).

(4) Funding and educational innovations to equip institutionalised staff to work in community settings have been inadequate.

(5) Fear of innovation and failure and an attachment to traditional working practices on the part of planners and providers has been evident. These features had been identified by the World Health Organisation in 1977 as being the greatest impediment to improving mental health services.

The above points were made in relation to policy prior to the 1990 NHS and Community Care Act being implemented. In the last section we drew attention to the criticisms made of this legislation by Carpenter (1994a). The introduction of quasi-markets is having a mixed impact on service development. On the one hand, divisive rivalries between agencies, which are instructed by the DoH to collaborate, have been amplified – they are in competition for contracts from purchasers (now called 'commissioners'). On the other hand, where commissioners have had a clear vision about proper community support services, which are needs-led not provider-led, they have been able to exert control over providers who have become entrenched in inpatient work. In other words, the reactionary role played by service providers (point 5 above) can now be disrupted by powers allocated to service commissioners.

Carpenter concedes that whilst current legislation based on notions of needs-led services quickly runs into resource difficulties, it is also the case that the provider-led emphasis of the past also disempowered service users. If marketisation has highlighted the question of good housekeeping of limited resources, the policy has also been able to claim a mandate in the face of previous provider domination. For this reason Carpenter has tried to develop a model of reform which is both 'user-centred and worker friendly' and which accepts the failure of the old provider-led NHS (Carpenter, 1994b).

If both resources and provider power determine service quality then the lives of users may be adversely affected on both counts. There is little point in the state allocating more money if it leads to the reproduction of provider-preferred services, which are medicalised and in-patient in emphasis, and which stigmatise and disable their clients. There is also little point in only financing reactive services, when mental health and distress are promoted by vagaries in the wider social policy framework of housing, employment and income maintenance.

The constraints and opportunities imposed by policies during the 1980s, characterised by privatisation, marketisation and managerialism, have altered the way in which people of all political persuasions argue about improving mental health care. The opponents, as well as the advocates, of the current long-serving Conservative administration now reflect carefully on the vested interests of service providers, as well as on the best way to allocate restricted funds. It is for this reason that the opposition parties have had to engage with arguments about user empowerment and citizenship. In the past, finance alone has tended to dominate debates. The days are also gone when politicians took at face value what clinical professionals advised about planning services. In the next chapter we examine the interests and influence of these professionals.

6

Mental Health Workers and the State

Introduction

This chapter will examine the relationship between the mental health workforce and the state. For reasons of space not every relevant occupation can be considered. We have selected five major groups: psychiatric nurses, psychiatrists, psychologists, social workers and the police. The first of these are the most numerous and are given the most attention here. The last, the police, is not a mental health specialism but it has taken on a particular salience in recent years with the emergence of community care.

As in other areas of health and welfare work, public policy defines which workers are qualified to carry out which tasks in the mental health system. Whilst the state regulates the work of professionals, the latter also shape the state policies which both constrain them and provide them with opportunities for the protection or expansion of their status and power. To give an example, it can be argued that there is no economic or scientific rationale for why one has to be a medical practitioner to prescribe drugs. Elsewhere in the NHS, where there is a shortage of particular skills, nurses perform tasks usually performed by medical practitioners. However, currently, medical practitioners retain and guard a monopoly over the prescription of psychotropic drugs. Consequently, other professions are prevented from prescribing them. Once the state operates regulatory policies relating to each of the professions, it is a major influence in setting the boundaries between occupational territories.

Thus, the relationship between mental health workers and public policy is not one-way but dialectical. Professional boundaries and mandates are not fixed but change over time, according to technological and

therapeutic changes and the power of each of the occupational [...]
in generating rhetorics of justifications. Some occupations m[...]
croach on the territory of other groups (see the case of comm[...]
mental health nurses (CMHNs) and social workers discussed b[...]
These encroachments may in certain circumstances be legitimis[...]
policy-makers both centrally and locally, which in time may infl[...]
the nature of the regulatory policies of mental health work. The[...]
also intervenes in the mental health labour market, in terms of the[...]
and functions of particular professions, through health care fina[...]
and organisation. For example, there has been a deliberate effo[...]
recent years to increase the number of CMHNs in the NHS.

These points will be elaborated and explored under the follo[...]
headings:

- The impact of marketisation
- The role of the mental health professions in therapeutic law
- Professional autonomy and power
- The workforce as a mirror of gender and class relations
- The composition of the mental health workforce
- Community care and the changes in professional work
- The policy option of introducing generic mental health workers.

The Impact of Marketisation

The 1990 NHS and Community Care Act has changed the traditional
territory of the mental health professions. An example of this can be
seen in the impact of the purchaser/provider split. This has entailed a
number of professions vying with each other for access to receive referrals. Clinical psychologists now regularly accept referrals from GPs
and may be commissioned as the providers of counselling or psychotherapy services. Two decades ago psychiatrists had a virtual monopoly of control over access to, and treatment of, patients, which
constrained the autonomous work of subordinate professions like clinical psychologists (Goldie, 1977).

One likely outcome of the new NHS structure is that the marketisation
of the health care system will result in local pay negotiations with
occupational groups replacing traditional nationally determined terms
and conditions. Local management of finances by health agencies
may also substantially change the numbers and influence of certain
professional groups. Two examples illustrate the point. Firstly, there

may be substitution of one expensive profession with a cheaper one. Psychiatric nurses are cheaper to employ than psychiatrists. However, they can perform many of the same functions and so they may grow in both numbers and power at the expense of the former superordinate profession. However, some recent reports about mental health services have suggested that the skill mix in the work of community mental health nurses is not cost-effective and CMHNs may themselves face challenges to their occupational territory from non-professional care assistants.

Secondly, the government's 'fundholding' initiative, which allows GPs to buy services in addition to their traditional role of providing services, is likely to increase the role of primary care workers. GPs may opt increasingly to buy counselling services from non-psychiatric professionals, because they are more popular with patients, assign mental health work to practice nurses, and substitute hospital psychiatric out-patient sessions for practice-based alternatives. GPs are likely to prefer these arrangements since they will have control over the employment of staff and services rather than being placed in a traditionally subordinate position to liaison or hospital psychiatry.

Education is another way in which governments intervene in the mental health labour market. For example, the sanctioning of Project 2000, through the the United Kingdom Central Committee (UKCC), engendered a different type of training for psychiatric nurses, in comparison with the previous Registered Mental Nurse course. The government's 'White Paper 10' also set nursing on a path entailing all future mental health nurses being educated in universities. Previously, training was mainly in colleges of nursing, which were under the auspices of health authorities.

The Role of the Mental Health Professions in Therapeutic Law

Unlike other health workers, the mental health occupations also regularly carry out a social control function, which is governed by legislation in relation to both the civil compulsory detention of patients and the assessment, treatment and detention of mentally disordered offenders, under various sections of the 1983 Mental Health Act. A rare example of this in another field is the 1948 National Assistance Act, which allows for the medical removal of patients in the community whose physical health is deemed to be in jeopardy. Even here, most of the cases dealt with under the legislation are older people with dementia.

Successive governments have allocated the main authority to compulsorily detain patients in hospital to the psychiatric profession. Other professions such as social work and psychiatric nursing take an important but secondary role. The emergence of therapeutic law in the mental health field has not been a one-way process. The struggle by psychiatry to become the dominant profession has been traditionally legitimised by its inclusion as the main profession charged with the implementation of mental health legislation for the last 150 years (see Chapters 3 and 4).

The social control function is also evident in the additional non-medical occupations, which have a right to lawfully intervene when a mental health problem is suspected. For example, police officers have only informal powers to act if someone is physically ill. But under Section 136 of the 1983 Mental Health Act they are authorised to detain for up to 72 hours, and refer for psychiatric assessment, anyone found in a public place who appears to them to be mentally ill.

The legislative mandate delegated by government within therapeutic law also has a peculiar impact on relationships between occupational groups. For example, the authority of the police, to identify who psychiatrists will see for assessment, threatens the traditional discretionary gatekeeping powers of the latter (Rogers, 1993). Thus, the existence of therapeutic law means that the state has delegated much stronger regulatory powers to mental health workers compared to other groups in the NHS. This of course is double-edged. Although the decisions of mental health professionals are *constrained* by specific legislation, the same law empowers them to intrude upon the lives of citizens in ways which would lead to other health workers being guilty of assault and false imprisonment. Mental health workers can lawfully intrude on resistant bodies and detain people without trial. In this sense they operate in an unusual way within the NHS. In other work contexts, such as social services, the social control function, for example in relation to child protection, is a common organisational norm.

Professional Autonomy and Power

A description of the various occupations within the mental health field emphasises differences in traditions, education, values, knowledge bases and skills. These factors are often cited as the core characteristics of the different professions. These attributes are often used to account for differences in status, occupational jurisdiction, remuneration and power over patients and other occupational groups.

Professionals claim a special mandate for their authority by referring to their educational standards, arcane skills and codes of practice. Thus, psychiatrists lead 'firms' of hospital teams on the basis of a purported set of expert traits, or their assumed expertise in co-ordinating and managing the work of others (Goldie, 1977). In other words, psychiatrists are superordinate in the division of labour because of their claimed unique knowledge. Their lengthy medical training, their incorporation of medical ethics, their clinical experience and their purported abilities to manage organisations, all figure in this formula to account for medical 'leadership'. However, studies of the work practices of the different mental health occupations indicate that what distinguishes one occupational group from another is the extent to which they have been able to secure governmentally endorsed autonomy over their work (Freidson, 1970). Thus dominance is an *outcome* of a successful bid for legitimacy. It is not an inevitable product of *a priori* claims to rational authority which are self-evidently valid.

Professional dominance also does not mean that one profession is superordinate against the wishes of others. Goldie (1974) showed how psychiatrists maintain their mandate of authority and how subordinate professions both challenge and *accommodate* that mandate. The latter resulted from, amongst other things, an acceptance of the medical model of mental illness as the only pragmatic basis from which to treat madness, a lack interest or concern to professionalise and a lack of enthusiasm about developing therapeutic skills. Nor does it mean that once a professional group has attained supremacy it will remain in that position. The picture of professional relationships painted by Goldie has changed significantly since the 1970s. Whilst it may still be the case that the psychiatric profession is superordinate over others it has a much more tenuous pre-eminence.

Professionalisation during the 1980s and 1990s has been a central concern of both psychiatric nursing and clinical psychology. Moreover, the ethos of multi-disciplinary working and the relocation of professional relationships outside of hospital walls has resulted in much more complex interprofessional power relationships. Some now argue that medical dominance in mental health work is substantially fragmenting (Samson, 1995).

The Workforce as a Mirror of Gender and Class Relations

The stratification within the mental health workforce reflects the divisions in wider society – particularly in relation to gender and social class. However, in the mental health field these factors have interacted in a slightly different way from that of the mainstream health workforce. For example, the gendered nature of general nursing owes much to the dominance, historically, of male medical practitioners. Garmanikov (1978) has suggested that the working relations between medical practitioners and nurses replicate the gendered nature of patriarchal society. The doctor assumes the role of patriarch, directing and determining the division of labour within the hospital setting. The nurse as a subordinate 'handmaiden' to medical practitioners, augmented by concerns of hygiene and caring, takes on the role of wife/mother. The patient, as the passive recipient of care, is placed in the role of child.

In contrast to this picture of the division of labour in general hospitals, psychiatric nursing developed in a different manner. Historically, social class appears to have been a major factor in shaping the hierarchy of mental health occupations. In the nineteenth century it was principally working-class men who were recruited as asylum attendants for their strength and ability to restrain patients, not middle-class women, who were typical in general nursing (Carpenter, 1980). These attendants worked under the auspices of asylum doctors whose ranks (as with other branches of medicine) were filled by 'gentlemen of independent means'. The male-working-class position of the asylum attendants is reflected in the strong trade-union affiliation of this sector of nursing compared with the preference for the 'professional organisations', such as the Royal College of Nursing, which represented the interests of general nurses (Carpenter, ibid). Given that in both medicine and general nursing men have come to dominate the higher echelons of the professions, the class background of psychiatric nurses is likely to have contributed to the view from within nursing that its psychiatric branch is inferior to the general branch.

Thus the history of nursing can be seen to be different for its two branches, but both were a product of the interaction of class and gender influences. At the outset, general nursing provided an opportunity of respectable employment for the large pool of genteel labour being produced by middle-class Victorian families (Veblen, 1925). Abel-Smith (1960) noted that, 'If nursing could be made respectable, it could provide an outlet for the social conscience and frustrated energies of the Victorian spinster.' In the general hospital the female middle-class matron displaced the lower-class male master of the poor-house. But she remained inferior in status and remuneration to the male medical superintendent.

At the turn of this century, nearly all of the male nurses were employed in asylums. The early nursing schools refused to admit them in case they might 'usurp the functions of doctors' (quoted in the Select Committee on Registration in 1904). Female nurses posed no such threat, even though their class background was closer to that of doctors. We will return to this question of class and gender again below when discussing psychiatric nursing in some more detail.

Whilst the male/female dichotomy appears to be at its strongest in relation to nursing, there is evidence that it occurs in other occupational groups. Women on average occupy lower-status positions within the 'psy' professions. Pilgrim and Treacher (1992) note that female clinical psychologists are less likely to occupy managerial and professional leadership positions than men. Moreover, they found that male elements in the profession also lamented the greater proportion of women to men on the grounds that this implies an inferior status and induces a decline in salary levels (e.g. Crawford, 1989). The recognition of sexism and the relative invisibility of women within the upper echelons of the profession has recently prompted the organisation of a separate Psychology of Women section within the British Psychological Society (Nicolson, 1992). Women also occupy an inferior status within psychiatry. Despite considerably more women medical graduates than men putting psychiatry as their first career choice and their over-representation in junior ranks, they are under-represented at Consultant level and in academic posts.

The Composition of the Mental Health Workforce

It can be seen from Table 6.1 that psychiatric nurses are the largest group of mental health workers, followed by psychiatrists. It can also be seen that the mental health workforce has increased substantially since 1981. For example clinical psychology doubled in size over a ten-year period.

Table 6.2 shows NHS staff by main staff group and sex for 1991.

TABLE 6.1   *The composition of the mental health workforce*

Staff group	1981	1991	Percentage change 1981–91
Psychiatric nurses	45,560	53,100	16.5
Psychiatrists	3,830	4,760	24.3
Clinical psychologists	1,230	2,500	102.4
Occupational therapists*	2,940	5,630	91.8
Child psychotherapists	120	290	139

* Includes a large percentage working in the non-psychiatric sector.

Source: Adapted from Department of Health, *NHS Workforce in England* (London: HMSO 1994).

TABLE 6.2   *NHS staff by main staff group and sex for 1991*

	Persons	Male	Female
Hospital medical staff*	42,610	31,070 (73%)	11,540 (27%)
Mental health nursing	53,100	16,980 (32%)	36,120 (68%)
Clinical psychology	2,330	840 (36%)	1,490 (64%)
Child psychotherapists	200	50 (25%)	150 (75%)
Occupational therapists	5,630	300 (05%)	5,330 (95%)

* Statistics only available for all medical specialties.

Source: Department of Health, *NHS Workforce in England* (London: HMSO, 1994c)

Psychiatrists

In Chapter 3 we noted that the rise of the psychiatric profession was closely linked to the establishment of the asylum system. Thus, its credibility and power was predicated on an administrative and managerial role, as much as it was on the skills of diagnosing and managing mental disorder. In fact, credibility about the latter skills has always been difficult to sustain. Psychiatry has tended to be treated with some suspicion by others (including other medical practitioners) and it remained, until late into the twentieth century, marginalised and isolated from mainstream medicine. The 1959 Mental Health Act is often considered to have been the greatest reformist measure placing mental illness, and to a large extent the activities of other mental health workers, firmly under the control of psychiatrists. The emphasis on treatment produced a corresponding increase in power, influence and autonomy, and the medical profession's position became uncontested for many years. However, this acquirement of a dominant role can be seen as state imposed. It was not something that was actively sought by the medical profession, rather it was 'thrust upon them by the Percy Commission' (Bean, 1979).

> In their evidence to the Percy Commission, the medical profession suggested a weak form of treatment where the courts would (a) retain powers to detain patients in hospital after they had been admitted for a period greater than two years, and (b) allow the courts to hear appeals from any patient compulsorily detained. Proposals which involved a weak form of treatment were not acceptable to the Percy Commission. They had in mind a more logical and more radical system. (Bean, 1979, p. 28)

The role assigned to the medical profession in this crucial piece of legislation, which was largely reproduced with few modifications in the Mental Health Act 1983, cemented and reinforced the dominant role of psychiatry more generally in the mental health field. Arguably recent changes have acted to dilute power derived from a legal mandate. The weakening of the territorial base of the hospital and reorientation towards primary care and community settings have, to an extent, shifted mental health care away from detention and treatment in hospitals.

By 1982 between 1 in 3 and 1 in 5 psychiatrists were working in a primary care setting. Much of this work centres on education, enhancing the skills of primary care workers and liaising between primary and secondary care settings (Strathdee and Williams, 1984). The multidisciplinary ethos of Community Mental Health Teams (CMHTs) also makes it more difficult to transfer to the community the traditional lead role played by psychiatrists.

The strengthening of other mental health professionals' autonomy and claims to skills and knowledge have also been a key factor in weakening the traditional role of psychiatrists. Fernando (1992), a consultant psychiatrist and a Mental Health Act Commissioner, claims that British psychiatrists currently feel under at-tack 'from a plethora of forces on several fronts'. He identifies these forces as coming from: the black community who criticise psychiatry for colluding with racist 'sectioning' practices; clinical psychologists who have attempted to take away the 'interesting' parts of psychiatric work, leaving doctors to deal with people deemed 'psychotic'; health services managers who have marginalised medical practitioners in decisions about the allocation of resources; and the public at large who are 'blaming psychiatrists for not curing the ills of society'. The response to these attacks, according to Fernando, has been for institutional psychiatry to:

> turn in on itself, going back to the traditional basics of medicine – emphasizing biological and genetic aspects of health and illness, concentrating on drug therapy (as an undeniably 'medical' form of treatment), devising more and more specialisms and refusing to address serious problems (such as racism) within its professional practices. (Fernando, 1992, p. 14)

Fernando goes on to note that despite some psychiatrists operating within a psycho-social framework, 'it is the bio-medical model of "mental illness" that is being pursued at most "centres of excellence"'. A retrenchment of this type has also been noted in the United States where de-medicalisation and community mental health took place at an earlier point than in Britain (see Chapter 8). Light (1980) notes that the de-medicalisation of community health, which has come about via the increased responsibilities of non-psychiatrists, has met with hostility from psychiatrists and a retrenchment into an organic medical model. We turn now to arguably the strongest challenge to psychiatry – the growth in professional strength of clinical psychology.

Psychologists

Clinical psychology is a relatively new profession. Its birth and growth have coincided with the NHS and for this reason it has closely followed the organisational contours, constraints and opportunities of the latter (Pilgrim and Treacher, 1992). Because a post-graduate qualification (which is now a doctorate) is required to practise, and its members claim a particular scientific mandate from their training, this has led to peculiar tensions arising with the psychiatric profession. At first, in the 1950s, when psychologists appeared in small numbers in the NHS, their psychometric assessment role posed no threat to medical dominance. A major problem emerged, though, when they made a bid to have autonomy about the behavioural treatment of people with neurotic conditions. This led to a prolonged conflict with psychiatry, which dissipated in the 1980s following the Trethowan Report (DHSS, 1977) about the role of psychologists in the NHS.

The 1980s also brought with it a shift in arenas of conflict. Clinical professions were now hedged around with the authority of general managers and so were less likely to fight amongst themselves. The relative scarcity of psychologists also gave them some advantage when the ethos of multi-disciplinary working began to take root within the health service. By the end of the 1980s remuneration of senior psychologists was catching up fast with their medical counterparts. Significantly perhaps, whereas clinical psychologists working in higher education are able to claim clinical scales of pay, alongside medical practitioners, this does not extend to psychiatric nurses, social workers or other professions allied to medicine.

Notwithstanding this challenge to medicine, in terms of knowledge and technical skills, because clinical psychology is the only main mental health profession without a formal legal mandate, it has a peculiar vulnerability. Psychiatrists, social workers and psychiatric nurses all have designated roles to play within the prescriptions of various sections of the 1983 Mental Health Act – psychologists do not. Also, the traditional division of labour of medicine – diagnosing and prescribing and nurses implementing treatment – has allowed the doctor – nurse relationship to have continuous stability, which is independent of site. With the emergence now of community mental health teams and centres, it is not clear what role a psychologist can adopt, which is free from potential encroachment from other occupational groups.

Thus, clinical psychology is currently in a contradictory stage of development (or decline). On the one hand, its numbers and remuneration increased significantly during the 1980s but, on the other, the new arrangements of employment, particularly in the wake of the 1990 NHS and Community Care Act, make its practitioners vulnerable. Their role can be eroded by others and their employment is no longer guaranteed. The latter is a result of 'treatment packages' being offered in modalities which potentially could be produced cheaper by other occupational groups (CMHNs or counsellors).

Psychiatric nurses

There has been a substantial increase in the number of community mental health nurses (CMHNs) in the last decade. In 1985 there were 3,000 CMHNs in the UK, projected to increase to 4,500 in 1990 and

7,500 in 1995. However, psychiatric nursing has its roots firmly embedded in the asylum system. As we noted above, the origins and development of psychiatric nursing differed in significant respects from that of general nursing. The former only became a recognised part of the nursing profession in 1914. Prior to that time there were more differences than similarities between asylum nurses and their counterparts in the general hospital. These can be viewed along a number of dimensions.

Isolation   Those working in asylums were, like their inmates, *geographically isolated*. Whereas many of the large teaching hospitals, which recruited large numbers of general nurses, were situated in major cities (most notably London), the deliberate building of asylums on the outskirts of urban conurbations restricted staff contact with external populations. This isolation was compounded by the long hours that asylum workers were required to work. In many establishments in 1912 the working day extended to 16 hours, with the added requirement of attendants sleeping in rooms next to the ward, and non-working days were restricted to only one per month (Carpenter, 1980).

According to Martin (1985) geographical isolation has been an important factor in explaining the origins and perpetuation of hospital scandals (see discussion earlier in Chapter 4). Geographical isolation engenders the privacy necessary for abuse to go unrecognised but, more importantly, it also ensures that staff are isolated from the norms, values and ethos of their core profession:

> Without knowing it, the world would pass them by and staff might very well accept bad working conditions without realizing how they had dropped behind. Even if staff realized they were not keeping up with progress elsewhere, it was easy to respond defensively, to enhance internal solidarity by sharing a feeling of being neglected by the powers that be of the outside world. (Martin, 1985, pp. 244–5)

Occupational status and remuneration   Perhaps the largest difference between general and asylum nursing has been in relation to occupational status. General nursing recruited its ranks from mainly single, middle- and upper-class women. General nursing has had a 'vocational' tradition, which has not been the case with mental nursing. The ideology of nursing as a profession and 'calling' was to prove attractive to a group of women who did not necessarily require high wages and were 'desperate to escape form stultifying drawing rooms' (Carpenter,

1980). Moreover, the 'product champion' of general nursing. Florence Nightingale, seems to have deliberately excluded asylum nurs-ing from her consideration.

The public status of asylum service, which was generally viewed as the lowest form of menial work, was far removed from the angelic stereotype of the general nurse. A large proportion of recruits were male and they received wages similar to those of agricultural workers. As we noted earlier, one of the reasons for establishing a principally male workforce was because men were deemed to have the physical strength needed to restrain patients. They literally manhandled them. Just as the tasks undertaken by general nurses mirrored female dom-estic tasks, so in middle-class Victorian England the supervision of asylum activity reflected the male division of labour of the wider society:

> While the duties of some nurses and attendants were confined to what would normally be described as 'nursing care' tending 'refrac-tory' and debilitated patients, or surveillance of those patients tak-ing exercise on airing courts, others spent much of the time supervising the work of patients. . . . Male inmates engaged in a wide diversity of trades and pursuits. For example, at Prestwich Asylum, during 1857, 158 out of 248 male patients were engaged in various trades, including working on the farm, assisting the asylum joiner, engin-eer, plumber and painter, tailor, upholsterer and baker. (Carpenter, 1980, p. 130)

Both asylum work and general nursing can be classified as 'dirty work' (Hughes, 1971). However, in the case of general nursing, difficult and dirty work was not imbued with stigma: quite the contrary – it added to the occupation's angelic image. There are two apparent rea-son why this did not extend to asylum work. Firstly, as we have seen in previous chapters, the insane were a marginalised and stigmatised group. They were not viewed as worthy of attention in the same way as the wounded heroes of the Crimean War – Nightingale's spring-board for the general profession.

Secondly, the ideology of professionalism with its sporadic appeals, that the nursing of the insane required both 'high calling' and 'the best qualities of heart and head', cut little ice with asylum workers. They had a class consciousness similar to that of other manual oc-cupations and required remuneration for their main means of subsist-ence. This was indicated by a sardonic communication to the asylum union's magazine in 1912:

Why should you grumble because a tradesman works 50 hours a week and you do 80 or 90 or more? Have you not your *dignity*? Cling to that precious position; feed your wife and children with it when pay-day is approaching; when the coalman comes with his bill, try paying him with a 'dignified' look. If the 'Super' has you up for some little offence, ask him how he does meddle with one engaged in a 'dignified profession'. Grievances vanish and sorrows fade before the wonderful zephyr of dignity. (Carpenter, ibid, p. 142)

Not surprisingly the working-class-male character of psychiatric nursing, together with the rejection of professionalism as an ideology, resulted not only in a class consciousness but in turn resulted in high rates of unionisation and conflict with employers. There is some evidence to suggest that asylum attendants were more than aware of the differences in status, power and remuneration that their medical overseers enjoyed:

At a time (1890s) when wages were under £50 a year, it was not uncommon for a medical superintendent of a large asylum to receive £800 a year and, in addition, a fine house and the pick of the farm's produce. Staff were not always slow to detect the hypocrisy of authorities who publicly expressed high ideals, but left staff to struggle on with minimal resources. (Carpenter, ibid., p. 140)

However, medical dominance was arguably more pronounced than in general nursing. The relationship between attendants and nurses was with the medical superintendent. Since there was a failure to recruit upper-class women in any great numbers, few asylums established the 'matron system' of general hospitals. Additionally, medical practitioners established their legitimacy in terms of the administration of the asylums as organisations, rather than via their surgical or medical skills (Scull, 1979). The jurisdiction of the medical superintendent extended into every area of nursing staff life. The rules governing the workforce were set by the medical superintendents and were harsher than in general hospitals. For example, asylum rule-books meant that such things as 'disobedience of elders' or intemperance (even outside of the asylum) were grounds for instant dismissal.

The division between a unionised psychiatric nursing force and professionally associated body of general nurses is still much in evidence. Although it is more common now for general nurses to belong to unions and psychiatric nurses to belong to the professional organisation the Royal College of Nursing, the Prison Officers Association (POA) is still the main representative of nurses in the Special Hospital system. There the 'security' and restraint of patients tends to be emphasised over therapeutic and nursing care. This picture is also a legacy of the particular role played by Broadmoor Hospital – the criminal lunatic asylum where the POA was established. Britain's main prison trade union began in a hospital not a jail.

The gradual shift of services to community settings in recent years has had an impact on the style and content of work undertaken by psychiatric nurses. The changing nature of mental health nursing has recently found official recognition in the setting-up of The Mental Health Nursing Review commissioned by the Department of Health in 1992 and headed by Tony Butterworth, Professor of Community Nursing at Manchester University. This was the first major review of mental health nursing since 1968, although the subsequent report *Working in Partnership* (DH, 1994), met with a lacklustre response from government representatives and the media. The recommendations of the review constitute something of a curate's egg, as a result of efforts to accommodate disparate views and interests. (User representatives and nurses from the old psychiatric hospitals were amongst those included on the review body.) In some ways the content of the report supported demands being promoted by the users' movement. For example, only limited support is given to District General Hospital Psychiatric Units as appropriate sites for nursing mental health crises and twenty-four-hour crises services were endorsed. At the same time, it suggested that greater attention needed to be given to the demands and needs of staff based in Victorian asylums.

In more general terms there appears to be a disjuncture between statements of policy and the practice and values of Community Mental Health Nursing (CMHN) on the ground. The assumption behind the investment in an expanded CMHN labour force has been that nurses should be focusing their attention on the needs of people with a serious and enduring mental illness (a euphemism generally for those diagnosed as suffering from chronic schizophrenia). The *Mental Health Nursing Review* called on nurses to prioritise their work with this group of people. Such a call is necessitated in part by the evidence that, contrary to the policy aim of targeting more chronic and severe cases, CMHNs have actually been directing an increasing attention to people with minor mental health problems in primary care settings with, according to standard psychiatric criteria at least, limited effectiveness (Gournay and Brooking, 1994).

CMHNs as an organised interest group have departed significantly

form their hospital colleagues as far as mental health policy is concerned. In particular, there is a desire from elements of the profession
to distance themselves from the use of compulsory legislative powers.
In contrast, hospital nurses have been keen to progress their role and
status, increasing their powers of compulsion. An example of this was
the inclusion in the 1983 Mental Health Act of a 'holding power',
which allows nurses to detain voluntary patients for up to 6 hours
(Section 5(4)). According to Bean (1986) this was not necessary and
reflected the use of trade-union tactics to gain increased state recognition for hospital nurses' status and role. This example contrasts starkly
with the failure of *community* psychiatric nurses to endorse the Royal
College of Psychiatrists' proposal for Compulsory Treatment Orders
(CTO). This could have entailed nurses administering forced medication, by injection, in patients' own homes. The failure of CMHN endorsement was an important factor in the proposed CTOs gaining legal
status. CMHNs argued that such a measure would adversely affect the
nurse–patient relationship. The government is now introducing other
legislative control measures, which do not centre directly on the administration of medication (Supervised Discharge Orders). Nonetheless, CMHNs are, at the very least, sceptical about becoming involved,
as indicated by this comment in an editorial in the *Nursing Times*: (in
Vol. 91, No. 18, 3 May 1995)

> New legislation could fundamentally change the relationships be-
> tween community-based mental health nurses and their clients. Un-
> less nurses get involved in the debate now, they will be in no position
> to snipe from the sidelines once the legal framework is in place.

Social workers and occupational substitution

Social workers have had an established and variegated role in mental
health, ranging from the introduction of a case-work approach in the
1950s heavily influenced by psychiatry and psychoanalysis, to the introduction of Approved Social Workers (ASWs) under the 1983 Act
with specified duties and responsibilities in relation to the compulsory
admission of patients to hospitals. The latter role acted to increase the
significance of mental health work within social work practice, as
indicated by the minimum requirement of two years' post-qualifica-
tion relevant experience, and the completion of a specialist training
course before becoming an ASW. Despite the increasing specialisation
of mental health work within social work in recent years, it has not

been immune from the threat of occupational substitution.

Competition between mental health workers is evident in relation to occupational territory. Occupational rivalry and encroachment can be found in most areas of health work. For example, in the area of childbirth there is the question over whether midwives should be allowed to act as independent practitioners, or whether doctors, who have a monopoly in this area, should direct the work and set the parameters of their practice. Often the state acts to resolve such struggles by agreeing to accept or reject the status claims of occupational groups, e.g. by agreeing to comparability with another group over pay, or changing policy.

Community care of people with mental health problems presents a current example in which two groups, social workers and CMHNs, are in competition. As mentioned above, social workers have a lengthy tradition of work in the mental health field. Community mental health nursing in comparison is a young occupation, which has become established in the last two decades. Both are increasing in importance, given the emphasis on community-based, as opposed to hospital-based, care. Both groups lay claim to similar roles with a similar client group (i.e. those experiencing mental health problems outside hospital).

On the face of things, the knowledge base and interventions with clients of the two groups differs only in emphasis (Sheppard, 1990). It may be remembered from the discussion in Chapter 1 that the knowledge base of social workers draws on a psycho-social model of mental health problems and the social sciences. CMHNs tend to adopt eclectic psychiatric ideologies, with little attention being given to conceptual issues. There have been suggestions that because the two professions share similar skills they are interchangeable. For example, Goldberg and Huxley (1980) claim that 'the community psychiatric nurse shares many skills with the social worker'. However, when longer-term contact with clients is considered, major differences do emerge:

> The differences confirm, to a considerable degree, expectations arising from the examination of occupational socialisation and discourse. Social workers define their clients primarily in terms of social problems, whereas mental health case definitions received a higher profile amongst CPNs [community psychiatric nurses]. Social workers, according to main incidators – role, context and indirect work – operated in a wider community context than CPNs. Social workers acted as advocate or resource mobilizers, worked with outside agencies and professionals, and tackled more practical, emotional and rela-

tionship problems indirectly to a far greater extent than CPNs. Indeed, in terms of active use of community resources and agencies, CPN work appears to have been negligible. (Sheppard, 1990, p. 83)

However, it may suit policy-makers and certain other professional groupings to promote the substitution of social work with psychiatric nursing. Increases in the number of CMHNs forms a major part of the government's policy of care in the community – particularly in relation to case or care management. Nursing remains a profession that medicine is easy with. CMHN's might more readily fit in with their nursing colleagues in the context of primary health care teams. A tradition of accepting the medical authority of psychiatrists is more established than is the case in social work (Bean, 1979). CMHN's may also be perceived to be more likely to respond readily to mental health crises in the community than social workers (Rogers and Rassaby, 1986). As health authority employees, funding for CMHNs comes from the main mental health budget, whereas social workers are funded out of the smaller allocated resources of social services departments. Finally, but perhaps most importantly, CMHNs are distinguished from social workers by being charged with the administration of depot (long acting) injections of neuroleptics. Much of community care policy for those with long-term mental health problems still relies on continued compliance with and uptake of 'maintenance' doses of neuroleptics. In the final chapter, we address this issue in terms of whether or not the limited handmaiden role of nurses in administering a chemical fix is now part of the crisis over the management of madness.

Police, psychiatrists and professional dominance

One of the oldest occupational groups to have a mandate in managing mental health problems is the police. Police involvement with mentally disordered people dates back to the founding of the police force in the early nineteenth century, and to its preceding constables (Walker and MacCabe, 1973). The police officer's role in welfare matters, such as mental health, has led some commentators to label them as 'the secret social service' (Punch, 1979). In this capacity, the police frequently act as an alternative to other mental health agencies. They may be the first port of call, before other services are involved, or at last resort, when alternative assistance is not forthcoming. Hospital-based mental health workers tend to work within the institutional boundaries of the hospital. Not all localities have crisis intervention teams and some social services do not have a 24-hour service, or they lack sufficient staff to cover psychiatric emergencies.

Until recently, police officers have not generally been viewed as legitimate mental health workers. However, with an increasing number of revolving-door patients and a greater number of people now spending less time in hospital and greater periods of time living in the community, police officers have become front-line emergency workers. Consequently, their role as mental health workers has become more visible. The police are the only professional group who are in a viable position to work as 24-hour community mental health workers. Unlike other community-based occupational groups, the police force operates seven days a week and on every day of the year.

The role of the police in psychiatric emergencies has been accepted as appropriate by successive governments and is enshrined in mental health law. Section 136 of the Mental Health Act 1983 empowers the police to remove a person they consider to be mentally disordered and in need of immediate care and control, from a public place to a place of safety. Under this legislation, a person may be detained for up to 72 hours for the purposes of being examined by a medical practitioner and interviewed by an Approved Social Worker and to allow suitable arrangements to be made for his or her treatment or care. Despite official endorsement of this police role, increasing challenges have been made to the use of these powers. Considerable disquiet has been expressed from different sources, not least from other professional groups, about the appropriateness of the police having and using this mandate.

Criticism has included that made by the British Association of Social Workers and sections of the psychiatric profession. These groups have expressed reservations about the ability of police officers to diagnose mental disorder and to handle patients appropriately. However, recent research suggests that across a number of indicators the police are generally able to diagnose the presence of mental disorder accurately and make appropriate referrals successfully (Rogers, 1990; Bean *et al.*, 1992). The negative evaluation of police officers' competence in this area may emanate from concerns about the image and occupational control and autonomy of other mental health professionals rather than any proven failure of the police to manage mental disorder (Rogers, 1993). Freidson (1970) identified three areas as being crucial to the attainment and maintenance of professional status. The requirements are that:

- Knowledge and skills are viewed as unique and effective
- There is a monopoly and control over a market for service
- There is close supervision of training and qualifications

The police role challenges two of the requirements that are necessary for psychiatrists to successfully maintain their professional legitimacy. In possessing a legal mandate to bring referrals for assessment, the police can challenge psychiatric control over a market for services, i.e. the right to choose who will be seen. Secondly, by making legally sanctioned decisions regarding whether a person is mentally disordered, on the basis of 'lay' judgements, the police may be in a position to challenge the claim that psychiatrists' knowledge and skills are unique and effective.

Police work with mental health problems is much influenced by the context in which they operate and differs considerably from designated mental health services. The importance and influence of members of the public is more pronounced, decisions have to be made in the absence of case notes or previous histories, and there are uncertainties which stem from the lack of prior cues and control over external events and resources (Rogers, 1990).

Community Care and the Changes in Professional Work

The police are not the only group in recent times to be given a more prominent role in the management of mental disorder. With the shift in the balance of mental health management away from inpatient provision, primary health care has come to occupy a more important position in relation to mental health care. Mental health professionals have made a shift, albeit a modest one, from hospital to primary health care settings. It has been estimated that in England and Wales more than 20 per cent of psychiatrists, 27 per cent of clinical psychologists and 22 per cent of psychiatric nurses spend some of their working time in general practice. The distribution of specialist mental health professionals is skewed, with most operating as Community Mental Health Teams (CMHTs) in larger 'training' practices (Kendrick *et al.*, 1993). Counselling services have also become widespread (Sibbald *et al.*, 1993). As will be discussed further in Chapter 8, general practitioners now have an increased role in the prevention and treatment of mental disorder and in the purchasing of community and acute psychiatry. The latter role is likely to increase significantly if the notion of 'total fundholding' (the purchase of all care for a local population) becomes more widespread in the NHS.

The shifting location of mental health services has had a major impact on how professionals organise their work and the way in which they relate to patients and each other. The territorial base of the asylum or hospital is to a large extent replaced by the need to negotiate one-to-one relationships in a domestic or community context. In many ways, this shift can be viewed as giving patients more autonomy and power to set the agenda for relationships with professionals. Mental health professionals are put in the position of having no automatic right of entry to a patient's home, and professional/client interactions no longer take place in a setting rich in colleagues. Thus, it may be that the client has a new control over who they see, when, and in what circumstances. Alternatively, faced with a choice between attending to those who are less able to negotiate a mutual relationship and client groups who are easy to engage and who are perceived as being most rewarding to treat, mental health workers may opt to treat the latter. Studies of community-based services show marked increases in rates of inception to care for less severe mental health problems (Onyett *et al.*, 1994a).

Clearly this re-balancing of power in the patient/professional relationship has posed problems directly for professionals, and indirectly for the state, in managing the activities of patients deemed to be a threat to themselves or other people. In other ways the relocation of community care provides new opportunities for abuse and neglect by a minority of staff to go unchallenged, in the absence of a well-developed system of monitoring and complaints procedures. This is particularly the case with the burgeoning growth of independent hostels and group homes for ex-patients, which are not subjected to official systematic inspection. In this regard, the privatised nature of much residential provision is in a similar position to the pre-regulated madhouses of the eighteenth century discussed in Chapter 3.

The myth of multi-disciplinary working

Mental health workers have also been faced with the need to change their working practices and the way that they interact. In particular, work outside of the hospital brought with it a philosophy of multi-disciplinary working, which had already operated, in theory at least, in inpatient settings. The basic tenets of multi-disciplinary working are: that each member of the mental health team has special skills to contribute to the management of patients; that these are contributed in co-operation and liaison with other mental health workers; and that this leads to the establishment of corporate consensual goals in delivering a service.

To a large extent the implementation of mental health policy, such as the aim to produce a 'seamless service' which overrides the division between primary and secondary care, is predicated on notions of communication and effective liaison. Multi-disciplinary working supposedly embodies these characteristics. However, just as corporate strategies have failed in other arenas of public life (most notably at governmental level and in NHS administration) there are a number of major impediments to effective multi-disciplinary working. There is much anecdotal evidence, and some research, to suggest that rather than entailing mutuality and co-operation, inter-professional relations are characterised by defensiveness, lack of role clarity and conflict. Much of the conflict centres around bids for professional dominance or autonomy.

Psychiatrists are loath to give up 'clinical responsibility' for patients. Psychologists are developing a training or consultancy role, seeking high levels of remuneration, adopting medical titles ('Consultant Psychologist') and developing the means for accepting direct referrals. When working in Community Mental Health Teams clinical psychologists are reported to have low team role clarity and team identification but high professional identification (Onyett *et al.*, 1994b). Threatened by de-professionalisation, psychiatric nurses have been busy collecting more 'therapeutic skills', which can be viewed as a means of countering claims of uniqueness of skills made by the other main groups of mental health workers.

Difficulties in ensuring multi-disciplinary co-operation and corporate goal achievement stem from the differing secondary socialisation and training of mental health workers. This has been succinctly described by Murphy (1993):

Professionals in both health and social services are taught almost exclusively in isolation from each other. Doctors, nurses, therapists, psychologists and social workers plough their own educational furrows, their courses focused almost exclusively on their own professional contribution to the care of individual patients. They are rarely taught about service development during their basic training years, and multidisciplinary team working is supposed to come naturally after graduation and with experience . . . It is not surprising then to find that community teams, primary care teams and hospital based community outreach teams and social work teams rarely develop a good overview of the total service or appreciate its broader objectives. (Murphy, 1993, pp. 20–1)

Onyett *et al.* (1994b) point to the problem that team work poses for professionals around role and identity once they have been fully socialised into distinct professional groupings:

The concentration of practitioners into teams places professional workers in a special dilemma. They become members of two groups: their profession and the team. As a result they may find themselves torn between the aims of a community mental health movement that explicitly values egalitarianism, role blurring and a surrender of power to lower status workers and service users on the one hand, and a desire to hold on to traditionally, socially-valued role definitions and practices on the other. (Onyett *et al.*, 1994b, p. 2)

Thus multi-disciplinary success is a poor bet for politicians, as each occupational group isolates itself during training and seeks to encroach on the work of others thereafter. Such a set-up is hardly propitious for mutual goodwill or efficient and rational co-operation. And yet these are expected by the present government when ministers exhort practitioners in the multi-disciplinary 'team' to improve service quality or learn from the mistakes of service failures. Such exhortations reflect a glaring double standard. Currently government departments are failing to co-operate to maximise the efficiency of community care (see Chapter 10).

The Policy Option of Introducing Generic Mental Health Workers

The alternative to multi-disciplinary working is the notion of a generic mental health worker. The last few years has witnessed a growth in the number of such workers. For example, in the last four years Community Mental Health Teams, have on average seen an increased input from generic mental health workers from 0.2 FTE (full-time equivalent) to 0.8 (Onyett *et al.*, 1994a). The impetus for a generic mental health worker has surfaced in a variety of forums about mental health. For example, the difficulties in recruitment of trained nurses led the trade union COHSE (now UNISON) to argue for their introduction. The recruitment of psychiatrists also still suffers from the stigma of psychiatry being viewed as a Cinderella service. This has been encouraged by auditing activities brought in by general management. There have been particular concerns around providing basic habilation and rehabilitation of long-term patients. At first CMHNs were deemed to be the most appropriate and accessible group to deal with the long-term needs of this group. However, the recent Audit Commission (1994) report marks a departure from this position in its suggested plan to shift responsibility for meeting the care needs of those with enduring problems to care assistants. This critique if effected could halt or reverse the growth in CMHNs and lead to their replacement with non-professional personnel. Whether the roles of the other mental health professionals are as easy to identify as being candidates for de-professionalisation is a moot point. However, given the flux, contradictions and changes in roles and relationships between and within mental health professionals which community working has brought about, this outcome can be considered as more than a remote possibility.

Conclusion

Uncertainty, conflict and continual change are the hallmarks of contemporary roles of, and relationships between, mental health workers. The structural separation of medical training, autonomous work practices and well-developed professional boundaries makes it unlikely that psychiatry will easily capitulate to the notion of generic working. Clinical psychologists too are in a strong position, given their limited numbers, to turn themselves into trainers, advisers or consultants to other mental health workers, rather than participate as generic mental health workers.

The prescribing of psychiatric drugs, which is the sole preserve of medical practitioners, is likely to prove a major hurdle to genericism, although there are signs in other areas of medicine of limited prescription rights being extended to other workers (e.g. practice nurses in primary care). On the other hand, the power of purchasers to set the agenda of services and an increasing recognition of the need for flexible working in community settings with clients with multiple needs may provide a stimulus for generic working. These considerations are about the maintenance or re-formulation of specialist work with those deemed to be suffering from mental health problems.

7

Questions of Effectiveness

Introduction

This chapter deals with questions of effectiveness. These have become important as a result of the accelerating impact of quasi-marketisation. The latter has been associated with both managerialism and the 'purchaser/provider split', now affecting both the NHS and, to a lesser degree, local authorities. Moreover, in an attempt to improve efficiency, there has been a government enthusiasm for an 'evidence based' NHS. This has translated into an NHS research and development programme which includes both new commissioned research work on effectiveness and reviews of existing evidence. To date this has tended to emphasise a traditional medical, randomised control trial approach to the production of knowledge. Over and above these government-encouraged initiatives, other policy events have engendered the need to discover whether services are effective. For example, consumerism which we will discuss in Chapter 9 may well have unleashed expectations about service effectiveness as well as citizenship.

Thus, the issue of effectiveness has to be understood within a wider context of changing expectations about health and welfare systems at the very time that those systems are undergoing rapid restructuring. For this reason, the concept of effectiveness will be discussed below in relation to a new vocabulary associated with a restructured welfare state. Following on from these conceptual clarifications, we will examine some of the research on the effectiveness of mental health services and psychiatric treatment. Because of the particular controversial relationship between psychiatry and women and black people, separate dedicated sections will be allocated for discussion. They highlight an anomalous feature of mental health services. Whereas most people would like to have equitable access to the NHS, the over-representation of women and black people in mental health services has led to criticism not gratitude from those groups.

Conceptual Clarifications

Quasi-marketisation

The effectiveness and efficiency of mental health services have to be understood in relation to quasi-marketisation. One of the main intensions behind quasi-markets is for the State to fund and enable services, not to directly supply them. The term 'quasi-markets' is used in preference to both the 'internal market', which would mean that the purchase and provision of services would remain internal to the NHS, and the traditional simple notion of 'market', because the organisations involved are not necessarily (or even typically at present) profit-making. A further difference is on the supply and demand sides. The purchasing of specific services is achieved through an earmarked budget, rather than money, and the purchasing decision is made via a third party (a GP or purchasing commissioning agency) rather than individual patients exercising choice. As we noted earlier, welfare consumerism does not entail individuals buying what mental health care they want. It is about proxy decisions made on behalf of local populations by service commissioners. The latter make their decisions after considering three interrelated concepts: effectiveness, efficiency and equity.

Effectiveness and efficiency

Effectiveness refers to the utility of interventions – put simply, do they work or do they do what we expect from them? Do anti-depressants relieve depression or not? And what are the relative utilities of different methods of treatment and management? Clinical effectiveness differs from the notion of cost-effectiveness. An expensive technique may be clinically effective in an individual case but a health economist might consider the cost to be too high for the health gain produced in a population or when compared to a cheaper but less effective alternative. Recently the arguments about the merits of different types of anti-depressants highlight this (Freemantle and Maynard, 1994). The new anti-depressants (SSRIs) are clinically effective and (their advocates argue) are more cost-effective because they do not lead to the accident rates associated with the old tricyclic drugs. The latter create greater sedation effects. However, the advocates of the old drugs point out that their substantial cheapness makes them a better buy, as they are just as clinically effective as the new drugs. Freemantle and Maynard are sceptical about the claims made on both sides and consider that a rational comparison of the drugs is made difficult by the research on the SSRIs being sponsored by their commercial producers.

Another controversial area is the cost of talking-treatments. The current cost to GPs of referral for psychotherapy is around £70 for a first visit compared with the cost of employing a counsellor which has been estimated at between £15 and £35 an hour (Trent Regional Health Authority, 1992). Clearly it would be desirable to purchasers of mental health services to establish whether the effectiveness of psychotherapy far outweighs the benefits of counselling. Currently there is no evidence that the longer training of psychotherapists does produce more health gain in its recipients than counselling.

For health economists, efficiency relates not just to the optimal treatment, in terms of clinical outcome, but the maximum social/health benefit of that treatment within the constraints of resource allocation. Le Grand and Robinson (1981) have defined efficiency as 'that output at which the excess of benefits over costs, called the net benefit, is largest'. This involves three associated concepts – benefits to consumers, the costs of production, and an efficient level of output. Efficiency, then, needs to take account of *costs* as well as the benefits of health care. For example, in relation to the treatment of schizophrenia, a number of economic evaluation studies have attempted to show that Clozapine (a new anti-psychotic drug) is cost-effective for use in relation to so-called 'treatment-resistant' patients. Despite the cost entailed in monitoring recipients for the known side-effect of agranulocytosis (a potentially fatal blood disorder), it is claimed that Clozapine performs well in comparison with other 'anti-psychotic' drugs. Its advocates claim that it reduces hospital admissions for a particularly expensive group of patients by enhancing both social functioning and quality of life.

Equity

Three common definitions of equity are used in a health care context:

1. a minimum standard of care for all of those in need;
2. equal treatment for equal need;
3. equality of access.

In relation to people with mental health problems, how these definitions of equity are operationalised will depend on who is doing the defining. The notion of need is likely to differ according to whether it is defined by purchasers, mental health professionals or users. For example in relation to point 3, the expressed need of a person to be referred to a counsellor may not accord with the opinion of a psychiatrist, if that person's problem is not viewed as severe enough to constitute 'clinical depression'. A minimum standard of care relates to whether or not someone in acute distress is offered *some* sort of help – such as admission to hospital. The second notion of equity above refers to the extent to which a type of treatment or facility is made available to people with the same or similar difficulties. An example is in relation to the availability of therapeutic communities. Not all those deemed to have a personality disorder by psychiatrists will have the option of such a treatment regime.

Acceptability

In addition to providing a cost-effective and equitable service, the notion of acceptability is also an emerging consideration. Acceptability is implicit in the concepts of effectiveness and efficiency – any attempt to measure benefits of treatments requires information as to the value placed on it in terms of improvements in mental health by those in receipt of service delivery. As we saw in the last chapter, this reflects the increasing credence being given to the expressed needs of service users. A good example of the conflicting pressures on purchasers in this regard is the controversy about the use of ECT (electroconvulsive therapy). Psychiatrists argue that it is a useful and legitimate treatment option and that it is clinically effective. By contrast, users find it frightening and often unacceptable (Rogers and Pilgrim, 1994). (MIND are currently campaigning to reduce its use in general psychiatry.) Twenty years ago the notion that treatments should be acceptable to their recipients was rarely if ever heard. Now it is commonplace.

Effective Treatments

Treatments are a component of services and so their effectiveness is important to consider. Claims of clinical effectiveness have been made for all of the main current interventions to be found in mental health services: major and minor tranquillisers; ECT; anti-depressants; lithium; and behavioural, cognitive behavioural, psychodynamic and other forms of psychological therapy (Bradley and Hirsch, 1986; Bergin and Garfield, 1994). That is, all of these interventions have been demonstrated, using randomised controlled trials, to be effective in reducing psychiatric symptomatology. In relation to the commonest form of treatment for psychotic disorders, neuroleptics, controlled trials have consistently demonstrated that most patients who receive these drugs experience fewer 'positive' symptoms and are hospitalised less often that patients receiving placebos or other kinds of medication (Green, 1988). However, it is only recently that trials have been conducted into the optimum dose levels to control symptoms and prevent relapse. These more recent studies suggest that small dosages of such drugs are as effective, or even more effective, than higher doses which have generally been prescribed (Bentall *et al.*, 1995).

With regard to talking-treatments being effective there are particular problems about applying a randomised control trial (RCT) methodology, which has been the main way of assessing the impact of impersonal interventions like drugs. The RCT model is increasingly being applied to talking-treatments, for instance in the NHS Research and Development initiative on health technologies. It is not that counselling or psychotherapy cannot be assessed in this way, it is that these interventions contain complex personal processes, some of which may be present in ordinary human relationships. If this is the case, then when talking-treatments are effective it may be because there is contact with someone who is conversing in a benign, attentive way, rather than it being a reflection of specific technical interventions boosted by a particular therapeutic orientation. This possibility is confirmed by the US research on therapist variables, which demonstrates that there are effective therapists in all therapeutic orientations and that there are wide variations of effectiveness *within* each orientation (Beutler, Machado and Neufeldt, 1994).

Despite an overall endorsement of mental health interventions from the RCT clinical literature, a number of recurring problems can be noted, which have been the focus of complaints by recipients of services. First, recipients have complained that some treatments have impaired their quality of life, or have created, as well as solved, problems. Complaints range from the unwanted physiological effects of drugs ('side-effects') to the sexual and emotional abuse of patients at the hands of psychological therapists. Moreover, treatments may be experienced as being helpful in some respects but harmful in others (Rogers and Pilgrim, 1994).

A second problem is that sometimes the degree of iatrogenic damage done by psychiatric treatments has been so profound that their overall utility is cast in doubt. For example, benzodiazepines are effective in the short term in reducing anxiety but they are very quickly addictive and ineffective. This has led to recipients needing to seek professional or self-help in withdrawing from their use. Another example is the death rate from major tranquillisers and the widespread prevalence of drug-induced movement disorders (Brown and Funk, 1986). In the final chapter the particular iatrogenic problems associated with major tranquillisers will be considered again.

A third problem with treatments is that because psychiatric knowledge is contested by some service users, and between professionals of differing theoretical orientations, there is no ready consensus on positive outcome criteria for interventions. For some people, symptom reduction defines effectiveness. For others (such as a psychodynamic therapist), criteria such as increased insight or even 'therapeutic regression' (getting worse symptomatically) may be deemed to be positive outcomes.

A fourth related problem is that recipients of treatments and other parties may disagree on the utility of interventions. For example, the high non-compliance rates for psychotropic drugs (Kane, 1985) can be contrasted with the enthusiasm that psychiatrists have for their prescription and the concerns that the relatives of patients have for their ensured administration (Finn *et al.*, 1990). Conflicts of opinion and interest about treatment compliance demonstrate that what patients and others consider to be effective is not always the same.

A fifth difficulty is that what is clinically effective may not be cost-effective. Cost-effective interventions must be clinically effective but not all clinically effective interventions are cost-effective. The earlier examples given about the merits of SSRI anti-depressants compared to the older trycylic drugs and the relative costs of psychotherapy versus counsellor referral in general practice highlight this point.

A sixth problem with psychiatric treatments is that their overall effectiveness is judged by comparisons between treated and untreated groups. However, even when treated groups show more improvement as a whole compared to untreated controls, within the treated group there will be some individuals who fail to improve or who deteriorate, and some in the untreated group who improve or fail to deteriorate. For the former sub-group of treatment 'non-responders' iatrogenic costs of treatment (the first and second problems discussed above) may be paid, whilst no symptomatic improvement is experienced. The converse also applies. For example, there is evidence to suggest that the scope for spontaneous recovery for people suffering from major depression is considerable. Patients in placebo groups of controlled trials receiving no treatment demonstrate a major improvement after four weeks of between 40 and 60 per cent (Freemantle *et al.*, 1993). These individuals improved without being exposed to the iatrogenic risks entailed in the treatment condition. 'Spontaneous' improvement from emotional problems may be a misleading misnomer – it implies a change which is in some sense remarkable or even mysterious. In fact, people untreated by a medical intervention may utilise lay relationships to ameliorate their distress. People in control groups continue to have relationships and some of these may be benign and supportive.

Effective Mental Health Services

Having introduced some concepts surrounding effectiveness in general and touched on the issue of effective interventions, we now turn to the literature on effective mental health services. This will be discussed under sub-headings which reflect the main emphases emerging within this research.

Comprehensive services

Huxley (1990) in his overview of the literature on effectiveness notes that the notion of a comprehensive service appears in three senses:

1. comprehensive response to the mental health needs of a population;
2. comprehensive provision of services;
3. comprehensive care of the individual client's needs.

These distinctions are important in relation to service evaluation. For example, it is possible for those in contract with services to be dealt with successfully in line with the third version above. At the same time in that locality there could be unmet need in the population (a failure by the first criterion). Patmore and Weaver (1991) interpret a 'comprehensive' service as being one which 'can address, as required, needs for money and housing, care for physical illness, leisure and social life, occupation, psychiatric medication, emergency support, liaison with family and help with daily living skills' (p. 4). Thus their definition is focused on the individual client (Huxley's third version above).

Huxley notes that co-ordinated and efficient services seem to be associated with greater benefit to clients, particularly those with long-term problems (1990, p. 197) and believes that this could be fostered by the use of case management. Both Huxley and Falloon and Fadden (1993), who also review the evidence about community mental health effectiveness, are aware of past shortcomings in community-based approaches. Huxley's recommendations are made in the light of an effort not to repeat the mistakes noted in the past in the US. Similarly, Falloon and Fadden advocate an approach that does not merely result in rehousing people with long-term mental problems in an alien community.

A shift from a medical inpatient to a psychosocial approach

One implication of a community focus for mental health work is that the appropriateness of a medical inpatient model of work is brought into question. Levine *et al.* (1993) claim that psychosocial rehabilitation models of care have superseded medical models in the US. They outline Assertive Community Treatment (ACT) which aims to prevent or reduce the re-hospitalisation of individuals with serious mental illness and increase their quality of life in the community.

ACT staff provide practical support services and focus on basic issues in day-to-day living such as domestic skills, medication, finances, housing and advocacy with other providers, and aim to increase client autonomy and access to services. Levine *et al.* claim that ACT is notable because it 'expands the concept of what makes an individual vulnerable to serious mental illness to include non-psychiatric factors . . . and gives explicit emphasis to non-medical community support interventions' (p. 528). They suggest that the improvement in adaption to community life in highly vulnerable individuals is more important than eliminating psychiatric symptoms, and report ACT's success with young adults, homeless people and substance abusers. The advantages of ACT is that it has been shown to reduce both hospital use and costs, although it has not had the same levels of success in terms of symptom reduction, improved social relationships or subjective quality of life.

Scott *et al.* (1990) detailed the development of a community-orientated mental health service, including the introduction of a community-based admissions unit. Due to limited resources, objectives were set for the first year only. These were: identification and assertive treatment of those individuals with severe long-term mental illness; crisis intervention for other individuals; a liaison-consultation input to primary care teams; and forging links with social service departments to set up inter-agency linkages.

Peck and Cockburn (1993) focus on the debate in the UK regarding preferred models of service for adults with mental health problems. They note that most of the research has addressed the 'apparent benefits' of the various models, while little has been undertaken to uncover their financial costs. Peck and Cockburn try to redress this by attempting to present initial costs for both innovative and standard models of service. Although initially the study sought information from 13 services which claimed to provide innovative community services, only 4 were able to provide adequate descriptions of service or sufficient financial information to allow comparison of costs to be made and this was then compared with a standard district general hospital based service.

Peck and Cockburn note that the major cost element of traditional mental health service is inpatient beds. They acknowledge the limitations of their methodology in so far as their sample size is small and they disregard capital charges. However, they claim that their study confirms the 'appetite' of such hospital beds for capital and revenue, and comment that in the light of such large sums being wasted in hospital services, the consequence will be a lack of funds to develop community services. They argue that services which do make an investment in community services, especially home treatment services, benefit financially as a result of not having to support large numbers of hospital beds. We will return to this question of resource imbalance between hospital and community services in the final chapter.

Both the American and British literature highlight the necessity of anticipating the needs of people with long-term problems ('continuing care clients') and to respond to them and others when in crisis. The role of a round-the-clock seven-days-a-week crisis service is central to this scheme. It implies responding to immediate client need as well as reducing impatient admission.

Case management

Case management is reported as being successful in providing care in the community for people with long-term problems and is widely used in the US. Huxley (1990) describes case management as a system in which care is provided through the individually planned combination of different sources of support. The whole care package is overseen by a single 'case manager'. The approach emphasises individual assessment and attempts to address the individual's needs rather that just fitting them into an existing service system.

Dietzen and Bond (1993) in their study of case management services and client outcomes observe that if the services are intensive enough, hospital use can be dramatically reduced. Whilst some studies bear this out (Olfsen, 1990) others actually show an increase in hospital use amongst clients who receive case management services (Curtis *et al.*, 1992). Dietzen and Bond's study found few associations between the intensity of services and client outcomes, although programmes that delivered very low frequencies of service were ineffective in reducing hospital use. This caused them to revise their assumption of the existence of a linear relationship at the programme level between intensity of services and client outcome. They deduced instead that programmes must maintain a minimum intensity of services to reduce hospital use amongst clients with frequent hospitalisations.

As with 'comprehensive' community care, Huxley points out that the role of a case manager is implemented with considerable variation and has different meanings in different settings. He suggests that a skilled case manager can detect early warning signs of client deterioration and claims that the technique combines practical and therapeutic forms of help, makes use of resources outside the statutory sector and extends the responsibility for costs of the service. Social workers are seen as playing an important part in case management in terms of co-ordination roles.

Despite the apparent advantages of case management, Huxley warns against its use as a quick fix for problems of mental health care in the community. He notes two main problems with the approach to date. First, there may be difficulties in ensuring that services which cross traditional boundaries remain accountable, particularly in a mixed system of funding. Second, the essentials of case management and the types of skills required to carry it out may not be properly understood by some professionals. A case manager must not only be able to perceive the gaps in the service but must also be able to create solutions, and must also possess a wide range of skills necessary to carry out assessment and care planning. Because of this broad role, Huxley suggests that GPs are not a suitable group to be chosen as case managers.

An extension of the case management approach has been the attempt to introduce into psychiatric nurse training the systematic application of skills which have been proved to be effective in reducing relapse and re-hospitalisation in people diagnosed as schizophrenic. This training package initiative, which currently operates in Manchester and London, include problem-orientated case management, family management and psychological interventions.

Cost-effectiveness

It was noted earlier that health economists emphasise that services or treatments that are effective may not necessarily be cost-effective. However, given the controversies about defining and meeting needs, which we discuss in Chapter 9, there may be a tension between managerial and service user emphases in this regard. For example, if a rigid regime is adhered to, treatment will take less time and absorb fewer resources, leading to a lower overall expenditure. Such a factory or production-line approach may be efficient organisationally and lead to cost minimisation but it may not be sensitive to user needs. Whilst there is no doubt that money alone does not create an effective service, an underfinanced service cannot succeed. The aim of cost-effectiveness in combination with good quality comprehensive care in principle will secure a consensus from all stakeholders. But views on what *is* cost-effective vary, as do approaches to 'cost-effectiveness' as a goal.

Blom-Cooper and Murphy (1991) describe the 'perverse funding system' (p. 67) which acted as a serious disincentive to collaboration between agencies, and to local authorities which have been discouraged from spending appropriately. Blom-Cooper and Murphy consider that patients and their families have insufficient money within their own control to make choices about how they wish to be helped. They acknowledge the contribution of specific welfare benefits to the care of individuals, but this is small in relation to the costs of providing residential or hospital care and they recommend welfare offices to aid clients to maximise their benefits. Blom-Cooper and Murphy stress that a key necessity for effective community care services is more government money, channelled by way of local government and the health service or going direct to sufferers and families through income support benefits.

Quality assurance

As well as debates over what services should be provided and how they should be implemented, there is a body of literature which examines ways of evaluating and measuring the effectiveness of these services: the 'quality assurance' debate. Parry (1992) reviews a number of service-based evaluative methods and clarifies the distinctions between service evaluation, operational research, professional audit, service audit, total quality management and quality assurance. Quality assurance models and programmes are discussed by Eppel *et al.* (1991), Hill and Leiper (1992) and Hoyt and Austad (1992).

Hill and Leiper (1992) define 'quality assurance' as the process by which the structure and functioning of a service is examined in order that achievements and limitations can be identified, and in such a way that some corrective action can be taken. They argue that quality assurance can be conceived of as either internal or external to a service but to be most successful it should be an amalgamation of the two approaches.

The challenge of quality assurance brings with it a variety of dilemmas for service purchasers, which have been summarised by Heginbotham and Ham (1992). These include whether to privilege an expert over a user view of what constitutes a good quality service and how to match the defined or expressed needs of service users with the inertia and constraints of a pre-existing service configuration. And of course an overriding consideration is that of financial constraints which, as we noted above, may mean that rapid throughput and minimal interventions are prioritised to bring about cost-containment. Such priorities would certainly militate against both offering a comprehensive response to all users and a guaranteed intensity of case management for those with long-term mental health problems.

The financial advantages of brief therpeutic contact have traditionally driven US service planning, and the quasi-marketisation of the British NHS now invites a similar approach. Currently this is waiting in the wings here rather than being centre-stage as in the US. The financial implications of service provision feature in a number of US papers. Whilst such considerations are often discussed in British articles, they do not assume the importance attached to them in the US, nor is their thrust so transparent.

Although the British literature is not as preoccupied with brevity of contact, there are already signs from some critical analysts of quality assurance that the latter is essentially a cover activity for service managers to contain costs and control clinicians. An overriding problem with quality assurance is that of seeking and finding a consensus definition of what 'quality' means.

This in turn links to the problem which we address in Chapter 9 about defining need. If psychiatric epidemiology is considered to be non-problematic, then it is possible to develop performance indicators to check that service inputs, service processes and service outcomes are having an impact on morbidity reduction in a population. Inputs refer to resources in a service. Process refers to provider activity within services. And outcome refers to changes in patients as a result of service contact. For example, within this framework Jenkins (1990) has argued that epidemiological data provides evidence of the incidence of schizophrenia. This, she argues, can be reduced by effective genetic screening and counselling. Similarly prevalence can be reduced by interventions including family management, education and support to reduce the probability of relapse. All of this entails a commitment to the assumptions of psychiatric knowledge – that schizophrenia is a valid diagnosis and that it is at least, in part, genetically determined. Such assumptions would be at odds with many in the service users' movement and so Jenkins's model of developing performance indicators may not find favour with them. Indeed, Jenkins concedes that what she calls 'subjective health indicators' (i.e. lay views of health state) may be at odds with professional views and yet they must be taken into consideration.

The overall problem of defining both service quality and need satisfaction is summarised succinctly here by Beazley (1994):

Legal definitions of need are fairly narrow and mainly refer to needs for particular services . . . rather than the wider view about the need for social care based on ideas about quality of life. The ability of a service to 'satisfy' a need is difficult to assess, as there are few examples of studies or effective systems yet in operation which draw directly on the opinions of service users.

Beazley's lament brings us to our next heading.

Acceptability to service users

One priority for purchasers of services is to secure those which are acceptable to those who use them. The research on this topic to date tends to damn impatient provision. The results of a national survey conducted by us for National MIND (Rogers *et al.*, 1993) showed that users often found inpatient services to be humiliating and the environment depressing and felt a loss of citizenship. Some of the sample, including informal patients, reported coercion and brutality from staff. Outpatient services were criticised for long waiting times, short consultation times, and inconsistent medical staffing, although some clients welcomed the access to psychiatrists and viewed the service in preventive terms.

Day care centres, still often linked to hospital sites, were seen as being inaccessible and extensions of the hospital regimen, with a lack of meaningful activity and continuing sense of coercion being commented on. Opening times were seen as inflexible. Clients enjoyed contact with other users and found staff to be more helpful than their hospital counterparts. Many clients who valued day care centres were concerned about cutbacks in services, which is at odds with the prioritising of non-inpatient services.

Recently a spate of studies point clearly to the conclusion that patients prefer to be treated outside of hospital. Rogers *et al.* (1993) found that the further services are from hospital the more they are appreciated by service users. McIntyre, Farrell and David (1989) found that 'the thing that inpatients most like about being in hospital is their ability to leave'. Marks (1992) found that the relatives of patients also prefer community care to hospital care. Other studies also indicate that community-based treatment is not only preferred but it is also a more effective method of care.

British patients with severe anxiety and depression were assigned to either day care or outpatient care in a study by Dick *et al.* (1991). Significant improvement occurred for most of the patients receiving day care, but for few of those who were outpatients. Day patients also rated themselves as coping more effectively and as being more satisfied with their treatment. These findings prompted Dick *et al.* to suggest that day treatment should remain an option for patients with persistent anxiety and depression resistant to outpatient treatment. Dean and Gadd (1990) investigated the outcome of UK community treatment of severe acute psychiatric illnesses that were traditionally treated in hospital. They found that home treatment was feasible option for most patients and that success of home treatment could be improved by a locally-based mental health resource centre, a 24-hour on-call service, an open referral system, and an active follow-up policy.

The limits of services

Whilst the preference for community- rather than hospital-based care is a consistent signal from research on users' views, the same research also highlights the problem of defining need satisfaction by service preference alone. Put simply, people with mental health problems are not just people who act oddly and/or experience distress, they are also devalued individuals with precarious rights of citizenship. Even *if* services were organised less and less on an inpatient basis, this would not in itself solve wider problems of social marginalisation and exclusion.

There are wide-ranging practical problems which affect people with mental health problems. Rogers *et al.* (1993) found that the issues of greatest concern were money, accommodation, a need for employment or occupation, as well as services and their staff. They also established that users' employment prospects were severely and irreversibly damaged as a result of having been a psychiatric patient. Many users find it very difficult to live on the money available to them and many are poorly informed about their rights to loans, grants, allowances and benefits (Hogman and Melzer, 1992). Choice of accommodation is often very limited to many users returning to the community, with a fair number ultimately spending time in group homes, hostels or other emergency housing.

Women, Men and Service Contact

Concerns about the discrimination and oppression of female patients culminated in the National MIND campaign concerning women and mental health, which at the time of writing is ongoing. An extensive recent review of services for women (Williams *et al.*, 1993) highlights a number of discriminatory processes. Services are prone to:–

- misdiagnose women's distress;
- fail to help women deal with the causes of their problems;
- mistreat women's distress by using inappropriate medication and ECT, and by inappropriately admitting them to hospital;
- be unsafe for women.

Williams *et al.* argue that distressed women who approach the mental health service are often automatically assumed to have biological or biochemical problems or interpersonal difficulties, which cause them to be mentally ill. They believe that what actually underlies women's distress is their experience of social inequality on a daily basis. Poverty, much more common amongst women than men, is associated with psychological distress (Bruce *et al.*, 1991). This situation is exacerbated when experienced in combination with the stress of caring for children and other dependents, which is an exacting experience in itself. Childbirth is estimated to be associated with depression in 10–30 per cent of cases (Nicolson, 1989), and domestic violence is similarly linked to long-term mental health problems. Williams *et al.* (ibid) identify older women, homeless women, lesbian women and black and ethnic-minority women as particular groups who are vulnerable to disadvantage and discrimination.

Older women are more likely to receive psychotropic drugs and less likely to be offered talking-treatments than any other group (Catalan *et al.*, 1988). Since they are the group that are most at risk from side-effects of drugs (Grohmann *et al.*, 1989) this is of significant concern. As 60 per cent of women over the age of 65 live below the official poverty line (Titley *et al.*, 1992), the links between poverty and mental distress are of particular relevance to them.

Williams *et al.* (ibid) cite research which suggests that homeless women are more likely than homeless men to report mental health problems or that they have been hospitalised in the past (Crystel *et al.*, 1986; Hagen, 1990). They also note that homelessness is on the increase amongst older people, especially women. There is much evidence which links sexual and physical abuse to mental distress, and Akilu (1991) found that such abuse can also be related to women becoming homeless.

Martin and Lyon (1984) and Rothblum (1990) argue that lesbian women are at a particular disadvantage due to mental health service providers assuming that all patients are heterosexual. They also argue that homophobia in services can cause additional stress and is associated with the idea that mental health problems stem from these patients' particular sexual orientation and lifestyle. (These pressures within the mental health system may well apply to homosexual men.)

The black and ethnic-minority community are particularly poorly served by the mental health service. Whilst many of the issues relating to this point will be discussed in the next section, it is important to emphasise that much of the literature fails to accentuate or differentiate the particular needs of black and ethnic women as opposed to black and ethnic minority men. One would surmise that the combined effects of gender and race place a double burden upon these women. However, the interaction between gender and race is complex. For example, whereas Irish women appear to suffer more mental health problems than their male equivalents, the reverse is true of Afro-Carribean people (see next section).

A number of studies conducted in psychiatric hospitals have found that a significant proportion of female patients (figures ranged from 46 to 72 per cent) have previously experienced abuse (Bryers *et al.*, 1987; Carmen *et al.*, 1984; Herman *et al.*, 1989). These findings coincide with the conclusions of community studies of women using psychiatric services or attending women's projects (Rose *et al.*, 1991; Mills, 1992). Williams *et al.* (1993) suggest that abuse is strongly linked with high service use. Women who have been abused are prescribed more medication, are admitted to hospital for longer periods of time and whilst in hospital are more likely to spend time in seclusion than women who have not experienced abuse. A history of sexual or physical abuse is also associated with depression, eating difficulties and heightened rates of self-harm and suicidal thoughts and attempts. Abuse can be experienced whilst patients are using mental health services, whether it be inflicted by staff, other patients or therapists (Nilbert *et al.*, 1989; Garrett, 1992; Edwards and Fasal, 1992).

These examples of discrimination and oppression experienced by female psychiatric patients can be considered against a different set of problems for male patients. Men's behaviour is more frequently recognised as dangerous than is women's, and this may have as much to do with stereotypical expectations as it does with fact. Women's behaviour is often associated with private, self-damaging acts, with aggression being directed inwards leading to self-mutilation, depression and eating disorders. Men's behaviour has been associated more with public antisocial acts such as drunken, aggressive behaviour and violent and sexual offences. As a result, men are more likely to be labelled as criminally deviant than are women. Therefore, women are seen stereotypically as being a danger to themselves, whilst men are seen stereotypically as being a danger to others; consequently within psychiatry men are more likely to have labels which refer to and incorporate the threat of their behaviour.

Women are more likely to be dealt with in primary health care settings at the 'soft' end of psychiatry, whilst men are more likely to be dealt with at that 'harsh' end, particularly at the interface between psychiatry and the criminal justice system. In 'special hospitals', it is men who are over-represented, despite the fact that in some instances they have not been convicted of a criminal offence. Men are subject to removal more frequently than women under Section 136 of the Mental Health Act, and the police use handcuffs and detention cells more frequently for men than women in these circumstances (Rogers, 1990). Thus although feminist researchers have accurately identified particular risks for women in relation to service contact, men also suffer risks but of a different type.

Race, Ethnicity and Service Contact

Compared to other groups in the population Afro-Caribbean (and Irish) people are over-represented in psychiatric admissions to hospitals. However, precise data on this is not always available since ethnic monitoring does not always take place consistently across health and social services. Afro-Caribbean people are much more likely than white people to make contact with psychiatry via the police, courts and prison system. They are detained under Section 136 of the 1983 Mental Health Act at two-and-a-half times the rate of whites living in the same locality, and they tend to be young and male (Bean *et al.*, 1991). McGovern and Cope (1987) and Cope (1989) found that migrant and British-born second-generation Afro-Caribbean men were found to be twenty-nine times more likely than white males to be referred under Part III of the Mental Health Act, which makes provision for dealing with patients involved in criminal proceedings or serving a prison sentence.

A study of people discharged from Special Hospitals found that there were higher proportions of 'non-whites' than would be expected from the general population and that the 'non-white' group had committed less serious offences prior to admission (Norris, 1984). Browne (1990) found that black defendants were less likely to be granted bail and more likely to receive court orders involving compulsory psychiatric treatment than their white counterparts. In contrast to this, there is evidence that black people are under-represented in outpatient and self-referred services (Littlewood and Cross, 1980), and are less likely than other groups to be referred by general practitioners (Hitch and Clegg, 1980).

There are a number of theories as to why black people are over-represented in psychiatric statistics. Some psychiatrists argue that it is simply a reflection of a greater incidence of severe mental illness in black people (Cope, 1989). By contrast, Francis (1989) views it as an indication of the way in which psychiatry forms part of a larger social control apparatus which regulates and oversees the lives of black people. Since black people, particularly young black men, are over-represented in all parts of the criminal justice system, both the 'criminalisation' and 'medicalisation' of black people may be closely connected processes.

This thesis is strengthened when we look at the type of service contact that black people have. Whilst most people enter psychiatric facilities informally, the chances that Afro-Caribbean people will do so are much smaller. Cope (1989) found that 20–30 per cent of Afro-Caribbean patients were detained involuntarily, compared with 8 per cent of the total compulsory admissions to the hospital system during the 1980s. Young Afro-Caribbean migrants were found to be admitted at 17 times the community rate for compulsory admissions and at 25 times the community rate for admissions via the criminal justice system (Cope, 1989).

Afro-Caribbean people are over-represented in locked wards and secure units (Bolton, 1984; Jones and Berry, 1986) and ECT is over-used in the treatment of Afro-Caribbean and Asian patients (Littlewood and Cross, 1980; Shaikh, 1985). Furthermore, black patients are more likely to: receive major tranquillisers and intramuscular medication (Littlewood and Cross, 1980); be seen by junior medical staff (Littlewood and Cross, 1980); and receive higher levels of medication over time (Chen *et al.*, 1991). Because of this coercive emphasis, it is not surprising that black people may avoid contact with statutory services and favour contact with black organisations in the voluntary sector (Goldberg *et al.*, 1993). Thus it would seem that statutory mental health services are not merely discriminatory in relation to black people but that they are not learning currently from good practice in the voluntary sector.

The alienation of the black community from statutory mental health services has been recognised by the NHS Executive Mental Health Task Force (DH 1994b) and its messages endorsed by John Bowis, junior Health Minister (DH, Press Release, 1994). The Task Force conclusions included that mental health service purchasers and providers should:

• Develop the role of the black non-statutory sector.
• Improve consultation and communication to bring black communities, including users and carers into the planning structure.
• Develop closer working relationships with local community forums.
• Acknowledge the work and experience of black professionals in statutory organisations.

• Build independent advocacy into service monitoring.
• Include culturally appropriate methods of assessment and intervention.

Discussion

The concerns expressed by black groups and feminist researchers about the over-representation of black people and women in psychiatric facilities raise an important point about mental health services. As we noted in the introduction to this chapter, whereas equity of access to the NHS is politically valued in relation to physical health problems, the excessive contact by some social groups is considered to be problematic in relation to mental health services. There are four possible explanations for this contradiction, which are not mutually exclusive. First, especially in relation to compulsory admission to hospital, service contact is often not about the expressed needs of patients being met but is about the resolution of social crises in public or domestic settings. As we noted in Chapter 2, it is difficult to determine who is the central client of psychiatry – the indentified patient or others affected by their behaviour? Second, psychiatric services are linked to the old lunatic asylum and have had an unbroken history of stigma. Third, psychiatric treatments (not just containment) are sometimes experienced as personally distressing or oppressive. Fourth, as part of a wider system of social control, psychiatry has become a site for the manifestation of institutionalised racism and sexism in society.

Taking these points together, it is not surprising that service contact is often seen by current and prospective users not as a right to be enjoyed but as an imposition to be suffered or endured. This may account for why, as we shall examine in Chapter 9, politicised service users often describe themselves as 'survivors' of the psychiatric system. Thus, the effectiveness of mental health services remains problematic. Although we have rehearsed an emerging consensus about good services being comprehensive and cost-effective, if contact with them is associated with stigma and with control not help, then will they ever be fully acceptable to recipients? This question does not imply that professionalised mental health services should be abolished. As will be seen in Chapter 9, only a small anti-psychiatric section of the mental health service users' movement advocate such a position. What it does imply, though, is that the limits on service effectiveness need to be appraised honestly. Moreover if, as it seems, psychiatric treatments and services can only claim modest success in terms of their impact on mental health problems, perhaps there is more mileage in attempting to reduce the prevalence of mental health problems at the level of population groups. This brings us to our next chapter which overviews the prospects of mental health prevention and promotion policy and the role of primary health care in the arena of mental health.

8

From Mental Illness to Mental Health?

Introduction

In this chapter, the place of mental health promotion, mental illness prevention and primary care will be examined. We noted in the preface that the term 'mental health services' is generally a misnomer. Most of what are called mental health services actually respond to people with a diagnosis of mental illness. The term 'mental health problem' may be used by some, as a less offensive version of the latter term. However, it still refers to a person's inner state or outward behaviour being deemed by themselves or others to be problematic. For this reason another alternative term, that of 'mental distress', fails to capture fully the behavioural features which provoke labelling from others − be they lay people or professionals. As with the National Health Service itself, which remains in the main an illness service, 'mental health' services signal the absence, rather than the presence, of well-being. Prevention has not been a central plank of government mental health policy. However, there are signs that this trend is changing and that mental health prevention and promotion and the role of primary health care are assuming increasing salience in policy-making. Thus, this chapter has little to say about policy initiatives *per se*, which, with the exception of *The Health of the Nation* (DH, 1992b), remain implicit in this area. Instead, what is outlined is the general context of health promotion and prevention within which an emerging focus on *mental* health promotion can be identified. The emergence of a primary health care service focus for mental health will also be explored.

The General Context of Illness Prevention and Health Promotion

Primary health care and preventative medicine were central assumptions which underpinned the establishment of the NHS. The anticipated effectiveness of this branch of the new health service led some of its advocates to predict optimistically that the health service would constitute a diminishing drain on public funds, as it reduced and prevented illness. However, the dominant resource position assumed by the hospital sector meant that acute services were prioritised over primary and preventative services. This imbalance has never been rectified (Berridge, et al. 1993). However, the trend in favour of the secondary care sector began to be reversed in the 1980s, when primary and preventive services were given greater priority within resource allocation and planning of the NHS. More recently, health promotion has been widely pursued as a policy goal. This can be seen as a reaction against the prevailing bias in the orientation and structure of the NHS towards curative medicine. It also reflects an increasing recognition of the importance of the role of environmental factors, dietary habits and stressful living in the generation of illness (Palmer and Short, 1989).

The area of health promotion and prevention is a highly contested one. Terminology is rapidly changing and signifies competing positions and orientations:

1. The *medical model* of health education and prevention is the most established and traditional approach. This focuses on bringing about attitudinal and behavioural changes in individuals. This individualistic emphasis is augmented by population-level interventions such as mass vaccination against infectious diseases.
2. The *educational model* is drawn from a more voluntaristic model in which information transfer encourages individuals to opt for more healthy habits. It is the style and orientation of these first two approaches that differs rather than their substantive content.
3. Criticism that these two approaches are too focused on individual behaviour, or 'victim blaming', has led some to try and shift the agenda to more socially orientated models of health prevention or a *'New' public health* model. This emphasises social and environmental factors influencing populations and places a priority on wider questions of social policy which can alter these factors.

The 1980s witnessed a change of emphasis away from a health education model to a health promotion approach. The Black Report on inequalities in health published in 1980 provided an impetus with its focus on the materialist causes of health inequalities. The promoters of this approach sought to distance themselves from the more traditional medical and educational model (e.g. Beattie, 1991). Instead this approach emphasises environmental, social and economic conditions and seeks to transcend the traditional boundaries of public policy (e.g. housing, health, transport). According to Dennis *et al.* (1982):

> Health promotion covers all aspects of those activities that seek to improve the health status of individuals and communities. It therefore includes both health education and all attempts to produce environmental and legislative change conducive to good public health.

A health promotion approach incorporates the activities of lay populations in setting agendas for health, and is directed towards action to tackle the causes of ill health. It is, necessarily, an eclectic approach to improving health, combining education, information, community development, local citizen participation, health advocacy and legislation. A health promotion approach has been reinforced at an international level by the World Health Organisation (WHO, 1985). This has initiated a 'Health for All' campaign, as an attempt to shift from a narrow medical approach to health prevention.

This approach has had variable success. At a local level, community initiatives, which involve 'healthy alliances', have started to emerge and have proved successful. However, notwithstanding these successes, the earlier preventative medicine approach still retains considerable salience and tends to set priorities within health policy. The interests of central power are often incompatible with a focus on the mobilisation of community groups and on the material causes of ill health (Little, 1990).

Mental Health Prevention and Promotion

Within the general approach to health prevention and promotion outlined above, the focus of policy has been predominantly on preventing physical ill health. Despite its aspirations to a holistic approach, the WHO strategy of 'Health for All' by the year 2000 gives a low priority to mental health within its statement on prevention. It includes only one mental health goal from the 38 identified: the reduction of the suicide rate (Thornicroft and Strathdee, 1991). Ironically, the choice of suicide is also a poor one. As we will discuss in a later section, it is open to question whether it unambiguously constitutes or reflects a mental health problem in all cases recorded.

The reason for this marginalisation of mental health within the WHO strategy is not altogether clear, but it may be related to the way in which services have been structured and mental and physical deviance dealt with historically. Both mental health and preventative medicine were a focus of nineteenth-century government reforms. Different strategies were adopted to deal with each of these. As we have seen in Chapter 3, the way in which Victorian society dealt with emotional deviance was by mass segregation in asylums. The threat of moral contagion posed by mental illness was dealt with by removing it from the sphere of civil society and community. A separate set of sanitary reforms constituted the basis of attempts to deal with the threat of infectious disease in Victorian society. Thus despite policies and action emerging over a similar time span, a clear demarcation between physical and mental health took place and the two policy topics were administratively separated. Similarly, in current times, government policy in the area of mental health has focused almost exclusively on community care, hospital run-down and de-institutionalisation, whilst health promotion strategies have emphasised the social causes and potential prevention of physical ill health. Questions about mental health have focused on organisational arrangements, not on environmental or lifestyle factors, as has been the case with the promotion of physical well-being.

An exception to this low policy priority about the promotion of mental health is the strategy adopted by the government in the immediate aftermath of the Second World War. As with many policy areas, war seems to focus government action in a way which eludes routinised peacetime policy-making. As we have seen the period within and around the Second World War was significant in introducing mainstream service provision, therapeutic communities and psychological treatments. Similarly, the government instituted Civil Resettlement Units (CRUs) to provide for ex-prisoners of war. As Newton (1988) points out:

Although the evidence as to their effectiveness is lacking they were clearly intended to be a preventative service. After three or four weeks with their family, the ex-prisoners of war were offered a stay of a few weeks or months at a nearby CRU. The centres provided an opportunity to rest and recuperate, to learn about post-war civil life, to get specialist advice and to rediscover their previous work skills or acquire new skills. The average stay was about five weeks and ex-prisoners were assisted in their efforts to reintegrate into the civilian community and especially their home environment. They were given vocational guidance and help in finding work. Furthermore, their families were offered advice on how best to respond towards and support their returning kin. (Newton, ibid, p. 13)

Newton's phrase 'clearly intended to be preventative' signals a connotation of the latter word which lay people would rarely use. It refers to the reduction of existing impairment or the chance of relapse (see discussion on tertiary prevention below).

Mental Health Promotion versus Prevention

It was seen earlier that there has been a variety of approaches to health promotion and prevention. A distinction between health promotion and illness prevention is also evident in the mental health field. A mental illness prevention approach has a narrow focus (Tudor, 1991). It derives from the natural sciences – in particular, medicine. Also, it has been located in the institutions of public health/welfare, at a particular historical time and place in the development of the welfare state. In other words, an emphasis on illness will inevitably tie prevention to the knowledge base, practices and institutional forms of a single profession – medicine. By contrast, mental health promotion is informed by a different set of assumptions, which underpin positive attempts to create or preserve mental *health*. This entails an inherently political strategy, which targets social and material aspects of society. It is also an approach which envisages the involvement of other groups of people apart from medical professionals:

Community mental health promotion is that work done to promote the positive mental health and well being of individuals, groups and communities, whether geographical or organisational work carried out by a range of professionals involved in the field of mental health and of health promotion as well as by members of that particular community – and mental health and well being as defined by those individuals, groups and communities. (Tudor, 1991)

The focus of British mental health policy has *not* to date been influenced by this broader tradition of health promotion. For this reason, what we report below mainly focuses on mental illness prevention strategies. Disease prevention has been classified by its medical advocates as primary, secondary or tertiary in type. *Primary prevention* refers to steps taken to anticipate and pre-empt disease occurrence. *Secondary prevention* entails intervening at an early stage in disease causation and or occurrence. *Tertiary prevention* is concerned with minimising the effects associated with existing illness and so refers to the prevention of relapse or the minimisation of subsequent impairment. For this reason, in practice it overlaps substantially with treatment. In psychiatry, treatment is often cited as having a prevention of relapse function.

This threefold categorisation is more appropriate when applied to physical ill health, where the chain of causal events and factors are generally (though not always) easier to define than in the case of mental illness. None the less, it provides a useful framework to analyse the policy and practice surrounding mental illness prevention.

Primary Prevention

The United States: a case study

In contrast to Britain, where there has not been a discernible primary prevention policy, North America has a recent history of such a focus. In the US, the 1960s saw the emergence of a movement which believed that mental health problems could be prevented through wide-ranging changes to the social structure. This radical primary prevention ethos was rooted in two traditions: the community mental health movement (CMHM) and psychiatric epidemiology. The CMHM emerged at the time of reforms which introduced community mental health centres (CMHCs) in the United States. These was designed as the main plank of a policy to shift the locus of care from state hospitals to the community. A national network of 2,000 CMHCs based on local catchment areas were set up.

The remit of the CMHCs was not only to provide alternatives to hospital care but to have a public health focus in preventing mental illness and promoting mental health. This philosophy was informed by a view that the cause of mental health problems could be located in society and social problems. Put another way, social structures and processes, rather than the individual, were deemed to be 'psychotoxic'. Accordingly, CMHC staff were to view themselves not only as clinicians but social activists.

If the reduction in the incidence of mental health problems is taken as an indicator of the success of primary prevention strategies, then the CMHM failed in its aspiration. This failure has been attributed to a variety of factors. Some argued that the commitment to a prevention strategy was hampered by the persistence of a medical model within mental health services. Certainly there was wide-scale opposition to this part of the CMHC's role from those adhering to a more conventional psychiatric position. Social activism was dismissed as a 'flight from the patient' (Dunham, 1967) and as a 'psychiatric band-wagon' (Burrows, 1969). There were other reasons for why innovative projects failed. In particular, there was a lack of clarity about the relationship of social factors and processes to mental illness and a simplistic notion of power in the community, which was deemed to be 'the therapeutic dyad writ large' (Wagenfeld, 1983).

This lack of focus had its roots in the knowledge base which provided the impetus and ideology for the CMHM. Community studies conducted in the 1950s and 1960s (Hollingshead and Redlich, 1958; Myers and Bean, 1968) suggested links between social conditions and disadvantage (e.g. unemployment, poverty and racism) and psychiatric morbidity. Whilst these studies were able to say something significant about prevalence rates (e.g. that rates of schizophrenia were far higher in 'lower' social classes than higher ones), there was a lack of data on the incidene of mental disorder. This meant that the linking factors between cause and effect were not established. In fact because causal pathways were never properly identified, few clues were provided properly as to where interventions could be most effectively targeted. The studies were also criticised for being over-social in failing to consider the contribution of endogenous (genetic) and other individual factors (Weissman and Klerman, 1978).

Despite the failure of this first primary prevention strategy, a second generation of US preventive initiatives has been identified (Wagenfeld, 1983). Whilst not forming the impetus of a new social movement (see Chapter 9) in the way that the first did, it was based on more clearly focused processes and objectives. The Task Force set up under the Carter administration to examine mental health differed in two major respects from the CMHC's approach. Firstly, a hierarchy of scope and specificity of interventions was identified. Secondly, there was a recognition that preventative strategies with their focus on the social, lay outside the remit and values of mental health professionals.

The underlying knowledge base emphasised a different level of analysis from that of the community studies discussed above. The approach was influenced by social epidemiology, which viewed the onset of mental distress as being linked to changes in life events and the social world of individuals (Dohrenwend and Dohrenwend, 1974). In other words, the emphasis shifted towards *precipitating* rather than predisposing factors and consequently sought to reduce the prevalence of mental health problems not necessarily their incidence. It may be remembered from Chapter 2 that prevalence refers to the aggregate number of cases recorded in a population at a point in time, or new plus old cases. Incidence refers only to recorded new cases. A model of prevention which seeks to identify and remove primary causes to reduce incidence is clearly more ambitious than one which seeks to lessen the stress on vulnerable individuals to reduce prevalence. Thus, preventing mental illness now focused on eliminating stressors or minimising their deleterious effects. The type of interventions implied by this model ranged from strengthening social networks to brief crisis counselling at the time of a threatening life event.

It has been pointed out that a shortcoming of this approach is that it ignores the social factors emphasised by the first generation of primary prevention – namely ageism, racism, sexism and classism. It seems that one of the major problems of primary prevention is that the level of analysis, where prevention is deemed to be crucial, excludes important factors operating at other levels.

A third conceptual framework for primary prevention is one which focuses on stages in the lifecycle, i.e. stressors pertinent to infancy, early childhood adolescence, adulthood and elderly people.

Targets for intervention involve socially, psychologically and biologically induced stressors. For example, the deleterious behavioural consequences of toxic psychoactive drugs on the CNS [Central Nervous System] for all ages are legitimate targets for public health interventions. For the elderly, preventative goals might involve the maintenance of cardiovascular, renal and pulmonary function as a means of retarding the onset of psychological symptoms; alteration of living arrangements to reduce the noxious effects of sensory deprivation; or targeted interventions to reduce the enormously increased risk of morbidity and mortality associated with widowhood. (Wagenfeld, 1983, p. 174)

Wagenfeld views this approach as complementing and strengthening the precipitating life event model of prevention, as it has the capacity to include biological factors.

It is interesting to consider why a strong tradition of primary prevention emerged in the US and not elsewhere. In Britain, there have been attempts to establish a prevention of mental illness agenda but these have not had a major impact on mental health policy formation. Three important factors appear to be the differences in Britain compared to the US in relation to: the radical politics of the 1960s; the community care focus of mental health policy-makers; and the nature of psychiatry.

The timing of community care initiatives began earlier in the US than elsewhere. The libertarian *Zeitgeist* of the 1960s entailed so-called 'anti-psychiatry' emerging in several countries (the US, Britain, France, Italy) in different forms. However, the fact that de-institutionalisation occurred earlier in the US than elsewhere is likely to have been an important factor. In Britain there was a politicisation of mental health but this mainly lay in a radicalisation of the therapeutic community movement. Consequently, in the US, it was understandable that radical mental health workers turned their attention to reversing what in the community seemed to be responsible for the creation of mental health problems.

A further factor in the US related to the presence of a segment of psychiatry which was dedicated to social epidemiology. This tried to uncover the social roots of mental health problems. Social psychiatry has a tradition in Britain too, but this has tended to focus on the production of secondary deviance generated by large mental hospitals (Barton, 1959), and secondary or tertiary prevention, as in the work on expressed emotion discussed in more detail below.

The Secondary Prevention Emphasis in Britain

General practitioners and primary health care services have been targeted as the agency for the secondary prevention of mental health problems. The rationale for this is that GP's are the officially designated gatekeepers of health services, and the first port of call for patients. Because of their ready accessibility, GPs are likely to have contact with most of their patients on an annual basis. Goldberg and Huxley (1980) suggested that over a period of a year, over 90 per cent of patients deemed to be suffering from a mental disorder made contact with their GP.

A focus of those advocating a concerted approach to secondary prevention is the screening and diagnosis of mental disorders. It has been estimated that through everyday consultations 'family practitioners are able to detect 60 per cent of all mental disorders'. However, formal screening devices are considered to yield higher detection rates (Falloon and Fadden, 1993). Mental distress is considered to be frequently masked by somatisation (the presentation of physical signs and symptoms) which may make detection more difficult. The use of formal diagnostic tools such as the Present State Examination and Mini Mental State Suicide Risk schedule are thought to increase detection rates, thereby allowing earlier intervention and referral to services.

However, different stakeholders hold differing views about the value of GPs accurately identifying the presence of psychopathology. Psychiatrists, who have been the main proponents of screening and have been instrumental in the design of tools specifically for this purpose, tend to view early screening as a self-evidently desirable goal. Moreover, they see GPs being guided in this task by the psychiatric profession. For example Creed and Marks (1989) state: 'Support and advice from psychiatrists enables GPs to improve their care of patients with psychiatric and psychological problems.' As a result of this input, the authors go on to say, 'the skills of general practitioners and their trainees are enhanced'. There has been a less enthusiastic response from some GPs who view the relationship between GPs and psychiatrists as an unequal and increasingly irrelevant one as GPs form new relationships with workers in other mental health disciplines such as psychology, counselling and social work (Ferguson and Varnam, 1994).

There is also evidence that users might not always place the same value on the screening and detection of mental illness as psychiatrists do. The fact that GPs are sometimes poor diagnosticians, as judged by traditional psychiatric standards, and hold views closer to lay definitions of mental health problems means that users may *prefer* them to specialists. Moreover it is interesting to note the discrepancy between the traditional psychiatric views outlined above about the tendency of GPs to miss mental health problems through somatisation, and the views of users in the same study who claimed that at times GPs fail to take seriously their physical complaints.

Reducing the suicide rate: a flawed secondary prevention strategy?

Contemporary government policy on mental health prevention emphasises a primary care focus. In the *Health of the Nation* (DH, 1992), for
example, primary health care workers, and GPs in particular, are identified
as the key people to reduce the suicide rate. The *Health of the Nation*
identified a reduction in the suicide rate as one of its primary aims, in
order to improve the mental health of the population. This is included
within targets to:

• improve significantly the health and social functioning of mentally
  ill people.
• reduce the overall suicide rate by 15 per cent by the year 2000 (from
  11 per 100,000 in 1990 to 9.4).
• reduce the suicide rate of severely mentally ill people by at least 33
  per cent by the year 2000 (from the estimated rate of 15 per cent in
  1990 to no more than 10 per cent).

Whilst government *Health of the Nation* targets have shown improvement overall the scope for reducing the suicide rate is limited, given
the present strategy. Moreover, it seems unlikely that a reliance on GP
skills and directing interventions purely at the symptoms of mental
illness will be effective in the longer term. The *Health of the Nation*
assumes that suicide is a direct manifestation of mental illness. The
rationale then goes like this: psychiatric morbidity needs to be detected
and treated, and this early intervention will reduce the incidence of
suicide. However, both the range of assumed causes and the official
categorisations of suicide are complex. Mental illness may not always
be an antecedent correlate, let alone a 'cause' of suicide. There are
many people who commit suicide whom any psychiatrist would not
label as mentally ill – for example those with a terminal illness or
those who, for existential reasons, consider their life to be over.
    Even for those who have had a previous history of mental illness,
their psychiatric condition may not be the main precipitating factor.
For example, pharmacists have one of the highest rates of suicide because of their access to the effective means of taking their own lives.
Similarly, many of the psychoactive drugs given to mental health service
users, if taken in overdose, are lethal. Hence, it may be ready access
to large amounts of toxic drugs which is primarily implicated in the
suicide of some social groups like pharmacists and psychiatric patients.
In the latter case, psychological disturbance may be compounded by

medical prescribing norms in relation to anti-depressants, major tranquillisers, anti-Parkinsonian agents and other drugs. If polypharmacy
(more than one drug being prescribed at the same time) is present,
then both intended and unintended self-harm increase in probability.

There are other possibilities too. Paradoxically, the detection and
treatment of a major mental illness may actually contribute to the suicide
rate. The pessimism surrounding the diagnosis of schizophrenia, the
iatrogenic impact of major tranquillisers, regular compulsory detention, and being unemployed and unemployable, might cumulatively lead
to a *rational* appraisal in patients that their lives are not worth living.
In other words, psychiatric patients are not just diagnosed as being ill,
they are subjected or exposed, in that role, to a series of events which
create depression and anomie. Indeed, many psychiatric patients diagnosed as schizophrenic, who are living in the community, struggle not
with active symptoms of psychosis but with the apathy and demorali-
sation arising from their social marginalisation (Barham and Hayward,
1991).

The *Health of the Nation* has also been criticised for paying 'little
attention to tackling the social conditions associated with this problem' (Baughan, 1993). The strategy emphasises screening and changing individual behaviour, whilst ignoring the structural influences
implicated in suicide. Baughan points out the importance of negative
life events – particularly attitudes towards and experience of unemployment in youth suicide. This analysis implies the need to reduce
youth unemployment and improve social conditions more generally. In
addition, greater consideration may need to be given to the provision
of counselling services in further and higher education rather than in
GPs' surgeries.

The cultural norms of machismo may make it less easy for young
men to admit to emotional problems either to informal networks or
more formal counselling services. Thus, anti-sexist education in schools,
together with education in dealing with personal troubles in the school
curriculum, might be an effective way of raising awareness of dealing
with intractable life situations and stressful life events (death, unemployment, divorce, etc.). It might also reduce the stigma of 'help-seek-
ing' amongst young men.

Labelling is also likely to play a significant role in who is, and who
is not, defined as a suicide risk. The recognition and labelling of the
act of suicide varies socially and culturally and is affected by the categorisations of a multiplicity of agencies, including medical practitioners, coroners and those who collate official statistics. One particular

consideration is who is likely to be labelled as a 'suicide risk'. For example, are depressed young white women more likely to be viewed as a risk than young black men diagnosed as schizophrenic? Does the latter diagnosis discourage professionals from formulating the problems of psychotic patients in personal and social terms? How are *attempts* at suicide viewed by health service personnel – genuine attempts, cries for help or manipulative gestures? All of these relevant factors are not addressed by a blinkered effort at diagnostic screening.

Tertiary Prevention

Whereas the hallmark of secondary prevention is accurate initial screening, tertiary prevention has a different focus. It is geared towards minimising the impact of mental illnesses on patients' lives and preventing the 'relapse' of recurring disorders such as 'schizophrenia'. The purpose of screening by mental health professionals here is to identify, and if possible intervene in, the determinants of psychopathology, in order to minimise the probability of distress recurring. Interventions are generally pitched at the level of the individual or their family and are based on the principles of cognitive psychology or operant conditioning. Most of these strategies are aimed at the individual adjusting to their social context.

There have been a number of important research findings in recent years which has suggested various ways of minimising recurrence of disorders. These are mainly social interventions. The identification of biological vulnerability is limited. However, acute episodes of mental distress are linked at times to nutritional variables, the effects of physical disorders, brain damage and the effect of drugs (Falloon and Fadden, 1993).

In the area of those with a diagnosis of schizophrenia, the work of Brown and his colleagues implies certain policy strategies to minimise the recurrence of acute mental distress. From this work two sets of findings about the social environment of vulnerable people suggest ways of reducing the prevalence of acute episodes and improving the quality of life of patients. A study carried out by Brown and Wing (1962) indicated that under-stimulation and total institutional settings were found to result in withdrawal and regression. On the other hand, over-stimulation was found to be detrimental too. Brown *et al.* (1966) noted that patients discharged to a hostel rather than back into a family setting often did better. Exploring this observation further, in subsequent studies, people with a diagnosis of schizophrenia are more likely to relapse where they are discharged to families expressing 'high expressed emotion' (a combination of critical comments, hostility and 'over-involvement'). Family therapy and educational models aimed at exploring family dynamics and reducing levels of expressed emotion have also been found to be successful.

Cross-cultural studies have also pointed to preventative strategies. In India, where long-term recovery rates are better, studies suggest that families with a member who has been labelled as schizophrenic are far less likely to show evidence of high expressed emotion than in Britain. A further observation implicating the broader social and economic environment has also been made by Warner. A study of the political economy of schizophrenia (Warner, 1985) suggests that developing countries are more conducive to recovery than Western nations. Developing countries appear to promote greater reintegration and the rehabilitation of social roles for people who have had a psychotic breakdown. This more successful re-socialisation seems to be linked to a combination of: family patterns of support, with low levels of expressed emotion; a return to valued work roles; and a lower level of stigma about mental illness. In the West, ex-patients often end up unemployed or confined to doing menial low-status jobs in occupational schemes with poor pay. A further indication that the social context rather than individual factors is important is the longitudinal study in Europe by Ciompi (1984), which has shown that social opportunities for worthwhile employment are a much better predictor of recovery than severity of diagnosis.

From the above discussion, it is clear that the social environment of people diagnosed as schizophrenic is a central feature in tertiary preventive policies. The reduction of expressed emotion in the family, the provision of adequate and suitable non-family-based accommodation and employment opportunities, and a flexible and tailored mental health management plan, which involves the patient's family, are all implicated. And yet there is little evidence that such approaches are widely adopted in contemporary psychiatric practice. There remains a reliance on large doses of major tranquillisers, coupled with the belief that 'schizophrenics' do poorly in response to psychological treatments. Thus there appears to be a major gap between the psychiatric literature on what is known about tertiary preventative practice and its actual implementation.

Barriers to Preventative Practice

We noted earlier that prevention has not been a high priority in British mental health policy. Examples of primary prevention come from the US and have impacted little here. Our secondary prevention strategies have proved modest in their remit and implementation in practice. Tertiary prevention is something that is widely discussed by social psychiatrists in Britain but there is little evidence of it being put into regular practice. We discussed the possible reasons for the emergence in the US of a strong primary prevention tradition and its absence in the UK in the context of the politics of mental health during the 1960s. Additionally, there appear to be a number of barriers to placing preventative practice at the centre of the mental health work.

Newton (1988) discusses some of the barriers to prevention. Firstly, *conceptual vagueness* is an impediment to the planning of preventative services, research and policies. The wide-ranging notions of prevention (primary, secondary and tertiary) mean that the concept covers everything from vulnerability factors and macro-social problems to the providing of treatment and care to prevent recurring crises. Additionally, 'mental illness' remains a catch-all phrase with little practical specificity. The second impediment Newton identifies is the lack of influence that research has had on practice, policy and the delivery of services. As we have seen from the US case-study described above, this may in part be accounted for by poor etiological specificity, which renders the design and implementation of effective interventions difficult. None the less, there are examples of conditions where the impact of interventions is marked, which strongly implicate a certain type of service provision.

The reason for this gap between research knowledge and service provision is not altogether clear. The separateness of the organisation of research and clinical services is likely to be an important factor (i.e. the university versus the 'clinic'). Policy-makers are on the whole influenced by practitioners, who have the main responsibility for setting up and running projects. Research which clearly points to a type of service is therefore easily marginalised because this knowledge is rarely known about or promoted by other stakeholders in the local planning and delivery of services. As Newton notes, 'Public policy has tended to be influenced more by enthusiasm than evaluated information and information has been generalised to problems it was never meant to solve' (Newton, 1988, p. 10).

Moreover, the planning of service provision makes prevention strat-

egies an unattractive proposition. Despite the drawing-up of long-term
plans of service delivery, until recently planning has been characterised by *ad hocism* and incrementalism (i.e. making minor adjustments
to existing arrangements). Planners are anxious to be seen to be 'doing something'. In contrast, reorientating towards prevention requires
extensive changes to existing arrangements and personnel, and the results of prevention policies are often difficult to measure. Managers or
purchasers of current services are under pressure to demonstrate a short-
term impact of their decisions – prevention may not fit well with this.
Also, they are now discovering the US lesson that prevention may
implicate social variables outside of the jurisdiction and potential control of health services. A problem related to this is the focus of clinicians. They have a vested interest in the identification and treatment
of disorders rather than prevention. The latter requires different approaches and personnel. The leap from being a medical practitioner to
a housing and employment 'broker' is a big one. The elitism, high
social status and treatment emphasis of hospital consultants militate
against such role flexibility. Do GPs then have more potential in this
regard? Will they be more prevention orientated? And will they cast
off the problems associated with a medicalised approach to mental health
work in the psychiatric hospital?

Primary Health Care

A primary care focus is an important trend in mental health policy. As
we have noted already, GPs are being expected increasingly to fulfil
both a secondary prevention and an after-care role (which subsumes
implicitly tertiary prevention). For some time after the setting-up of
the NHS, GPs operated in the shadows of their hospital counterparts
and so they attempted to emulate hospital medical practice:

> The recurrent concern about trivial demands, the desire for hospital
> work, and the emphasis on academically acceptable foundations are
> all examples of the continuing influence exerted by the consultants
> over their generalist colleagues during this period. (Calnan and Gabe,
> 1991, p. 145)

The relationship of general practice to mainstream hospital provision
is also embedded in the legislative and other arrangements pertaining
to mental patients during the two decades after the setting-up of the

NHS. This is clearly reflected in the part that GPs assumed in connection to the procedures for the assessment of patients for compulsory admission to hospital. Compulsory admissions under the 1983 (and previously the 1959) Mental Health Act generally require two medical recommendations. One of these is a psychiatrist (usually a consultant) and the other should be a registered medical practitioner with personal knowledge of the patient which is usually for this reason their GP.

The thinking behind this combination was that each of the medical practitioners could bring something different to the assessment – the psychiatrist his or her specialist knowledge and the general practitioner his or her personal knowledge of the patient. In theory, the idea envisaged by the designers of the mental health legislation specifying medical recommendations (under the 1959 Act) was that the GP could act as a corrective to the psychiatrist's assessment, if the need arose. In practice, however, GPs probably rarely challenge the authority of psychiatrists, who, as the 'specialists', are likely to be the key decision-makers (Bean, 1986).

Certainly there is evidence to suggest that GPs tend to defer to a psychiatrist's opinion. For example, in a recent study, a comparison of GPs' and psychiatrists' decision-making showed that GPs' decisions were strongly influenced by the presence of a previously acquired psychiatric label in making referrals, whereas there was no similar influence on psychiatrists in their decisions about clients (Farmer and Griffiths, 1992). This suggests that in relation to mental health legislation and referral, GPs may still view themselves as subordinate to their hospital colleagues. Certainly, as we discussed earlier in this chapter, in relation to diagnosis and ability to detect and manage mental disorder, specialists currently view GPs as inferior psychiatrists, and appropriateness of referral and treatment remains a construct defined and operationalised by psychiatry.

During the 1980s, this negative view of GPs was also prevalent in the wider community, in relation to the prescribing of benzodiazepines (minor tranquillisers). During the 1970s and 1980s these drugs, which were widely prescribed by GPs, came to be associated with addictive and dependency-inducing properties. Young or middle-aged women suffering from anxiety and depression were portrayed in the media as the victims of inadequate care by GPs (Bury and Gabe, 1990). Despite both litigation and vociferous campaigning from addicted campaigners and cautions from professional bodies, such as the Royal College of Psychiatrists, the number of prescriptions of these drugs fell by only a third between 1979 and 1989 (from 31 million to 22 million) (Medawar, 1992).

Notwithstanding this view of the GP's inadequacies as a mental health practitioner held by psychiatrists, and by the public over the prescribing of minor tranquillisers, the pattern of mental health provision is changing. This has been brought about as a result of the need to provide for the medical requirements of ex-patients and for new patients residing in the community as opposed to hospital, as well as by other organisational factors.

A shift in the subordination of general practice to hospital specialisms started to take place in the 1960s and 1970s. On the whole, the principle advocated by the World Health Organisation in 1978 was adopted. GPs in the UK were to view themselves as allies of their patients, giving basic health care advice and providing as much of a service outside of a hospital setting as possible. There was greater organisation of practices from single-handed to group practices. Primary health care teams, which included nurses and health visitors, began to emerge and general practitioners became employers of clerical and other staff.

There was also a shift in the knowledge base of general practitioners towards a biographic approach to medicine. This stressed the need to engage with the patient in a holistic manner and to view their illness in the framework of their biography and current circumstances (Armstrong, 1979). These changes were important in terms of incorporating mental health within the ambit of primary health care. They built on innovative minority practices already in operation. For example, the Tavistock Clinic pioneered the attachment of social workers and others in primary care, and the group-case seminar approach of Balint (1957). Currently, the biographic approach, which places an emphasis on the psychological needs of patients, is advocated by the profession's leaders, even if the profession itself is divided in the extent to which it applies the model in practice (Calnan and Gabe, 1991).

In relation to mental health provision, the role of primary care has been significantly strengthened in recent years. The creation of Family Health Services Authorities (FHSAs) in place of Family Practitioner Committees in 1990 fortified the provisions for directing the activities of GPs. The FHSAs brought with them the power to allocate funds for new developments. Mental health is one of the new developments to benefit from such funding and some FHSAs are opting to directly fund independent mental health workers to work in primary health care (Goldberg *et al.*, 1993).

The balance of power is also shifting under the reforms introduced by the NHS and Community Care Act 1990. Many GPs are now budget-holders and can act as purchasers as well as providers of services. This places them in a strong position to purchase the type of mental health services they think most fits their patients' needs. Thus, GPs may decide to buy psychological services direct from clinical psychologists or employ counsellors on a sessional basis in their surgeries. However, the disadvantage of this new arrangement is that it may create a form of anarchy with fund-holders failing to conform to a local mental health strategy.

One of the aims which can be identified in the direction of community mental health policy is the intention of creating a 'seamless robe' between the primary and secondary care sectors. Some have argued that what is required is not so much a shift from secondary to primary care but a more 'balanced service'. It has been suggested, for example, that mental health staff such as CMHNs should be allocated to GPs but that these staff should be based in community mental health teams from the mainstream psychiatric services. It is argued that this will provide improvements in community care and bring primary and secondary services closer together (Goldberg *et al.*, 1993). This can also be viewed as a strategy of those in the hospital specialist sector to retain traditional control over an area which is being encroached upon by another health specialty.

Traditional primary and secondary care arrangements between specialist and generalist medical practitioners have been further disrupted by two other community mental health policy developments. The first is the introduction of Community Mental Health Teams (CMHTs) which act as the focal point of most local services. These multi-disciplinary teams are increasingly becoming the main referral point through which GPs and other primary care sources gain access to specialist services and psychiatrists. In effect this replaces the traditional referral arrangements operating between the primary and secondary sector where arrangements are principally made between the GP and hospital-based psychiatrist. Secondly, primary care workers are also being expected to become full participants in the Care Programme Approach (CPA) which was introduced in 1991 as a means of overcoming poorly co-ordinated and fragmented service delivery. The CPA works on the principle of a single plan in which the needs of an individual are assessed and the contributions from each service identified. A single 'key worker' keeps in contact with that individual with the aim of ensuring that all the necessary elements of that care are delivered.

These new working arrangements in a rapidly changing mental health world may already make primary health care workers and GPs in particular vulnerable to a number of accusations about their potential lack of success as (part-time) mental health workers:

(1) As a medical grouping they may simply carry over some of the shortcomings of a medicalised approach to mental health work. For example, they cannot rectify the social difficulties impinging on their patients.

(2) The fundholders amongst them may fail to work within a locality-wide mental health strategy (as they will all make their own idiosyncratic purchasing decisions).

(3) Lacking a history of specialist knowledge about mental health policy, they may be overwhelmed by the administrative expectations from central government about such issues as involvement in care and case management, supervision registers and referral to CMHTs. Their traditional role within sections of the Mental Health Act will encourage a continued subordinate role in relation to psychiatrists. Rather than taking a lead in community mental health they may prefer to allow secondary care specialists to retain their dominance on new sites.

(4) They have had the role of being medical co-ordinators of community care thrust upon them by *Caring for People* (HMSO, 1989), the White Paper preceding the 1990 NHS and Community Care Act. They reacted badly to this imposition, feeling that it would disrupt their traditional work patterns and bring with it new onerous responsibilities. This is not a propitious starting point for them to be enthusiastic about their role in mental health work in the community, whether it be about prevention or treatment.

Of course the above points are mitigated by the finding that psychiatric patients seem to prefer relating to GPs than they do to psychiatrists. However, this favourable expectation from service users is no guarantee in the long term that GPs will prove to be agents of change in community mental health practice.

Conclusion

This chapter has reviewed a set of debates about mental health promotion and the prevention of mental illness. It is clear that to date neither of these have been high on the agenda of the mental health policy formation process in Britain. Organisational changes are now bringing GPs into the spotlight as gatekeepers, agents of prevention and overseers of the care of people with a range of mental health problems living in the community. Apart from this primary care focus (the success of which is in doubt for reasons discussed above) there is little other evidence that either a promotion or prevention emphasis is waiting in the wings of current mental health policy in Britain. By contrast, in the next chapter, we turn to a feature of recent policy which is both new and impactful.

9

Consumerism and Mental Health

Introduction

In Chapter 5 we addressed the triple development of privatisation, marketisation and managerialism during the 1980s in Britain. At first sight, consumerism flows naturally from the underlying market ideology of these three policy features. However, the notion that services governed by such an ideology *necessarily* lead to recipients being treated as 'customers', is flawed in a number of respects. On the other hand, as we noted earlier, user views of services are now part of the discourse about mental health policy, both nationally and locally. This chapter will address the constraints and opportunities for psychiatric patients, which have been associated with consumerism, under the following headings:

- 'Anti-psychiatry' and patients' rights
- The rise of the mental health service users' movement in Britain
- The professional response to users' views
- Consumerism and the labour movement
- The problem of need definition
- Identifying the needs and interests of 'carers'

'Anti-Psychiatry' and Patients' Rights

Concerns about the protection of the human rights of asylum inmates date back to the last century. But, as we noted in Chapter 3, those anxieties were essentially about the inappropriate detention of the sane and they have recurred in recent years. For example, in the 1990s

television documentaries have focused at times on the use of psychiatric
services to unjustly detain and control sane people in Australia and
the US. In the case of the former USSR, Western psychiatrists themselves have compiled critiques of the 'misuse' of forced psychiatric
detention for political ends (e.g. Bloch and Reddaway, 1977). This
conception of psychiatric abuse assumes that 'normal' psychiatric practice
is benign and legitimate – that it is 'non-abusive'. Within this view,
coercive control in the form of detention and treatment is only deemed
inappropriate for those 'falsely' diagnosed as being mentally ill. Similarly diagnostic categories like 'sluggish schizophrenia' are criticised
for their pseudo-scientific status, but similar diagnoses in Western psychiatry are considered to be non-problematic. An example here is the
diagnosis of 'pseudo-neurotic shizophrenia', a form of psychosis mas-
querading as neurosis, which only a trained psychiatrist can detect.
Leaving these questions of the overlap between Western and the old
Soviet forms of psychiatric knowledge aside, a much simpler question
is begged about 'normal' psychiatry. If the detention and treatment of
sane people is offensive and unacceptable, why is the same detention
and treatment, but of insane people, inoffensive and acceptable?

The view that 'normal' psychiatry is acceptable and legitimate has
been contested by both dissident psychiatrists in the US (Szasz, 1971;
Breggin, 1993), Italy (Basaglia, 1981) and Britain (Cooper, 1968; Laing,
1967) and latterly by clinical psychologists hostile to biological psychiatry (Johnstone, 1992). The term 'anti-psychiatry' has often been
used to describe this collection of dissenting professionals, although
only Cooper (ibid) used the term about his own work. The psychiatric
service users' movement emerged internationally at various points in
time in the wake of these professional critiques dating back to the
1960s. We will look at the particular features of the British Mental
Health Users' Movement later on in this chapter.

A number of common concerns emerged across these national developments which included hostility to electroconvulsive therapy (ECT),
major tranquillisers and the use of therapeutic law to detain citizens
without trial. These aspects could also be found earlier in the writings
of dissenting psychiatrists, along with other connecting threads such
as a twin concern for individual freedom and social justice. The current *libertarian* aspect of user campaigning was also common in prior
right- and left-wing critiques of psychiatry. For example, Thomas Szasz's
work on the myth of mental illness (Szasz, 1961) and on the oppression

of institutional psychiatry (Szasz, 1971) is commonly cited with enthusiasm by user critics, who share little in common with his wider political ideology, which is right-wing. He is committed to the free-market principle in relation to any commodity, whether it be opiates or personal therapy.

Professional dissent within the mental health industry focused mainly on: the conceptual weaknesses of psychiatric knowledge; the inadequacy of biological responses to social and existential problems; and infringements of the human rights of psychiatric patients. Given that these areas of dissent came to find favour with disaffected service users, it is little surprising that the latter recognised and respected the authority of the 'anti-psychiatrists'.

The Rise of the Mental Health Service Users' movement in Britain

The work of Laing and of Cooper in Britain was largely ignored and occasionally dismissed indignantly by psychiatrists during the 1970s (e.g. Hamilton, 1973; Roth, 1973). One exception in this regard was Anthony Clare, who essentially expanded traditional theory and practice by conceding some of the arguments of anti-psychiatry (Clare, 1976). By and large, psychiatry carried on regardless in practice and consequently remained a target for criticism.

Moreover, after the 1960s a whole series of radical critiques of traditional authority had emerged which were separate from the established struggles of opposition between capital and labour. The latter was centred on industrial tensions and had been bureaucratised in most Western countries via employers organisations and conservative parties on the one side and trade unions and social democratic parties on the other. The separate opposition movements have come to be known as the new social movements, to distinguish them from the older labour movement. The new social movements are exemplified by struggles to advance the interests of marginalised and oppressed groups in modern society (e.g. the women's and black movements). In the case of animal rights, this has now even extended to other species. New social movements have been contrasted with the labour movement broadly on two grounds. First, they exist in a post-industrial context – the labour movement was a product of an industrial mode of production. Second, the new social movements use different forms of political organisation and action. In Britain, as in other countries, the labour movement was bureaucratised and sought gains through trade-union negotiations and parliamentary representation.

By contrast the new movements often operate outside of these bureaucratic forms or even explicitly criticise hierarchy and mandated authority – libertarianism is a strong and recurrent motif in these movements. One central feature of new social movements is the role of identity. Being black, being a woman, being disabled, etc. often represents both a ticket of entry to the movement and an ongoing source of motivation and group solidarity. However, some members may not have that particular identity (e.g. 'allies' in the mental health service movement). Another feature of these movements is that they have no definitive or stable programme of action or even organisational goals. They change, often in response to new contingencies. Moreover, within the same broad grouping there may be quite varied ideologies operating. Apart from politics being typically personalised within new social movements, their other characteristic feature is the emphasis on direct action demonstrations, local and national lobbying, artistic events and forms of protest idiosyncratic to the particular cause.

With these general characteristics in mind, let us now look briefly at the rise of the British mental health service movement, which we discuss in more detail elsewhere (Rogers and Pilgrim, 1991). This movement was late in developing compared with the US, Canada and the Netherlands. It eventually gained noticeable momentum by the late 1980s. For example, it took direct action to campaign against the moves by the Royal College of Psychiatrists to introduce some version of Community Treatment Order in 1987. Around the same time it lobbied the Advertising Standards Authority to remove a series of stigmatising posters produced by SANE (Schizophrenia A National Emergency). In 1988 the most significant demonstration of organisational capability was the parliamentary lobby of the shadow health minister. This entailed the co-ordinated efforts of 56 different users' groups nationwide.

The service users' movement is variegated in a number of ways. First, different groups vary in their attitude towards psychiatric orthodoxy. Some believe in the abolition of psychiatry. Others seek to reform it and a small minority adhere to an illness framework and seek only to improve the treatment of 'sufferers'. Second, groups vary in their attitude towards 'allies'. By and large the latter are welcomed but there is also a current of opinion that they are a threat to the integrity of self-advocacy. Third, views vary about the extent to which energy should be expended on service development. Involvement in local consultant action has been a demand of elements of the users' movement, which is now legitimised by government directives and guidance about user involvement. However, some argue that involvement of this type diverts time and energy from wider campaigns.

What this last point highlights is a possible unintended consequence of government reforms which emphasise consumerism. The old Labourist form of health policy tended to be provider-dominated and emphasised issues of equitable access and workers' rights within the NHS. The Conservative agenda has thus provided opportunities for new social movements struggling to advance the interests of the users of health and welfare services. What may not have been anticipated is that Conservative intentions about the rights of individual consumers (embodied in, for example, the Patient's Charter, with its telling apostrophe) have created a political space for the collectivist and anti-Tory aspirations of radical groups. At times this outcome has been amplified by the building of alliances between the new managerial elite in the NHS and users' groups to usurp or challenge the traditional authority of medical elites (Thompson, 1987).

The Professional Response to Users' Views

The views of mental health service users are potentially at odds with a professional viewpoint for two broad reasons. First, psychiatric patients are characterised, by definition, by some degree of temporary or permanent irrationality. As credibility is bound up with reason, then those deemed to have lost the latter also tend to lose their credibility in whole or part. The views of anti-psychiatrists described earlier challenged this logic by introducing the notion that conduct which lacks immediate intelligibility may, in fact, be understandable if the person's inner world and social context are explored properly. For their part, users more recently have suggested that their actions are provoked by various sources of oppression. This was captured in the title of the user-made TV documentary *We're Not Mad We're Angry* in 1988. Both these approaches to rendering the irrational intelligible tend to cut little ice with orthodox psychiatry and with most forms of psychodynamic therapy. A second challenge for professionals in accepting users' views is that they may be (and often are) hostile to current psychiatric theory and practice.

Thus mental health professionals have had a number of difficulties in conceding the viewpoint of their patients. This is also the case with some social policy researchers and commentators as well. We have examined the ways in which the views of psychiatric patients have been resisted or ignored in some detail elsewhere (Rogers *et al.*, 1993). Essentially four professional responses have been present:

1. Users' views unsupportive of professional interests are rejected.
2. The irrationality of patients is emphasised.
3. Patients and their relatives are deemed to have the same interests and to hold the same views.
4. Patients' views are re-framed to suit those of professionals.

More recently there are signs, however, that clinical professionals are beginning to shift over the issue of the legitimacy of service users' views. This is noticeable in the increasing number of short reports of local audits of mental health services, which include within them a sampling of patients' views of service satisfaction. This may be a reflection of clinicians conceding a loss of power to the inevitable new order dominated by a new elite of service commissioners. The traditional resistance to allowing patients a legitimate voice may well now be collapsing in the face of new political forces being brought to bear in each locality.

Notwithstanding these new concessions to 'patient power', it would be incautious to read too much into the potential that the emerging picture holds for patients' rights. It is the case, as we have noted earlier, that marketisation and privatisation have been important determinants of recent consumerism. However, as far as mental health services are concerned, consumerism has only a limited potential in favouring shifts of power and interests to service users. If taken to its logical conclusion, allowing markets to regulate social relationships would always privilege the consumer. The latter would opt for better forms of care, and inferior versions of the latter would wither from lack of demand. However, the NHS, the main supplier of the bulk of mental health services, has not been abolished or been seriously privatised despite recurrent fears and claims of this from the left. Thus it is still questionable as to whether or not any NHS patient can act like a proper consumer. That is, the marketisation of the NHS by creating a split between purchasers and providers means the latter have a monopoly most of the time, in most localities, and the former are not patients but managers in purchasing authorities or are fundholding GPs.

Marketisation has introduced new ideological expectations of consumerism, particularly in terms of the patient perspective being included in audit and service planning. But this influence, relatively, has been limited in its impact. This may be due to the contradictory position of health consumers generally as manipulated components of a marketing enterprise and as radical opponents to a medically dominated health care system. Because 'commissioning' agencies make proxy decisions on behalf of patients, one professional discourse, that of clinical professionals, has been displaced by another, that of service purchasers. What impact there has been about taking the 'customer's' view seriously has arisen because in making their proxy decisions, purchasers may be genuinely concerned to get a 'good buy' on behalf of patients. These good intentions have to be supported by an informed confidence on the part of purchasers when challenging conservative providers. The wishes of the latter will still predominate if their purchasing managers are uneducated about the shortcomings of psychiatric theory and practice, or insecure about challenging medical interests.

These general cautions about consumerism triumphing in the NHS are reinforced by the particular position of psychiatric patients. A consumer model can only retain coherence if the supply of a service is regulated by demand from those wishing to use that service. But many psychiatric patients do not ask for what they get – it is imposed on them. Various sections of the 1983 Mental Health Act, like its legal predecessors, are utilised to lawfully impose restraints and treatments on resentful and reluctant recipients. In such circumstances, mental patients could only be construed to be consumers if being dragged off of the street and forced fed was a feature of being a customer in a restaurant. Whether or not the principle of coercion in mental health law is deemed to be fair and reasonable, it is clear that no logical case can be made for calling detained patients 'consumers' or 'customers' – the cornerstone of contemporary Conservative health policy.

Thus the ideology of consumerism, with its attendant assumption that the market is the key determinant of good social policy (be it about schools, transport or health facilities), has generated a number of difficulties for Conservative ministers. In recent years the latter have supported or issued a number of policy statements which are directly at odds with consumerism. Two in particular illustrate these contradictions. They highlight that government's main concern was not to support the consumer rights of patients but was instead to hold professionals responsible for self-harm and anti-social acts.

As we noted in Chapter 8, the *Health of the Nation* (DH, 1992b) set a target of reducing suicide in both the general and the psychiatric populations by set amounts by the year 2000. Re-framing social problems which culminate in personal anger and despair as an individual health problem (suicide), and then holding health professionals responsible for its incidence, is clearly politically convenient. If professionals fail in their task in this regard, then politicians can devolve blame for individual acts of self-harm. These acts are rooted in the problem with, not the solution of, the market. The largest increase in suicides has been in the very group (young men) whose identity has been most marred by the absence of long-term employment.

The second policy initiative of relevance here has been the push for Supervision Registers, which the DoH demanded were in place in every locality by October 1994. Groups such as SANE and the NSF had been lobbying for the enforcement of community treatment for a number of years. It is ironical that the users' campaign against the Royal College of Psychiatrists in 1988 about Compulsory Treatment Orders (CTOs), noted above, was striking at an ambivalent opponent, as the College membership was split about their desirability. Even the College's own recent endorsement of the weaker measure of supervision orders has been issued alongside complaints that new legal powers are not a substitute for better resourced mental health services. The issue of community surveillance will be discussed further in Chapter 10.

Consumerism and the Labour Movement

At the time of writing (1995) Britain remains under a Conservative administration and has done so for sixteen years. During that long absence from office, the Labour Party and the public service trade unions have had the time and obligation to reflect on and modify their policy on a number of matters including the rights of service recipients. One of the boldest policy shifts and reviews in this regard came from COHSE (now part of UNISON) which, during the mid-1980s, began to support community- rather than hospital-based care. By the late 1980s it was encouraging collaboration with user groups (Read and Wallcraft, 1992). COHSE also commissioned policy critiques such as that by Carpenter (1994b) which we noted in Chapter 5.

In 1993 John Smith instigated a series of policy reviews ('forums') inside the Labour Party about a number of topics, one of which was mental health. The latter invited a wide membership which was not dominated by service providers but included user representatives, academic researchers and people working in the voluntary sector of care. The overall impact of these adjustments to the previous labour movement trajectory which was unambiguously provider-led has been that mental health policy from the labour movement is showing a greater sensitivity to the rights of service users than was previously the case. In this regard, if user campaigning has had an influence on Labour policy it raises some interesting conceptual questions about making a neat separation between old and new social movements. A relevant existing example of the mixing of parliamentary and extra-parliamentary political forms was the common overlapping membership of CND and the Labour Party. With the collapse of Leninism in much of the East and the political diversification of the aims of Western social democratic parties beyond the demands of labour organisations, it may be that old and new social movements are being brought together rather than being separated. What is currently missing in regard to the influence of the mental health service users' movement is the opportunity of a Labour government to be tested in its commitment in practice to a new pluralistic health and welfare agenda.

The. Problem of Need Definition

The shifting power balance between providers, purchasers and service users is one framework for understanding the current picture about the impact of consumerism on mental health policy and practice. Likewise the intermingling of old and new social movements on the left has possibly generated a new pluralistic agenda, which moves mental health debates away from the views of the workforce only and towards wider questions of citizenship. However, such a singular focus on shifting power relationships may also obscure an associated but separate problem: that of need definition.

This is a conceptual not just a political question. The pragmatic imperatives of those commissioning and running services may obscure some unresolved underlying difficulties, which continue to exist about defining the need for mental health services. One of these, already noted, is that some people receiving services are forced (usually lawfully) into the role. In what sense are they in need of a service? And according to whom – their treating professionals, their relatives, anxious strangers in public places? One framework that helps us to clarify this type of dilemma is that put forward by Bradshaw (1994). He makes a distinction between four types of need. The first of these is 'defined' or 'normative need', which is identified by professionals. The second is 'felt need' which is a subjective state of desire or want. This may be converted into the next category – 'expressed need'. Basically, this refers to people saying or asking for what they want from services. The fourth category which Bradshaw describes is that of 'comparative need'. This refers to identifying whose needs should be prioritised – the question of equity.

These distinctions are useful, not because they solve unending debates about how to define need and how to respond to or reduce it. What the distinctions do is highlight the potential tensions which exists between the four categories. They also suggest that policies designed to respond mainly to one type of need may fail to address needs defined in a different way. Let us take some examples in relation to mental health. First, returning to the example of the coerced recipient, we can see that services at present are shaped, at least in part, by decisions based upon normative not expressed need. If the latter completely determined service utilisation then no patient would be held formally under the Mental Health Act. Detained patients are in hospital because some other party has engineered that outcome (responded to normative need) not because they have requested admission – they have not experienced a felt need and then expressed it as request for admission.

Another example is the finding that although patients prioritise talking-treatments when asked to identify which psychiatric interventions they prefer (Rogers *et al.*, 1993), the treatments are actually biased towards chemotherapy and ECT. This example highlights that need definition also underpins styles of service practice. Moreover, it raises a consideration about need which lies outside of Bradshaw's typology. If clinicians defend their right to clinical freedom about choice of treatment or their right to treat (see Chapter 4), are they expressing their *own* needs, under the guise of defining the needs of others? In other words, the current debates about need definition and needs assessment focus very much on a problematic category of 'them' (patients) and evade relevant questions about the needs of 'us' (non-patients). In practice, the latter group make decisions about the former group in the light of the needs of *both or either* party.

A third example is in relation to comparative need. A number of policy analyses have pointed out that unrewarding long-term service users are often not prioritised by service providers. The latter opt to work with more rewarding groups of patients (see Chapter 10). An example of how expressed needs and comparative needs may be met separately is the existence of private psychotherapy. Those patients with the ability to pay for this will have their expressed needs met (at least when the outcome is positive); however, private practice is *ipso facto* discriminatory on grounds of wealth. It excludes many people wanting it and so it is iniquitous.

Each of these examples show something of the problem of naively assuming that services can be planned on the back of psychiatric epidemiology. They can of course be planned in this way but they would be built solely on normative need. Once expressed need is brought into play then a different service configuration might be implied. This is most clearly seen in the example of the 'Hearing Voices' campaigning/self-help group. This group of people would on the basis of presenting with symptoms of auditory hallucinations normally be diagnosed as schizophrenic, according to traditional psychiatric criteria. However, if their expressed needs arising from the experience of hearing voices were taken into consideration, then a singular response (aimed at suppressing the experience) would be inadequate. It would be replaced instead by a responses including tolerance and various ways of negotiating meaning about the experience with the people involved.

Currently service purchasers are making *ad hoc* judgements based upon both types of input. A normative approach to planning a service inevitably will reflect professional interests, as it is built upon medical categories of information gathering. An approach based primarily on expressed needs is more likely to reflect user interests. This might explain why users, who want the help required to live an ordinary life, get frustrated with providers, who tend to see need narrowly in terms of providing services and treatments for the illnesses they diagnose.

Bradshaw summarises the tension between a medical and social model of needs assessment by pointing out that:

> Needs assessment has emerged from and quickly settled into the language of priority setting, economic efficiency, cost-effectiveness and the market-orientated preoccupations of the political right . . . If we are to adapt a social definition of health, then we have to be involved in research on a much wider range of issues than merely the assessment of the prevalence of medical conditions. (Bradshaw, 1994, p. 55)

A tolerance of the co-existence of the two models of response to need is commonplace. An example of this is the stance of the Mental Health Foundation, which defines the overall scale of need for service by referring to psychiatric epidemiology but also emphasises the rights of citizenship demanded by service users (see Chapter 10). At times, the implications of the two models are identical. An example here is the convergence of the two models about the cost-effectiveness of community-based service models. However, at other times the two models are clearly incompatible. The use of normative need to justify enforced hospitalisation is at odds with the expressed needs of people to retain their freedom.

The tension between a social model of need built upon the views of ordinary people and an official epidemiological approach also reflects a recent tension about which accounts about illness are to be privileged. When lay and professional accounts coincide then policy-makers can proceed with some confidence in their decisions. However, a problem undoubtedly arises when the views diverge. Another problem can arise when academic analysts, who are committed to an objectivist framework of population-level need analysis, remain reliant on medical knowledge, which may be distrusted by service users.

An example recently is that of the work of Doyal and Gough (1991) in their *A Theory of Human Need*. The commitment of the authors to defining need properly, in order to justify equity, leads them to reject the implications of relativism and constructivism. The latter approaches (currently popular in medical sociology) emphasise the problem of objective definition: needs, like other phenomena studied, are deemed to be relative to time and place and are understood as being the product of negotiated meanings between parties with different viewpoints. By contrast, Doyal and Gough attempt a defence of the universality of needs. This leads them to identify what they consider to be objective indicators of 'basic need-satisfaction'.

When this model is applied to people with mental health problems it falls back squarely on to medical epidemiology. Doyal and Gough discuss 'mental disorder', along with 'cognitive deprivation' and 'opportunities for economic activities', under a notion of 'autonomy', which is separated from 'physical health'. Their indicator as to whether or not a society is responding to mental disorder is 'the prevalence of severe psychotic, depressive and other mental illness' (Doyal and Gough, ibid., p. 190). At no point do they concede conceptual problems about psychiatric knowledge nor analyse the oppressive role professionals may play at times. For the time being, there appears to be an unre-

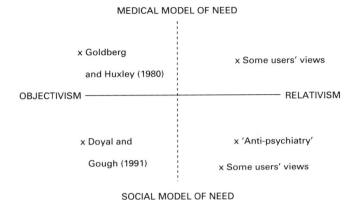

MEDICAL MODEL OF NEED

x Goldberg   x Some users' views

and Huxley (1980)

OBJECTIVISM ————————————————— RELATIVISM

x Doyal and   x 'Anti-psychiatry'

Gough (1991)   x Some users' views

SOCIAL MODEL OF NEED

FIGURE 9.1   *Different approaches to need assessment*

solved debate between social determinists like Doyal and Gough and
the relativist critiques of psychiatric knowledge, which have been associated with both 'anti-psychiatry' and the mental health service users'
movement. Both emphasise a social approach to need, but they differ
along an objectivism–relativism dimension. Thus, we could situate different approaches to need assessment within four boxes produced by the
intersection of two dimensions, as in Figure 9.1.

It can be seen that we have placed 'some users' views' in two places
in Figure 9.1. This is to indicate that the users' movement contains a
mixture of ideologies. Most of the users' movement can probably be
situated in the bottom right box. The largest users' organisations like
Survivors Speakout and United Kingdom Advocacy Network (UKAN)
are examples in this regard. They are consistently critical of medically
dominated services and they emphasise rights of citizenship. However,
some are in the top right box. An example here would be that of the
small users' group associated with the National Schizophrenia Fellowship (Voices). This accepts the medical label of schizophrenia, describes
users as 'sufferers' and accepts the likelihood that the condition is biologically caused. However, these people also defend their right to be
heard about the quality of service delivery from their own experience
and perspective.

What is clear is that the top half of the diagram implies a response
to need dominated by *services*. By contrast, the bottom half of the
diagram implies a response to need based mainly around social rights.

The right half of the diagram emphasises a *lay* perspective, whereas the left half emphasises the views of *experts*. These different emphases highlight and return us to a point made at the start of this section: definition of needs are contested and they reflect underlying tensions about knowledge, as well as power.

The issues of knowledge and power, and their expression through interests, is a focus of the recent analytical work on consumerism in the NHS by Williamson (1993). She makes the valid point that an emphasis on interests takes us further than power and knowledge alone:

> Consumerism in health care is often discussed in terms of knowledge or power, as if it were consumerism in commerce. I think that looking at consumerism in health care in terms of interests offers a more liberating analysis. It allows the dynamics of the convergences, conflicts and interchanges between consumerism and professionalism to be understood with sympathy towards both sides. It recognises that although some people lack power or knowledge, they always have interests and that when their interests are met, they do not need to secure them through knowledge or power. It takes account of the existential and not merely the political weakness of patients. (Williamson, 1993, pp. 2–3)

Williamson extends the work of Alford (1975) about structural interests in health care (see Chapter 2) in order to unpack the ways in which the interests of professionals and those of patients can be antagonistic or complementary. Her two main dimensions of analysis are synergistic/non-synergistic interests and dominant/repressed interests (see Figure 9.2). Synergistic interests are compatible or concordant ones.

For example for our purposes we might think of the depressed patient successfully seeking help from a psychotherapist or a GP prescribing anti-depressants. In this case the interests of the patients (to be helped) and those of the professional (to be paid a salary and deploy a treatment they like) are both being met. However, at other times interests may be incompatible or discordant. An example here might be the person who is depressed and reluctantly agrees to ECT. The person feels under duress but is too low to protest and goes through a frightening and unhelpful experience. The professional prescriber of ECT on the other hand has their interest met (by using a treatment of their choice).

The other concept Williamson (1993) uses is that of dominant interests. This is a rephrasing of the established work on medical dominance

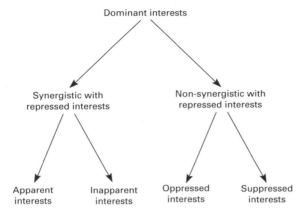

FIGURE 9.2   *Synergies and non-synergies between dominant and repressed interests*

Source: Williamson (1993).

within medical sociology (Freidson, 1970; Turner, 1990). Basically, clinical professionals – especially, but not only, medical practitioners – have interests which prevail over patients. There are clearly degrees of this. The surgeon faced with patients who for crucial periods of time are unconscious has more opportunity to exert his or her dominance (both before and during operations) than a general practitioner who relies on building a long-term, voluntary and compliant relationship with patients. In the case of psychiatry, as well, a range of contingencies may arise along this dimension. When therapeutic law is used to detain or treat patients against their wishes then it is clear that their interests are being repressed. By contrast, the patient who works out a treatment plan with their psychiatrist does not have their interests repressed.

To complicate matters Williamson also notes that people are not always aware of their interests being met or denied. Figure 9.2 outlines her view of the four different outcomes in practice when the dominant interests of professionals are either synergistic or non-synergistic with repressed interests. Applying this set of outcomes to mental health we could envisage the following examples:

1. *Apparent interests*: A CPN carefully checks with a patient about their morale and asks whether they require any extra home visits.

The patient is fully aware of this activity, is grateful to the professional for their consideration and gratefully accepts the invitation for more contact.

2. *Inapparent interests*: A social worker spends an hour ringing various housing agencies to find a placement for a patient awaiting discharge from a secure hospital. The patient is not aware of this activity.

3. *Oppressed interests*: A service users' group campaigns without success to have a leaflet they have produced on the hazards of psychotropic medication made available to all patients in a local district general hospital (DGH) psychiatric unit. The users are fully aware of what is happening but, for the time being at least, professional power has blocked their demands.

4. *Suppressed interests*: A patient new to the psychiatric system is given major tranquillisers but not told anything about the iatrogenic risks involved in their use. Here staff withhold important information, which keeps the patient in ignorance and jeopardises their health and well-being.

The strength of Williamson's analysis lies in it going beyond a simplistic conceptual and political opposition between consumerism and professionalism. The latter two *are* opposed at times but at other times they are not. This returns us to the question raised by Carpenter (1994b) in Chapter 5 about the possibility of a mental health service which is both user and worker-friendly. Without a framework for examining the ways in which the interests of users and professional may in various ways either coincide or clash, one is left having to be either pro- or anti-professional. Williamson's framework for this reason has a sophisticated explanatory potential. For example, to return to the range of user group views we mentioned above, it is rare to find users who believe that psychiatry should be abolished (the Campaign for the Abolition of Psychiatry, CAPO, has but a handful of members in Britain). Equally, the NSF (National Schizophrenia Fellowship) users' group which adheres conventionally to a medical model of illness is a minority position within the users' movement as a whole. This framework also contains the possibility of a convergence of the collective interests of users and professionals.

Having reviewed the issue of needs and then re-framed it as one of interests, it becomes apparent that the meeting of various needs and interests can be analysed as a *dynamic* between groups of social actors (in our case mental health workers and service users in the main). The problem with limiting the discussion to needs alone is that it is always vulnerable to the problem of individualism. Needs ultimately are defined and explained in terms of states inside individuals, who are always patients or clients and very rarely professionals. Clearly these needs do exist – people are distressed and some of them want and may obtain help. But the states are only part of a wider picture in which interests are also in play *between* groups of individuals. The collective interests of these groups can be analysed separately from individual needs.

Identifying the Needs and Interests of 'Carers'

Throughout this chapter we have discussed users' needs, interests and demands. Informal carers have also been identified as an important interest group in both the provision and the burden that caring imposes on mainly women (Finch and Groves, 1980). There is a particularly large body of literature about the provision of forms of community care by the family which entails tending and nursing tasks. However, informal care in the area of mental health is not the same as that associated with carers of people with physical illness or disabilities or of children or elderly people. The distinctions that have been used by social scientists to analyse carers' role (i.e. the distinction between caring for and caring about) are not altogether transferable to mental health. More than any other group of carers, the relatives of people with mental health problems, particularly those diagnosed as schizophrenic, have been implicated in the identified patients' symptom presentation. This is not only true of the arguably sexist view put forward by 'anti-psychiatrists' (Laing and Esterson, 1964) that schizophrenia is primarily related to the 'double-binds' that mothers impose on their children, but also of more mainstream research which illustrates the importance of Expressed Emotion in 'relapse rates' (discussed in Chapter 8).

The relationships between psychiatric patients and their relatives are complex. Situations may arise in which relatives may care about a person but at the same time be very distressed or frightened by their actions. A person who will not get out of bed or acts in a chaotic and menacing way is clearly not easy to live with and will undoubtedly upset their relatives. Whether the strain and distress the latter experiences and is expected to tolerate constitutes caring for the identified

patient is a moot point. As Perring *et al.* (1990) point out, the most
important question in this regard is 'What is it like to live with someone who is diagnosed as mentally ill?' Psychiatric patients may at times
need others to tend to their physical needs but more frequently need
others to tolerate, adapt to or cope with their oddity. The latter can be
both distressing and disruptive to family life. In consequence, relatives of people with mental health problems often develop psychological distress of their own. Indeed, relatives express the need for
psychological support and clear information from statutory services in
this coping role (Goldberg *et al.*, 1993). Given this complexity about
the notion of informal care in mental health, the needs of relatives
should have separate consideration within mental health policy and
provision. It cannot be assumed that their needs and difficulties are
the same as those of the carers of other groups of people, nor can it be
assumed that their needs are the same as those they care for.

Whilst the simple distinction between being a carer and being a disabled person is ambiguous in relation to physical disability (for example
disabled women may care for their children and/or vice versa), it is
even more complex in the case of people with mental health problems.
A psychiatric patient may live at home and care for either children or
older relatives. Also, the relatives of psychiatric patients may be angry
and resentful about the intimate contact which is imposed on them
because they share the same household. Relatives feel obliged to care
for the person with problems in their midst. However, intense domestic
relationships may then aggravate the mental health of both parties. But
sometimes the reverse will apply, and family support will be enabling
to people with mental health problems, as for example in patients returning to the community from secure facilities (Norris, 1984).

A final peculiarity of the carers' role in relation to mental health
problems is at the collective level. Whereas carers' groups in the area
of physical disability are usually marginal or powerless in relation of
social policy, this has not bee the case in relation to mental health
policy. Groups dominated by the interests of relatives such as the NSF
and SANE have often engaged in high profile campaigns which have
overshadowed the public profile of patient-centred groups such as MIND
(Manthorpe, 1994).

Notwithstanding this complexity of roles, recent research on the impact
of community-care mental health reforms in Italy on female relatives
living with psychiatric patients reported results which indicated surprisingly low levels of 'burden'. The findings of this research suggest
that economic prosperity and employment opportunities for women

outside of the home may act as important social support mechanisms in cushioning the negative aspects of living with someone with a severe and enduring mental health problem (Samele, 1993).

Conclusion

This chapter has explored the emergence of consumerism in general and its particular relevance for mental health policy. The sources of consumerism as an ideology may be linked narrowly to the New Right agenda about shaping public services in the image of businesses in a market-place. However, as we note elsewhere in the book, this process has been incomplete and it has led to unintended consequences. It would seem that it has spurred or reinforced the growth of a new social movement of disaffected service users. In turn, the latter has challenged the worker orientation of the labour movement in relation to health policy, as well as traditional medical elites. For different reasons all the major political parties now support a users' voice in the policy formation process.

The chapter then turned to conceptual points about need definitions and interest work. Politicians now have to take account of two competing models in this regard. One emphasises psychiatric services and the other demands for citizenship. At times the service implications of the two guiding models are the same. However, at other times they are different. Consequently the tensions between the two models have to be acknowledged by service purchasers as well as national politicians. Currently it is not clear (to us) whether or not either of these parties are fully recognising the different implications of the two models.

10

Failures and Prospects

Introduction

As we approach the end of the century, there is a continuing debate about the future organisation and arrangements of mental health services. In previous chapters we have discussed the radical shifts of policy, service provision and authority from medical and institutional to non-medical and community stakeholders. The latter include purchasing managers, local authorities and service users. Such changes have involved new political and ethical controversies about madness and liberty, and posed academic problems for policy analysts about notions of both 'community' and 'care'. This final chapter will draw together some of the main strands of our arguments about mental health services to date, and draw out some implications for their future.

It is clear that during most of this century, services have been unimaginative, and institutionally orientated. Overall, these services have been insensitive to the expressed needs of their users. Over the past ten years, a consensus of opinion about such a state of affairs being unsatisfactory has emerged. Accordingly, we are now going through a transitional phase to a post-institutional world, where questions about defining mental health problems and envisaging appropriate responses are being raised by many interested parties. The legacy of the Victorian British segregative policy on lunacy is now grating against a new order of community mental health. For this reason, the dead weight of the former, as well as the emerging features of the latter, need to be discussed together. Accordingly, this chapter begins with a brief review of three recent official reports which highlight the problems, inadequacies and dilemmas of contemporary service provision and policy.

Waiting for Community Care?

Moving from institutional to community settings has triggered a whole new mental health enterprise. As we saw in Chapters 5 and 6 community care remained a concept to be wheeled out in all manner of legislation and government documents after its original inclusion in the 1930 Mental Treatment Act. But it has only moved from rhetoric to some form of reality with the closure of a number of key hospitals at the beginning of the 1990s. This change, in turn, has triggered a burst of official reports that all try to identify the nature, problems and approach to be adopted in a post-institutional mental health context. For British mental health policy 1994 was a year of diagnosis. No less than ten reports from official policy bodies emerged about the problems of securing efficient community care for people with mental health problems. In this section we will summarise points arising from three of these, which illuminate a recurring analysis of why, in recent times, the mental health system has failed its recipients.

The report of the inquiry into the care and treatment of Christopher Clunis (Ritchie *et al.*, 1994)

This report was requested by the Chairs of North East and South East Thames Regional Health Authorities in July 1993 and was submitted in February 1994. The inquiry examined the way in which services failed to respond adequately to Christopher Clunis, a young black man with a diagnosis of paranoid schizophrenia. He stabbed a stranger (Jonathan Zito) to death on 17 December 1992 at Finsbury Park underground station in London. Clunis was subsequently committed to Rampton Special Hospital.

The investigation of the service response to Clunis highlighted a number of problems which are relevant to our discussion here of inadequate community support for people with severe mental health problems. A unique aspect of this case was that the widow of the dead man, Jayne Zito, was an experienced psychiatric social worker. Accordingly, despite losing her husband, she retained a strong interest in campaigning for proper community support for patients. The inquiry highlighted a number of features in the case:

(1) Although Clunis had been in recurrent contact with services since the mid-1980s, there was poor communication by professionals about each admission. In other words, there was a lack of continuity of care – a motif of the case up to the tragic killing. Prior to him becoming

violent in the early 1990s neither he nor his family had been given any systematic help or support by either NHS or social service staff.

(2) No discharge plans were made for his care in the community under Section 117 of the Mental Health Act. He was often homeless and out of touch with relatives or services. For seven months between September 1988 and April 1989 he was 'lost', with no record being available of his existence anywhere. In June 1989 the first violent incident was recorded, when he attacked the manager of a bed-and-breakfast hostel. This was the first of a series of incidents, mainly involving him threatening or actually carrying out knife attacks on those around him.

(3) During the latter part of his psychiatric career, the inquiry discovered further evidence of a fragmented and under-resourced system with professionals being ignorant or poorly aware of prior events and the opinions or concerns of others. Between 1987 and 1992 Clunis had been admitted to four major metropolitan psychiatric units – each of them lost contact with him. A bed in a secure facility was not always readily available when indicated for Clunis during this period. At one point to save money he was transferred from a secure to a general psychiatric bed.

(4) Despite Clunis making violent attacks with a screwdriver on strangers in public places on two consecutive days in the week before the killing of Jonathan Zito, and the police being given clear evidence about his identity and whereabouts, they failed to make an arrest.

The main lessons from the Clunis case are that:

- Professional liaison within the NHS and between it and other agencies like the police, housing authorities and social services, are inadequate.
- S117 of the 1983 Mental Health Act is not being implemented, and other strengthening policies such as the Department of Health's Care Programme Approach (which, incidentally, does not apply in Wales) are not being put into practice properly.
- A range of facilities, from secure psychiatric beds to supported housing in the community, is not currently being resourced properly.
- Even when and if services have procedures in place to receive and treat difficult-to-manage people, they fail to deliver long-term support after or between crises.

Other implications from this inquiry are the failure of professionals to rationally appraise dangerousness and the problems of an over-reliance on medication, with the consequent neglect or exclusion of personal and social support for patients and their families. An interesting post-script to this inquiry is that at the time of writing, the lawyers acting on behalf of Christopher Clunis are preparing to sue the Regional Health Authorities involved for his lack of care.

Creating community care (Mental Health Foundation, 1994)

This report was being prepared at the time of the release of the Clunis Inquiry Report and concurred with and extended its implications, when submitted in September 1994. The brief of the inquiry commissioned by the Mental Health Foundation (MHF) was to assess the current state of community care for 'people with severe mental illness'. Early on in the MHF Report there is a recognition that the latter term currently finds no official definition. It will be remembered that mental illness is not defined under the 1983 Mental Health Act. The inquiry appealed to the Department of Health to provide a working definition. The recent attempt by the DoH to do so has produced a rambling and over-inclusive response and service commissioners are none the wiser for it. What is helpful about the MHF Report, by contrast, is that it sets out a clear value-led position about responding to the needs of people with mental health problems in the community. These are listed as:

- An appropriate place to live
- An adequate income
- A varied social life
- Employment and other day activity
- Help and support
- Respect and trust
- Choice and consultation

The report is also clear about separating the needs of patients and those of carers. Also, as well as the citizenship emphasis for patients in the list above, the report notes that 'Everyone should be able to have a sense of safety in the community.'

The problem checklist it offers about current inadequacies points the finger firmly at central government and even stipulates that the Prime Minister should take the lead regarding a comprehensive strategy, the provision of sufficient resources and organisational change.

The report also notes two other major problems: a lack of under-standing of mental illness and diffuse responsibility across agencies. The latter observation could be read as both a traditional lament about professionals not communicating well with each other (as exemplified by the Clunis case) and as a governmental failure to engender co-operation and collaboration. In recent years, Conservative health ministers, when faced with criticisms of community care policies, have tended to stress the failure of professionals to collaborate and liaise properly. However, both the Clunis and MHF Inquiries complain of the failure of central government to give a clear lead to local services about strategy. At times there has been confusing guidance issued about the implementation of three overlapping policies, which separately and together are not working efficiently: Section 117; the Care Programme Approach (CPA); and care management. The confusion these have placed at a local level are being added to by current demands from the DoH for supervision registers to be kept in every locality. The MHF inquiry recommended that people currently being placed on Supervision Registers should have access to an advocate. Presumably it would make a similar plea for those to be placed under the jurisdiction of the proposed Community Supervised Discharge Orders.

The issues of lack of organisational stability and inadequate resources together are traceable to central government policies – marketisation, and shifting responsibility for community care to local authorities, without providing them with the financial support to operate a needs-led service. These have made for an uneasy, patchy and faltering transition to a community-based system of care. Inadequate co-ordinated joint commissioning of care between local and health authorities is one problem the inquiry highlighted. This difficulty indeed is likely to be made worse now by another government policy in the wake of the 1990 NHS and Community Care Act – the introduction of GP fundholding.

It has been problematic enough for two large commissioning bodies (local and health authorities) to co-ordinate their efforts. Now it will be even more difficult to carry through any strategy with the anarchy created by a fragmented group of separate GP purchasers in every locality. GPs are not fully trained up in the complexities and dilemmas of mental health policy and practice. Also, as independent practitioners they have a culture of autonomy and so they may or may not submit readily to demands for strategic compliance from local or central government. Indeed, the latter has actively encouraged an individualistic attitude by installing the fundholding scheme. If strategic compliance is to entail financial or political costs, which GP fundholders do not wish to bear, they will simply evade the demand.

Overall, the MHF Report can be seen to combine a critique of the current government's lack of mental health policy strategy with an

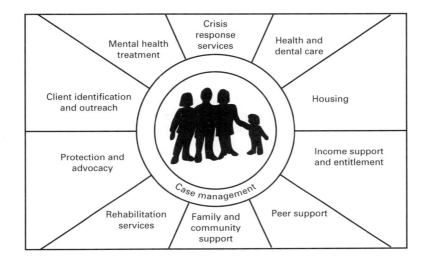

FIGURE 10.1 *The elements of an appropriate community service*

Source: Strathdee, personal communication, 1995.

attempt to offer positive advice to purchasers and providers about making the best of current resources. Its view of an integrated mental health service can be seen in Figure 10.1.

Finding a place (Audit Commission, 1994)

This constitutes a critical overview of the success of recent government mental health policy. It is not clear from the report whether this was an intended or an unintended consequence. Either way, health ministers indicated their profound irritation with its analysis, probably for the following reasons. First, the report (like that from the MHF) holds the government responsible for a lack of clear vision of, and responsibility for, a co-ordinated mental health strategy. Second, it tells the government how it can save money to progress community developments – by implication a cost-sensitive administration is not doing its job properly. Third, it refers to the backlash to community care created by events such as the fatal stabbing of Jonathan Zito. Former Health Secretary Virginia Bottomley is pointedly cited (but not supported) as complaining that 'the pendulum has swung too far' (p. 7). Fourth, given these three features of the report, its overall message is very negative about government success.

By contrast, health ministers have been keen to emphasise how much thought, care and resources they put into community care. Examples of this that were regularly cited by Virginia Bottomley and her junior minister John Bowis were statements on the increase in the number of specialist staff (especially CMHNs) and those emphasising supervision registers. *Finding A Place* pointedly queries whether the skill mix of community nursing staff is currently appropriate and cost-efficient. Also claims by the current government that they hold the strategic reins about mental health are disingenuous. The overall welfare policy since 1979 has been about devolving blame to local authorities, whilst with-holding the resources required for them to take responsibility for efficient community services. The role of central government has been to oc-casionally lay down the law, metaphorically in relation to registers and literally in relation to the stronger community supervision orders. But such sporadic shows of authoritarianism do not constitute strate-gic leadership. *Finding A Place* is a detailed appraisal of current ser-vices. Even a summary is beyond the scope of our space here, but some of its key points or features include:

1. Two-thirds of the £1.8 billion spent on mental health in 1992/3 went to inpatient facilities.
2. Given that community mental health services are more cost-effec-tive and preferred by users and their relatives, a strategy needs to put in place to break the current inertia about inpatient work.
3. Government should be more directive about re-balancing resources. Some districts need more money than others (especially the large urban areas containing inner-city problems). These should have more resource allocations taken from other localities.
4. Savings can be made to move forward on community developments in a number of ways:

   (a) by employing unqualified staff to carry out tasks currently be-ing done by more expensive trained staff in the community;
   (b) by the reduction in bed use being accompanied by more efficient home-based assessments and treatment, which would lead to fewer admissions and shorter stays in hospital;
   (c) by reducing the current over-utilisation of 24-hour-staffed ac-commodation.

Sub-point (a) above relates to the finding of the inquiry that expensive and highly trained CMHNs are carrying out work that could be done by less-qualified people. In some cases CPNs were also found to be failing to prioritise those with the most severe needs. Sub-point (b) relates to one we have already made (Chapter 7), that there is empirical evidence that home-based care is more cost-effective and yet currently services are not putting this evidence into practice. The final sub-point is a function of the tendency of employers to re-deploy staff from the old asylums. This policy was thus provider-driven not needs-led.

The savings suggested in the report by these three measures (per annum, at the time of costing in 1992/3) would be: £100 million from a 12 per cent reduction in inpatient services; £42.5 million from rationalising accommodation staffing; and £13.3 million from changing the community nursing skill mix. Thus, over £155 million could be reinvested in improving community care by this formula. By avoiding demands for *extra* resources (the emphasis of the MHF report), *Finding A Place* paradoxically posed a threat to government authority. Conservative administrations, since 1979, have been used to warding off (often with pride) opposition demands for more public spending. Consequently, a report which offers a critical analysis without this extra spending agenda demands a new type of riposte.

A series of points raised by the MHF report were also made by the Audit Commission. These included the need for collaboration with housing authorities; the caution about resources leaking from hospital closures away from mental health facilities; making care programming work efficiently; and the responsibilities of local purchasers and providers to improve collaboration and liaison about assessing and responding to needs. The shared responsibility of local authorities, health purchasers, NHS trusts, GP fundholders and statutory providers was highlighted. The report endorses the concept of a comprehensive set of activities to respond to the range of needs of people with mental health problems.

Together, these three reports, bunching, as they have done, at the time of writing, highlight and analyse some of the difficulties that community care is currently encountering. In the next sections we look at some of the specific issues related to contemporary mental health policy and management which underlie the analyses in the three reports. These are:

- The management of madness
- Risk assessment
- The illness model as a weak basis for policy
- Institutional inertia and accommodation rights

The Management of Madness

A shift to community settings has exposed a new set of debates about the limitations of, and cautions about, major tranquillisers as a form of treatment. One common concern of clinicians and policy-makers alike is the apparent lack of compliance by people with diagnosis of psychosis with their prescribed medication. When major tranquillisers were first introduced in the late 1950s they were given in low doses. Subsequently, dose levels increased until, by the 1970s, the limitations of these drugs became apparent. In particular, iatrogenic tardive dyskinesia – the drug-induced movement disorders – emerged as a major hazard for psychiatric patients. Instead of being used in low doses and on a temporary basis, it became commonplace for major tranquillisers to be used at high doses and permanently, using maintenance depot injections. The risk of tardive dyskinesia increases with both dose level and chronicity of use. A reliance on high-dose depot maintenance policy is thus a formula for drug-induced brain damage for many of its recipients. As we noted in the chapter on effectiveness, recent RCTs (randomised control trials) confirm that low-dosage regimes are optimally effective. Progressive social psychiatrists have for some time advocated carefully tailored minimal dose levels in combination with good family management (Falloon and Fadden, 1993). A complaint of these writers (as well as of disaffected service users), is that chemotherapy is used all too often by clinicians in an impersonal, over-zealous manner within a conveyer-belt routine.

The disabling impacts of these drugs were, until recently, contained in hospital settings. Now they are manifest in the community. Patients themselves will be hampered by the iatrogenic effects of drugs, and their stigma in the eyes of others will be made greater by the effects. Major tranquillisers have a dual disabling effect. They impair concentration and volition and so pose problems for people in daily living. Also, the disfiguring movement disorders they trigger make their recipients very obvious to those around them. This increases perceptions of difference or oddity in the eyes of non-patients. The stigma of having a psychiatric diagnosis is then amplified by the iatrogenic physical impact of psychiatric treatment.

Tardive dyskinesia in patients living in the community is only one part of the iatrogenic problem. The other is the use of major tranquillisers to control disturbed patients in both acute and secure psychiatric settings. Sudden death from high doses of the drugs is now accepted as being a risk by professionals (Kellam, 1987). This risk increases if the patient is physically and emotionally disturbed and has to be restrained (which is often the case in such circumstances). The risk also increases if major tranquillisers interact with other drugs in the patient's body. The chances of this are high, given that patients admitted to acute psychiatric units are often already medicated (Hemmenki, 1977). In secure settings, the sudden deaths in seclusion recorded at Broadmoor have been associated with deliberate polypharmacy (the use of a cocktail of drugs to sedate disturbed patients).

The adverse effects of neuroleptics pose a dilemma for those responsible for the development and implementation of mental health policy in the 1990s. This is particularly so in a cultural context which is becoming increasingly sensitive to risk (Giddens, 1991). On the one hand, people with a diagnosis of schizophrenia are often portrayed in the media and in the public imagination as potentially violent. The official reports discussed above emphasise strategies which ensure that patients receive medication as the means of preventing violent acts. On the other hand, emerging concerns about the iatrogenic effects of neuroleptics (Brown and Funk, 1986), together with the evolution of consumer-orientated approaches to health care, which promise to give due regard to patients' views of services and treatment, make the risks associated with neuroleptic therapy less acceptable. In some way, policy-makers have to steer a path which reflects sensitivities about both of these two sources of risk.

With the closure of large mental health hospitals, more psychotic patients have become visible in public spaces. Although psychiatry extended its remit from madness to include neurosis after the First World War, the continued use of Victorian asylums during most of this century separated one psychiatric sub-population ('psychotics') from another living in the community ('neurotics'). The physical separation of these groups has been replaced increasingly with a conceptual separation. The recent shifts in mental health policy have been associated with a different public and mass media response to these two groups. The recipients of minor tranquillisers became the focus of consumer campaigning and attracted substantial public and media sympathy (Bury and Gabe, 1990). By contrast, the media attention on madness has been about dangerousness and threat. Those diagnosed as being schizophrenic are just as (if not more) prone to iatrogenic risk when receiving major rather than minor tranquillisers, but they receive little public sympathy. Thus the social problem associated with neurotic distress has been psychiatric *treatment*, whereas the social problem associated with madness has been psychiatric *patients*.

A final point to note about the shifting discourse about community-based psychiatric populations is the expanding remit of professionals for 'minor' psychiatric problems. With the increased detection of anxiety and depression in primary care settings, and a commitment of the Royal Colleges of Psychiatrists and General Practitioners to 'Beat Depression', the psychiatrisation of the community has become substantial. Community psychiatric epidemiology is now identifying large groups in the population, particularly women, as suffering from some form of psychiatric morbidity. From this perspective, 'worry' 'anxiety' and 'stress' are symptoms affecting, it seems, a large minority of the British population. It is not clear at the time of writing how far this psychiatrisation of hitherto everyday distress will be taken. Policy questions are raised by this enthusiasm for detection, which may, in part, be seen as an attempt to find a new role for professionals like psychiatrists whose traditional roles are changing and being challenged by other stakeholders. If such large numbers in the general population are deemed to be psychologically distressed, what is to be done? How will attaching a psychiatric label to distress (which cannot easily be separated out from social circumstances) help those people and affect the other informal means by which people resolve or cope with problems in everyday life? Will they all be given medication or offered counselling? If not, how will decisions be made to prioritise need within a health service so conscious now of cost containment? If rationing is to take place, what criteria will be used and who will be charged with responsibility for their implementation?

Risk Assessment

People with a psychiatric diagnosis make a minimal contribution to violence in society (Monahan, 1992). Male gender, low social class, youth, and drug or alcohol abuse, are much better predictors of violence than mental state. Even so, violence and mental disorder is an issue which has appeared on the recent mental health policy agenda, partly as a result of concerns which have arisen about a number of cases involving violence and psychiatric patients living in the community (see discussion of Christopher Clunis case above). A focus on risk assessment and management is likely to assume an increasing part of the future mental health policy agenda. In 1994 concerns about violence and mental disorder led to a government-supported Confidential Inquiry into Homicides and Suicides by Mentally Ill People, which submitted a preliminary report. The introduction of supervision registers and supervised discharge also reflect political concern about risk assessment. Following the introduction of community supervision registers in England from 1st April 1994, directives from the NHS Management Executive were sent to all provider units to set up a register to identify and provide information on patients liable to be violent, suicidal or prone to serious self-neglect. The Queen's Speech at the opening of Parliament at the end of 1994 included a proposed Mental Health (Supervised Discharge) bill which will endeavour to intensify the supervision powers of the Mental Health Act.

In the 1970s, research demonstrated the limitations of mental health professionals assessing the dangerousness of people. In the 1980s this picture did not improve because of the failure of professionals to adequately theorise either mental disorder or violence. Consequently, it came to be accepted that there is poor predictive validity in the assessment of dangerousness by clinicians and that attempts to predict violence within psychiatric populations was futile or misjudged. However, currently there appears to be a number of persuasive arguments for increasing the validity and utility of predicting dangerousness.

In the absence of efficient and proven methods of assessing the risk of violence many people are being incarcerated unnecessarily. They are treated as potentially dangerous based on the dubious or contestable speculations of mental health professionals. The Special Hospitals are a case in point, where everyone is treated as posing a maximum degree of threat, when this is not the case for a significant proportion of detainees. Better prediction mechanisms would allow more rational targeting of secure facilities and would remove unnecessary and unfair restraints on inappropriate cases.

A related problem exists about community surveillance. Apprehension about being held accountable for untoward acts on the part of patients released from hospital is likely to lead to the over-surveillance of some patients who may pose little or no threat. Professionals responsible for

putting at-risk patients on to the newly introduced supervision registers will want to avoid errors. Because they will not want to be ac-
cused of letting someone who is at risk slip through the net, faced
with uncertainty they are likely to overestimate the number of patients
who are likely to pose a threat to themselves or other people. The
reverse problem may also occur, albeit rarely. A few dangerous patients,
are erroneously discharged and under-supervised. This situation needs
to be predicted and prevented as far as possible. Currently, as was
seen in the discussion about Christopher Clunis, information is not
being utilised efficiently for this purpose.

The existing research about violence and mental disorder has largely
been undertaken in institutionalised settings and is therefore of limited
applicability to the focus of contemporary mental health policy, which
is orientated towards community care. For instance, there is evidence
which suggests that institutional settings may predispose residents (and
staff) towards violence. The highest prevalence rate for hospital patient
violence is reported from Rampton (Larkin, Murtagh and Jones 1988)
where 36.6 per cent of the patients were found to have assaulted staff
or fellow patients in a six-month interval. This is one of the hospitals
where staff violence has also been an officially recorded feature (DHSS,
1980a).

The inverse can also occur. Some violent acts are situationally specific
to open settings. The arsonist, the rapist or the predatory paedophile
will not be surrounded by relevant triggering contingencies inside a
secure hospital, and so the assessment of risk would be undertaken on
an inappropriate site.

Violence also needs to be seen as a characteristic of the person but
a feature of context and group interaction. Discharging patients to high-
risk situations should be avoided. Care should be taken to discharge
people to non-violent, non-threatening social situations. There is emerging
evidence that hostility and threat from interpersonal networks provokes
violent reactions. There are suggestions that domestic violence and sexual
abuse require greater attention than they have received to date (Estroff
and Zimmer, 1994). Family relationships should also become the focus of attention. The implications of research on 'expressed emotion'
have been consistently ignored by successive generations of policy-
makers. It is also emerging that adult-child to parent relationships may
predispose towards the occurrence of violence:

It is clear from our investigation and others that mothers bear not only considerable responsibility for caring for relatives with mental illness but a concurrent risk for being the targets of repeated violence by these relatives. (Estroff and Zimmer, 1994)

In some cases, friends may also function more as instigators of violence than as sources of social support (Klassen and O'Connor, 1988).

A new generation of research might well lead to better prediction. This requires the abandonment of inadequate classification systems, e.g. psychotic versus non-psychotic. The diagnosis *per se* of schizophrenia is not a good predictor of violence. However, some types of active paranoid symptoms are associated with a higher probability of violence. New research initiatives from the US suggest the need for theoretically coherent indices of risk, which take into consideration: dispositional factors (personality variables); clinical factors (specific symptoms rather than global diagnoses); and historical and contextual factors (past history of violence, social stressors and support) (Steadman *et al.*, 1994). Patients' insights about their own violent tendencies should be given greater weight in risk assessment, as should the reports of significant others. Including self-reports of violence increases predictive accuracy by 28 per cent (Klassen and O'Connor, 1987).

Some but by no means all of the above set of considerations about risk assessment are currently recognised by the Department of Health (see e.g. NHSME, HSG (94) 27, 1994). Supervision registers and the imminent supervision orders, which are aimed at minimising risk, find little favour with either service users or many providers. This suggests that central government may encounter substantial resistance to its attempts at increasing community surveillance and control. User critics of the supervision registers (Crepaz-Keay, 1994) point out that funds used for their set-up (estimated at £77 million) would be diverted from services; bad providers who lose contact with patients would be the ones keeping the most inefficient registers; patient confidentiality would be threatened; and those on the register would lose their right to a mental health review tribunal. The registers were supposed to be set up and running in every provider unit by October 1994 but many units failed to meet their obligation.

To conclude in this section, two challenges face future mental health policy-makers. Firstly, they will need to justify the separate treatment of psychiatric patients from others who are deemed to be potentially dangerous in society. Previously, legal control has been focused around detention in hospital; policy-makers will need now to justify such measures in community settings. Secondly, if legal control in the community is to stand a chance of being workable and acceptable to mental health stakeholders, the complex ethical and empirical problems discussed above in relation to risk assessment will increasingly need to be reflected in the decisions of central government, local health policy-making and the everyday work of clinicians.

The Illness Model as a Weak Basis for Policy

The illness model which has characterised mental health policy for most of the nineteenth century and the twentieth has proved more resilient than its opponents have anticipated, but it remains precarious. The relevance of the illness model to policy is that psychiatric epidemiology, which is predicated on the use of diagnostic categories, remains a common starting point for estimating population-level need. However, the medical discourse of 'illness' is giving way slowly but surely to an administrative one of 'disability' and 'mental health problems'. The illness model has not been so much abandoned or refuted as subtly displaced and augmented. Current shifts from hospital to community settings have exposed a number of the difficulties inherent in the use of an illness model. Indeed, the knowledge base of psychiatry has in many ways been marginalised as a consequence. For example, policy documents are becoming less concerned with diagnostic groups (like 'schizophrenics') and more concerned with an alternative administrative discourse about of demand on services ('the continuing care client' or 'people with an enduring or severe mental illness'). Such an administrative rather than medical discourse reflects in part the shift of authority from clinicians to managers during the last decade. But it may also reflect an unintended consequence of shifting from segregation to de-segregation in mental health policy.

Community care has done much more than open the doors of the old asylums before knocking them down. It has also opened up a new set of questions about how to conceptualise what actually constitutes a problem (of psychological distress or oddity). The coherence of an illness framework (which was the target of much criticism within institutional psychiatry) is being tested out further in the community. Given this emerging pattern, it is likely that future policy-makers will continue to review the degree of coherence that the illness model now contains and address its utility for decision-making when drawing up legislation or endorsing ways to help people with mental health problems.

Institutional Inertia and Accommodation Rights

Despite the recent shifts in services and the conceptualisation of mental health problems, and the accelerated hospital closure programme, one of the paradoxes about contemporary psychiatry is that it is still hospital-orientated whilst also experiencing a crisis of legitimacy (Pilgrim and Rogers, 1994). With the closure of the Victorian asylums, there has been a strong tendency for psychiatric theory and practice to be re-sited in District General Hospitals. Developments in community mental health service have been patchy, and investment levels from central government reflect a strong inertia about hospital-centred interventions. State mental health spending on hospitals has over the past twenty years remained around the 90 per cent mark (DH, 1994 and OPCS, 1994). Put another way, spending on community facilities, be it for accommodation or treatment, has not compensated for loss of hospital bed or inpatient treatment – since hospitals still absorb the bulk of funding on mental health. The failure to shift from hospital to community funding has been compounded at times when monies gained from hospital run-down have not been protected for reinvestment in community services. This inertia about hospitals creates problems on several fronts for future policy-makers which reflect and constitute a vicious circle. Resources have become trapped in hospital services and denied to community support services. The lack of community support in turn exposes people living outside of hospital to stressors or crisis triggers (poor social support, poverty and homelessness). Resource mobilisation to reduce poverty and homelessness is made difficult if care budgets are locked into institutional facilities. And the problem goes round and round.

The failure to meet the accommodation rights, particularly of those entering the mental health system for the first time, is becoming increasingly evident. A recent report on community care and single homeless people makes a number of critical points about the failure of central government to reduce the stress of poverty and homelessness on vulnerable people, including those with mental health problems (Leigh, 1994). These points include:

1. There has been poor co-ordination between the Departments of Health, Environment and Social Security to maximise the income maintenance of those in residential care homes and those in low-paid work.
2. Community care is conceived too narrowly as service delivery to individuals. Instead it should entail poverty reduction strategies.
3. In 1993 the Parliamentary Health Select Committee recommended the need for an inter-departmental committee to plan and co-ordinate community care. This was ignored by the DoH.
4. The current range of affordable housing options for people with mental health problems has been limited by government housing policies and by a lack of imagination at a local level about alternatives to hospital admission (like sanctuary houses).

Another recent report (Nuffield Provincial Hospitals Trust, 1994) has also emphasised the failure of government to generate a stock of affordable and adequate housing and the negative consequences this has for both physical and mental health problems. Housing which is damp or cold brings with it particular stressors which increase the probability of both depression and anxiety in inhabitants (Hyndman, 1990). Likewise, overcrowding, a hallmark of temporary bed-and-breakfast accommodation offered to poor families by local authorities, creates tensions, and can culminate in psychological distress (Hunt, 1990). What these points signal is the challenge of providing forms of accommodation which protect people from, rather than predispose them to, mental health problems. Both homelessness and bad housing are threats to mental health.

A separate issue is that of accommodation rights in a post-institutional world. The old asylums were warehouses for madness. Acute psychiatric units cannot serve the same function, although, in practice, the speed of discharge of patients can be currently influenced by the lack of availability of appropriate accommodation. Consequently, hospitalisation is a solution for neither homelessness nor inadequate housing for people with mental health problems.

Policy-makers need to separate out their wider responsibilities for ensuring that all citizens have access to places of residence in the community, from the technical advantages that can be offered by hospitalisation. Moreover, the frequency of demand for the latter needs to be appraised in the light of the poor resources currently available for support for people with severe mental health problems in the community.

There are signs that some health service managers are beginning to plan service re-configuration around a holistic set of principles. Heginbotham and Bosanquet (1995) report a strategy for a 'care guarantee', devised by twelve inner city trust chief executives which emphasises community support, a 24 hour seven day a week crisis service, staff re-training, assertive outreach work for the most disabled clients, housing support and employment schemes. The twelve managers point out that at current costs these necessary innovations would require around £50 million from the Department of Health.

One difficulty at present is that British mental health policy is mainly characterised by incrementalism- small adaptations to the status quo. But given that this is an over-burdened yet over-financed acute hospital service, what is required is a bold plan to break the hospital centred emphasis of the past. For example, in Birmingham one service has been organised successfully around home treatment. This exceptional development, with a product champion with a clear vision of community work, the Clinical Director, a psychiatrist, Sashi Sashidaran, is noteworthy precisely because the majority of services are still principally based around DGH psychiatry and revolving door patients who receive inadequate community support. The Birmingham service, along with those devised in South East London by two other psychiatrists, Graham Thornicroft and Geraldine Strathdee, are the exception when they should be the rule.

Probably the most difficult problem for policy analysts at present is trying to answer the question: has community care succeeded or failed? The honest answer is that currently we do not know because the systematic monitoring of services is absent. A report prepared for the Mental Health Task Force in 1993 about hospital run-down finished as follows:

> The task of monitoring 130 large mental illness institutions has exercised many organisations over the past two hundred years. However, the task of monitoring the wide range of services for the mentally ill that are provided, both in hospital and in the community, is likely to prove much more difficult. The challenge for the next century is not simply to provide more appropriate care for the mentally ill, but also to establish how such a service can be monitored. (Davidge *et al.*, 1993, p. 11)

This leads us to our final discussion. Without proper monitoring, community care cannot be fully evaluated. However, the consistent attack on inadequate community resources from disparate stakeholder groups is underpinned with strong evidence and argument.

Discussion

Given all of the problems rehearsed above, this final chapter finishes
on a cautionary note. Over the past twenty years a consensus has gradually
emerged about the desirability of community care. For this reason,
journalistic accounts often simplistically allude to 'the government's
care in the community policy', as if the latter is the sole and unsavoury
property of the former. An assumption is then set up in the naive reader's
or listener's mind that community care is simply a cost-cutting Conservative policy, which lacks advocates outside of government ranks.

However, as we noted earlier critics of institutions, and latterly service
users, have rejected the inherited Victorian segregative social policy
and emphasised instead the right to live an ordinary life. Whether or
not hospital run-down saved money for the state, the problems of segregation were so palpable, that in the face of increasing expectations
of citizenship, parties other than penny-pinching governments were going
to demand the demise of the total institution.

Thus, the consensus between right and left about the principle of
de-institutionalisation means that the substantive policy arguments now
are not about whether we should return to large-scale hospitalisation.
Instead, they are about how we might understand why community care
has not yet been fully implemented and how we might rectify this
problem. For example, one resistance, which the Conservative administrations have spawned, is the failure to offer wider supportive social
policies for community care to work. Examples here are the run-down
in the affordable stock of both public and private rented accommodation and the favouring of the private nursing home sector of care within an engineered 'mixed economy of welfare'.

Together these two policies have actively undermined proper and
successful community care because they have failed to provide the
needed range of housing resources for systematic and sensitive community reintegration. They have favoured re-institutionalisation rather
than ordinary living in the community. The current government policy
in relation to housing and community is consequently decidedly contradictory. In the midst of the policies which have engendered re-
institutionalisation, the White Paper which preceded the 1990 NHS
and Community Care Act (HMSO, 1989) talks of 'suitable good quality housing' being central to social care packages. Means and Smith
(1994) describe the practical tasks which face policy-makers and ser-

vice providers if independent living is to be properly achieved via a range of affordable and available housing options. The wider challenge of providing opportunities for ordinary living rather than re-institutionalisation is discussed by Ramon (1991, ch. 7). As we noted earlier in relation to the Housing Campaign for Single People (CHAR) (Leigh, 1994) and Nuffield Provincial Hospital Trust Reports, government commitment to delivering the housing resources to support successful community care has been weak or absent. Thus, currently academic research and housing charity lobbying repeatedly draw attention to the pivotal role of housing policy in successful community care – but government departments are not providing the action they imply.

With re-institutionalisation, there is an attendant danger of a return to an eighteenth-century scenario of an extensive network of private madhouses, which defy public regulation and which could lead to a scattering of abusive and negligent acts hidden from public view. The risk of abuse in community settings is made all the more likely given the rate of mistreatment in large institutions, which have been formally under the gaze of the Mental Health Act Commission. The Commission, which has had problems enough controlling abuse in these hospitals with detained patients, has no powers of jurisdiction over voluntary patients. This means that those living in residential or nursing homes will be offered no protection by the main state-funded mental health service watchdog. Thus, there is a danger at present of mental health policy regressing to the problems experienced two hundred years ago.

Whilst private sector nursing home care has been actively encouraged by central government and its regulation evaded, local government has been budget capped. Consequently, community care for all groups, and other locally provided facilities from state education to the fire service, have all had their allocated budgets from central government reduced. Thus an overarching problem at present is simply a lack of protected finance to implement proper community care. Whilst money does not guarantee the latter, adequate finance is a *precondition* of it being achieved. The tendency of the current government to deflect attention from poor resource allocation is evident in a recent pronouncement (August, 1995) by Stephen Dorrell, Secretary of State for Health. When faced with criticisms from the Social Services Inspectorate and Clinical Standards Advisory Group about the 'patchy' provision of adequate community care, his response was to demand that health authorities should demonstrate improvements within a three month period. The professional resistance to community care we have noted throughout this book provides cost-containing governments with an alibi for their own inadequacies.

Another important contradiction in government mental health policy in recent years is about patients' rights. The government has not squared a policy embodied by documents like the Patient's Charter and Working for Patients with that of mental health law. As we have discussed earlier in this chapter, latterly attempts have been made by central government to strengthen community surveillance and control with the introduction of supervision registers and community discharge orders. The pragmatic and ethical problems these risk in their wake have led professional groups (psychiatrists and CMHNs), as well as service users, to be either lukewarm or actively hostile in response.

Bean and Mounser (1993) described an earlier suggestion in 1991 of Community Treatment Orders as 'an ill considered attempt to transfer the whole of the hospital into the community'. Supervision registers, and supervision orders likewise, are likely to come to be viewed by many as a futile and diversionary bureaucratic measure and no substitute for the proper resourcing of a full range of community services for people with a variety of mental health problems. In this light, it is clear that within government ranks there is an unresolved ideological tension between a libertarian emphasis on citizenship and an old-fashioned authoritarian demand for direct state control of pauper deviance. Currently, the fear of the violent reputation of psychiatric patients has led to the contradiction of former Health Secretary Virginia Bottomley championing a community care policy at one moment and at the next complaining of 'the pendulum swinging too far', as an overture to introducing new legislation to enforce community surveillance. What remains untested at the time of writing is the commitment of an incoming Labour government to improve the current policy problems about both resources for community care *and* the lack of a bold vision about patients' rights as citizens.

This chapter has summarised the main problems facing mental health policy makers in the future. Currently there are difficulties at three main levels- clinical, political and cultural. As the service level, with a few exceptions, there has been resistance from clinical professionals whose practices and vision have been limited to hospital based work. At the political level, central government has failed to provide adequate wider supportive social policies to ensure citizenship for people with mental health problems. At the cultural level, citizens, mental health professionals and politicians alike have not been able to break free from the totalising character of the asylum. All, to some extent, have remain trapped in the discourse of a mental health system which was in the ascendancy over a hundred years ago. Hospitals need to be left behind conceptually as well as physically by all parties as we enter the twenty first century.

In conclusion, rights of citizenship for people with mental health problems will only improve with changes in three spheres. First, adequate resources must be rationally targeted to maximise the efficiency of community care, by breaking the inertia of hospital dominance and by offering supportive wider social policies of housing and income maintenance. Second, the prediction of dangerousness needs to be improved and implemented rationally and fairly. Third, the 1983 Mental Health Act needs to be seen primarily as a threat to patients' rights and only secondarily (if at all) as a means of access to service access or treatment.

Bibliography

Abel, B. (1988) *The British Legal Profession* (Oxford: Blackwell).

Abel-Smith, B. (1960) *A History of the Nursing Profession* (London: Heinemann).

Abramson, M. (1972) 'The criminalisation of mentally disordered behaviour: possible side-effects of a new mental health law', *Hospital and Community Psychiatry*, 23(3), pp. 101–5.

Akilu, F. (1991) 'Women's experience of homelessness', *Newsletter of the Psychology of Women's Section of the British Psychological Society*, 8, pp. 1–12.

Alford, R. (1975) *Health Care Politics* (Chicago: University of Chicago Press).

Allderidge, P. (1979) 'Hospitals, madhouses and asylums: cycles in the care of the insane', *British Journal of Psychiatry*, 34, pp. 321–34.

Allsop, J. (1984) *Health Policy and the National Health Service* (London: Longman).

Andreason, N. (1989) 'The scale for the assessment of negative symptoms (SANS): conceptual and theoretical foundations', *British Journal of Psychiatry*, Supplement 7, 155, pp. 49–52.

Armstrong, D. (1979) 'The emancipation of biographical medicine', *Social Science and Medicine*, 13, pp. 1–8.

Armstrong, D. (1980) 'Madness and coping', *Sociology of Health and Illness*, 2(3), pp. 393–413.

Ashton, J. (1990) 'Creating healthy cities', in C. Martin and D. McQueen (eds), *Readings for a New Public Health* (Edinburgh University Press).

Atkinson, P. (1983) 'The reproduction of the professional community', in R. Dingwall and P. Lewis (eds), *The Sociology of the Professions* (London: Macmillan).

Audit Commission (1986) *Making a Reality of Community Care* (London: Audit Commission).

Audit Commission (1994) *Finding a Place* (London: Audit Commission).

Balint, M. (1957) *The Doctor, His Patient and the Illness* (London: Tavistock).

Barham, P. and Hayward, R. (1991) *From the Mental Patient to the Person* (London: Routledge).

Barker, I. and Peck, E. (eds) (1987) *Power in Strange Places* (London: Good Practices in Mental Health).

Barnes, M., Bowl, R. and Fisher, M. (1990) *Sectioned: Social Services and the 1983 Mental Health Act* (London: Routledge).

Barnes, M. and Maple, N. (1992) *Women and Mental Health: Challenging the Stereotypes* (Birmingham: Venture Press).

Barton, W.R. (1959) *Institutional Neurosis* (Bristol: Wright & Sons).

Baruch, G. and Treacher, A. (1978) *Psychiatry Observed* (London: Routledge & Kegan Paul).

Basaglia, F. (1981) 'Breaking the circuit of control', in D. Ingleby (ed.), *Critical Psychiatry* (Harmondsworth: Penguin)'.
Bassuk, E., Rubin, L. and Lauriat, A. (1984) 'Is homelessness a mental health problem?', *American Journal of Psychiatry*, 141, pp. 1546–50.
Baughan, R. (1993) *Suicide: A Summary of Different Approaches and Perspectives* (Banstead: COHSE).
Bean, P. (1979) 'Psychiatrists' assessments of mental illness: a comparison of Thomas Scheff's approach to labelling theory', *British Journal of Psychiatry*, 135, pp. 122–8.
Bean, P. (1980) *Compulsory Admissions to Mental Hospital* (Chichester: Wiley).
Bean, P. (1985) 'Social control and social theory in secure accommodation', in L. Gostin (ed.), *Secure Provision* (London: Tavistock).
Bean, P. (1986) *Mental Disorder and Legal Control* (Cambridge University Press).
Bean, P. and Mounser, P. (1993) *Discharged From Mental Hospitals* (London: Macmillan).
Bean, P., Bingley, W., Bynoe, I., Faulkner, A., Rassaby, E. and Rogers, A. (1991) *Out of Harm's Way* (London: MIND).
Beardshaw, V. and Morgan, E. (1990) *Community Care Works* (London: MIND)
Beattie, A. (1991) 'Knowledge and control in health promotion: a test case for social policy and social theory', in J. Gabe, M. Calnan and M. Bury (eds), *The Sociology of the Health Service* (London: Routledge).
Beazley, M. (1994) 'Measuring service quality', in N. Malin (ed.) *Implementing Community Care* (Buckingham: Open University Press).
Bebbington, P.E., Hurry, J. and Tennant, C. (1981) 'Psychiatric disorders in selected immigrant groups in Camberwell', *Social Psychiatry*, 16, pp. 43–51.
Beliappa, J. (1991) *Illness or Distress? Alternative Models of Mental Health* (London: Confederation of Indian Organisations).
Bentall, R., Day, J., Rogers, A., Healy, D. and Stevenson, R. (1996) 'Side effects of neuroleptic medication: assessment and impact on outcome of psychotic disorders', in S. Moscarelli, A. Rupp and N. Sartorius (eds) *The Economics of Schizophrenia* (London: Wiley).
Beresford, P. and Croft, S. (1986) *Whose Welfare? Private Care or Public Service* (Lewis Cohen Urban Studies).
Bergin, A.E. and Garfield, S.L. (1994) *Handbook of Psychotherapy and Behavior Change* (New York: Wiley).
Berridge, V., Webster, C. and Walt, G. (1993) 'Mobilisation for total welfare 1948–1974', in C. Webster (ed.), *Caring for Health: History and Diversity* (Buckingham: Open University Press).
Beutler, L., Machado, P. and Neufeldt, S. (1994) 'Therapist variables', in A.E. Bergin and S.L. Garfield (eds), *Handbook of Psychotherapy and Behavior Change* (New York: Wiley).
Bion, W. (1958) *Experiences in Groups* (London: Tavistock).
Blaxter, M. (1990) *Health and Lifestyles* (London: Routledge).
Bleuler, E. (1911) *Dementia Praecox or the Groups of Schizophrenias* (New York: International Universities Press) (English edn, 1955).
Bloch, S. and Reddaway, P. (1977) *Psychiatric Terror: How Soviet Psychiatry is Used to Suppress Dissent* (New York: Basic Books).

Blom-Cooper, L. and Murphy, E. (1991) 'Mental health services and resources', *Psychiatric Bulletin*, 15, pp. 65–8.
Bluglass, R. (1985) 'The development of regional secure units', in L. Gostin (ed.), *Secure Provision* (London: Tavistock).
Bolton, P. (1984) 'Management of compulsorily admitted patients to a high security unit', *International Journal of Social Psychiatry*, 30, pp. 77–84.
Bowlby, J. (1969) *Attachment* (London: Hogarth Press).
Bradley, P. and Hirsch, S. (eds) (1986) *The Psychopharmacology and Treatment of Schizophrenia* (Oxford: Oxford University Press).
Bradshaw, J. (1994) 'The conceptualisation and measurement of need: a social policy perspective', in J. Popay and G. Williams (eds), *Researching the People's Health* (London: Routledge).
Breggun, P. (1993) *Toxic Psychiatry* (London: Fontana).
Brown, G.W. (1959) 'Experiences of discharged chronic schizophrenic patients in various types of living group', *Millbank Memorial Fund Quarterly*, 37, p. 105.
Brown, G.W. (1973) 'The mental hospital as an institution', *Social Science and Medicine*, 7, pp. 407–21.
Brown, G.W. and Harris, T.O. (1978) *The Social Origins of Depression* (London: Tavistock).
Brown, G.W. and Wing, J.K. (1962) 'A comparative clinical and social survey of three mental hospitals', *The Sociological Review Monograph*, 5, pp. 145–71.
Brown, G.W., Birley, J. and Wing, J.K. (1972) 'Influence of family life on the course of schizophrenic disorders: a replication', *British Journal of Psychiatry*, 121, pp. 241–58.
Brown, G.W., Harris, T.O. and Bifulco, A. (1986) 'Long term effects of early loss of parent', in M. Rutter, C. Izard, and P. Read (eds), *Depression In Childhood: Developmental Perspectives* (New York: Guildford Press).
Brown, G.W., Bone, M., Dalison, B. and Wing, J.K. (1966) *Schizophrenia and Social Care: A Comparative Follow-Up of 339 Schizophrenic Patients*, Maudsley Monograph no. 17 (London: Oxford University Press).
Brown, P. and Funk, S.C. (1986) 'Tardive dyskinesia: barriers to the professional recognition of iatrogenic disease', *Journal of Health and Social Behaviour*, 27, pp. 116–32.
Browne, A. and Finklehor, D. (1986) 'Impact of child sexual abuse: a review of the research', *Psychological Bulletin*, 99, pp. 66–77.
Browne, D. (1990) *Black People, Mental Health and the Courts* (London: NACRO).
Bruce, M.L., Takeuchi, D.T. and Keaf, P.J. (1991) 'Poverty and psychiatric status', *Archives of General Psychiatry*, 48, pp. 470–4.
Bryers, J.B., Nelson, B.A., Miller J.B. and Krol, P.A. (1987) 'Childhood sexual and physical abuse as factors in adult psychiatric illness', *American Journal of Psychiatry*, 144, pp. 1426–31.
Burrows, W. (1969) 'Community psychiatry – another bandwagon?', *Journal of the Canadian Psychiatric Association*, 14, pp. 105–14.
Burstow, B. and Weitz, D. (eds) (1988) *Shrink Resistant: The Struggle Against Psychiatry in Canada* (Vancouver: New Star Books).
Bury, M. and Gabe, J. (1990) 'Hooked? Media responses to tranquillizer

dependence', in P. Abbott and G. Payne (eds), *New Directions in the Sociology of Health* (London: Falmer Press).

Busfield, J. (1982) 'Gender and mental illness', *International Journal of Mental Health*, 11(1–2), pp. 46–66.

Busfield, J. (1986) *Managing Madness* (London: Hutchinson).

Busfield, J. (1988) 'Mental illness as a social product or social construct: a contradiction in feminists' arguments?', *Sociology of Health and Illness*, 10, pp. 521–42.

Busfield, J. (1989) 'Sexism and psychiatry', *Sociology*, 23(3), pp. 343–64.

Busfield, J. (1994) 'The female malady? Men, women and madness in nineteenth-century Britain', *Sociology*, 28(1), pp. 259–78.

Byalin, K. (1991) 'The quality assurance dilemma in psychiatry: a sociological perspective', *Community Mental Health Journal*, 28, pp. 453–9.

Calnan, M. and Gabe, J. (1991) 'Recent developments in general practice: a sociological analysis', in J. Gabe *et al.*, *The Sociology of the Health Service* (London: Routledge).

Campbell, T. and Heginbotham, C. (1991) *Mental Illness, Prejudice Discrimination and the Law* (Aldershot: Dartmouth).

Carmen, E.H., Ricker, P.P. and Mills, T. (1984) 'Victims of violence and psychiatric illness', *American Journal of Psychiatry*, 141, pp. 378–83.

Carpenter, I. and Brockington, I. (1980) 'A study of mental illness in Asians, West Indians and Africans living in Manchester', *British Journal of Psychiatry*, 137, pp. 201–5.

Carpenter, M. (1980) 'Asylum nursing before 1914: a chapter in the history of labour', in C. Davies (ed.), *Rewriting Nursing History* (London: Croom Helm).

Carpenter, M. (1994a) 'Community Care: the "other" health reform', *Medical Sociology News*, 19(2), pp. 30–3.

Carpenter, M. (1994b) *Normality Is Hard Work* (London: Lawrence & Wishart).

Castel, F., Castel, R. and Lovell, A. (1979) *The Psychiatric Society* (New York: Columbia Free Press).

Catalan, J., Gath, D.H. and Bond, A. (1988) 'General practice patients on long term psychotropic drugs: a controlled investigation', *British Journal of Psychiatry*, 152, pp. 263–8.

Chamberlin, J. (1988) *On Our Own* (London: MIND).

Chen, E., Harrison, G. and Standen, P. (1991) 'Management of first episode psychotic illness in Afro-Caribbean patients', *British Journal of Psychiatry*, 158, pp. 517–22.

Chesler, P. (1972) *Women and Madness* (New York: Doubleday).

Ciompi, L. (1984) 'Is there really a schizophrenia? The long term course of psychotic phenomena', *British Journal of Psychiatry*, 145, pp. 636–40.

Clare, A. (1976) *Psychiatry in Dissent* (London: Tavistock).

Clausen, J.A. and Kohn, M.L. (1959) 'Relation of schizophrenia to the social structure of a small city', in B. Pasamanick (ed.), *Epidemiology of Mental Disorders* (Washington DC: American Association for the Advancement of Science).

Clegg, S.R. (1990) *Modern Organisations* (London: Sage).

Clements, J. (1994) 'Comment', *Open Mind*, 3, p. 70.

Cobb, A. and Wallcraft, J. (1989) 'Women's needs', in A. Brackx and

C. Grimshaw (eds), *Mental Health Care in Crisis* (London: Pluto Press).

Cochrane, D. (1988) '"Humane, economical, and medically wise": the LCC as administrators of Victorian lunacy policy', in W. Bynum, R. Porter and M. Shepherd (eds), *The Anatomy of Madness: Essays in the History of Psychiatry* (London: Routledge).

Cochrane, R. (1977) 'Mental illness in immigrants to England and Wales: an analysis of mental hospital admissions 1971', *Social Psychiatry*, 12, pp. 2–35.

Cochrane, R. and Bal, S. (1989) 'Mental hospital admission rates of immigrants to England: a comparison of 1971 and 1981', *Social Psychiatry*, 24, pp. 2–11.

Community Psychiatric Nurses Association (1988) *The Patient's Case* (London: CPNA Publications).

Cooper, B., Harwin, B. and Depla, C. (1975) 'Mental health care in the community: an evaluative study', *Psychological Medicine*, 5, pp. 372–80.

Cooper, D. (1968) *Psychiatry and Anti-Psychiatry* (London: Tavistock).

Cooperstock, R. (1978) 'Sex differences in psychotropic drug use', *Social Science and Medicine*, 12, pp. 179–86.

Cope, R. (1989) 'The compulsory detention of Afro-Caribbeans under the Mental Health Act', *New Community*, 15(3), pp. 343–56.

Copeland, J., Dewey, M. Wodd, N., Searle, R., Davidson, I. and McWilliam, C. (1987) 'Range of mental illness among the elderly in the community', *British Journal of Psychiatry*, 150, pp. 815–23.

Coulter, J. (1973) *Approaches to Insanity* (New York: Wiley).

Crawford, D. (1989) 'The future of clinical psychology: whither or wither?', *Clinical Psychology Forum*, 20, pp. 29–31.

Creed, F. and Marks, B. (1989) 'Liaison psychiatry in general practice', *Journal of Royal College of General Practitioners*, 39, pp. 514–17.

Crepaz-Keay, D. (1994) '"I wish to register a complaint . . ."', *OpenMind*, 71, pp. 4–5.

Crompton, R. (1987) 'Gender, status and professionalism', *Sociology*, 21(3), pp. 413–28.

Crystel, S., Ladner, S. and Towber, R. (1986) 'Multiple impairment patterns in the mentally ill homeless', *International Journal of Mental Health*, 14, pp. 61–73.

Curran, W. (1979) 'Comparative analysis of mental health legislation in forty-three countries: a discussion of historical trends', *International Journal of Law and Psychiatry*, 1(1), pp. 79–92.

Curtis, J.L., Millman, E.J. and Struening, E. (1992) 'Effect of case management on re-hospitalisation and utilisation of ambulatory care services', *Hospital and Community Psychiatry*, 43, pp. 895–9.

Dabbs, A. (1972) 'The changing role of clinical psychologists in the National Health Service', *Bulletin of the British Psychological Society*, 26, pp. 123–7.

Dalley, G. (1988) *Ideologies of Caring* (London: Macmillan).

Davidge, M., Elias, S., Jayes, B., Wood, K. and Yates, J. (1993) *Survey of English Mental Illness Hospitals* (University of Birmingham: Inter-Authority Comparisons and Consultancy Health Services Management Centre).

Davidhazar, D. and Wehlage, D. (1984) 'Can the client with chronic schizophrenia consent to nursing research?', *Journal of Advanced Nursing*, 9, pp. 381–90.

Davis, A., Llewellyn, S.P. and Parry, G. (1985) 'Women and mental health: a guide for the Approved Social Worker', in E. Brook and A. Davis (eds), *Women the Family and Social Work* (London: Tavistock).

De Boer, F. (1991) 'Sex differences in the construction of mental health care problems', paper presented at the British Sociological Association Medical Sociology Conference, York.

De Swaan, A. (1990) *The Management of Normality* (London: Routledge).

Dean, C. and Gadd, E.M. (1990) 'Home treatment for acute psychiatric illness', *British Medical Journal*, 301, pp. 1021–3.

Dean, G., Walsh, D., Downing, H. and Shelly, P. (1981) 'First admission of native-born and immigrants to psychiatric hospitals in South-East England 1976', *British Journal of Psychiatry*, 139, pp. 506–12.

Dennis, J., Draper, P., Holland. S., Snipster, P., Speller, V. and Sunter, J. (1982) 'Health promotion in the reorganised NHS' *The Health Services Journal*, 26 November.

DH (1994) *Working in Partnership: A Collaborative Approach to Care* (London: HMSO).

DH, Press Release 94/526 (1994) *Two new publications on mental health needs of people from ethnic minority communities* (London: Department of Health).

DH (1994a) *Health and Personal Social Services Statistics for England.* NHS Workforce in England Edition. (London: HMSO).

DH (1994b) *Mental Health Task Force, Local systems of support: a framework for purchasing for people with severe mental health problems* (London: HMSO).

DH (1994c) *NHS Workforce in England* (London: HMSO)

DH (1992a) *Health and personal social service statistics* (London: HMSO).

DH (1992b) *The Health of the Nation* (London: HMSO).

DH (1989) *Health and personal social service statistics* (London: HMSO).

DHSS (1971) *Enquiry Into the Practice and Effects of Scientology* (The Foster Report) (London: HMSO).

DHSS (1977) *The Role of Psychologists in the Health Service* (The Trethowan Report) (London: HMSO).

DHSS (1980a) *Report of the Review of Rampton Hospital* (London: HMSO).

DHSS (1980b) *Organisation and Management Problems of Mental Illness Hospitals* (The Nodder Report) (London: HMSO).

DHSS (1987) *Mental Illness and Mental Handicap Hospitals and Units in England: Legal Statistics 1982–85,* DHSS Statistical Bulletin 2/87 (London: HMSO).

Dick, P.H., Sweeney, M.L. and Crombie, I.K. (1991) 'Controlled comparison of day patient and outpatient treatment for persistent anxiety and depression', *British Journal of Psychiatry*, 158, pp. 24–7.

Dietzen, L.L. and Bond, G.R. (1993) 'Relationship between case manager contact and outcome for frequently hospitalised psychiatric clients', *Hospital and Community Psychiatry*, 44, pp. 839–43.

Dohrenwend, B. and Dohrenwend, S. (eds) (1974) *Stressful Life Events: Their Nature and Effects* (New York: John Wiley).

Donnelly, M. (1983) *Managing the Mind* (London: Tavistock).

Donzelot, J. (1980) *The Policing of Families* (London: Hutchinson).

Doyal, L. and Gough, I. (1991) *A Theory of Human Need* (London: Macmillan).

Dunham, H.W. (1964) 'Social class and schizophrenia', *American Journal of Orthopsychiatry*, 34, pp. 634–46.

Dunham, H.W. (1967) 'Community psychiatry the newest therapeutic bandwagon', *Current Issues in Psychiatry*, 5, pp. 612–3 (New York: Science House).

DYG Corporation (1990) *Public Attitudes Toward People with chronic Mental Illness* (Elmsford, NY: DYG Corporation).

Earl, L. and Kincey, J. (1982) 'Clinical psychology in general practice: a controlled trial evaluation', *Journal of the Royal College of General Practice*, 32, pp. 32–7.

Easton, D. (1953) *The Political System* (New York: Knopf).

Edwards, M. and Fasal, J. (1992) 'Keeping an intimate relationship professional', *OpenMind*, 57, pp. 10–11.

Ennis, B. and Emery, R. (1978) *The Rights of Mental Patients – An American Civil Liberties Union Handbook* (New York: Avon).

Eppel, A.B., Fuyarchuk, C., Pheips, D. and Tersigni-Phelen, A. (1991) 'A comprehensive and practical quality assurance program for community mental health services', *Canadian Journal of Psychiatry*, 36, pp. 102–6.

Estroff, S. and Zimmer, C. (1994) 'Social networks, social support, and violence among persons with severe, persistent mental illness', in J. Monahan and H. Steadman (eds), *Violence and Mental Disorder: Developments in Risk Assessment* (Chicago: University of Chicago Press).

Falloon, I. and Fadden, G. (1993) *Integrated Mental Health Care* (Cambridge: Cambridge University Press).

Farmer, A. and Griffiths, H. (1992) 'Labelling and illness in primary care: comparing factors influencing general practitioners' and psychiatrists' decisions regarding patient referral to mental illness services', *Psychological Medicine*, 22, pp. 717–23.

Farris, R.E.L. (1994) 'Ecological factors in human behaviour', in R.E.L. Farris and H.W. Dunham, *Mental Disorders in Urban Areas: An Ecological Study of Schizophrenia* (Chicago: Chicago University Press).

Faulkner, A. (1992) 'Planned Provision Blues' *Community Care,* 22, Oct. pp. 20–21.

Fennell, P. (1991) 'Diversion of mentally disordered offenders from custody', *Criminal Law Review*, 4, pp. 333–48.

Fenton, S. and Sadiq, A. (1991) *Asian Women and Depression* (London: Commission for Racial Equality).

Ferguson, B. and Varnam, M. (1994) 'The relationship, between primary care and psychiatry: an opportunity for change', *British Journal of General Practice*, 44, pp. 527–30.

Fernando, S. (1988) *Race and Culture in Psychiatry* (London: Routledge).

Fernando, S. (1992) 'Psychiatry', *Open Mind*, no. 58 (Aug/Sept).

Field Institute (1984) *In Pursuit of Wellness: A Survey of California Adults* (Sacramento: California Department of Mental Health).

Finch, J. and Groves, D. (1980) 'Community care and the family: a case for equal opportunities', *Journal of Social Policy*, 9, p. 4.

Finn, S.E., Bailey, M., Schultz, R.T. and Faber, R. (1990) 'Subjective utility ratings of neuroleptics in treating schizophrenia', *Psychological Medicine*, 20, pp. 843–8.

Forsythe, B. (1990) 'Mental and social diagnosis and the English Prison Commission 1914–1939', *Social Policy and Administration*, 24(3), pp. 237–53.

Foucault, M. (1961) *Folie et deraison: histoire de la folie a l'age classique* (Paris: Plon).

Foucault, M. (1964) *Madness and Civilisation* (New York: Random House).

Francis, E. (1989) 'Black people, dangerousness and psychiatric compulsion', in A. Brackx and C. Grimshaw (eds), *Mental Health Care in Crisis* (London: Pluto).

Francis, E., Pilgrim, D. Rogers, A. and Sashidaran, S. (1989) 'Race and "schizophrenia": a reply to Ineichen', *New Community*, 3, pp. 161–3.

Franklin, J.L., Solovitz, B. and Mason, M (1981) 'An evaluation of case management', *American Journal of Public Health*, 4, pp. 674–8.

Frederick, J. (1991) *Positive Thinking for Mental Health* (London: The Black Mental Health Group).

Freemantle, N. and Maynard, A. (1994) 'Something rotten in the state of clinical and economic evaluation', *Health Economics*, 3(2), pp. 63–8.

Freemantle, N., Song, F., Sheldon, T., Watson, P., Mason, J. and Long, A. (1993) 'Managing depression in primary care', *Quality in Health Care*, 3(2), pp. 58–62.

Freidson, E. (1970) *Profession of Medicine* (New York: Harper & Row).

Gabe, J. and Lipshitsz-Phillips, S. (1982) 'Evil necessity? The meaning of benzodiazepine use for women patients from one general practice', *Sociology of Health and Illness*, 4(2), pp. 201–11.

Gabe, J. and Thorogood, N. (1986) 'Prescribed drug use and the management of everyday life: the experiences of black and white working class women', *Sociological Review*, 34, pp. 737–72.

Gamanikov, E. (1978) 'Sexual division of labour: the case of nursing', in A. Kuhn and A. Wolpe (eds), *Feminism and Materialism: Women and Modes of Production* (London: Routledge & Kegan Paul).

Garrett, T. (1992) *National Survey of Clinical Psychology Practitioners' Sexual Contact with Patients* (London: PROPAN).

Gelinas, D. (1983) 'The persisting negative effects of incest', *Psychiatry*, 46, pp. 312–32.

Gerard, D.L. and Houston, L.G. (1953) 'Family setting and the ecology of schizophrenia', *Psychiatric Quarterly*, 27, pp. 90–101.

Giddens, A. (1991) *Modernity and Self-Identity* (London: Polity).

Ginsberg, G., Marks, I. and Waters, H. (1984) 'Cost benefit analysis of a controlled trial of nurse therapy for neuroses in primary care', *Psychological Medicine*, 14, pp. 683–90.

Glover, G., Farmer, R. and Preston, D. (1992) 'Indicators of mental hospital bed use', *Health Trends*, 22(3), pp. 111–15.

Goffman, E. (1961) *Asylums* (Harmondsworth: Penguin).

Goldberg, D. and Bridges, K. (1988) 'Somatic presentation of psychiatric illness in primary care settings', *Journal of Psychomatic Research*, 32, pp. 137–44.

Goldberg, D. and Huxley, P. (1980) *Mental Illness in the Community* (London: Tavistock).

Goldberg, D. and Huxley, P. (1992) *Common Mental Disorders* (London: Routledge).

Goldberg, D. and Morrison, S.L. (1963) 'Schizophrenia and social class',

British Journal of Psychiatry, 109, pp. 785–802.

Goldberg, D., Sharp, D., Strathdee, G., Thornicroft, G., Mann, A., Pilgrim, D. and Rogers, A. (1993) *Developing a Strategy for a Primary Care Focus for Mental Health Services for the People of Lambeth, Southwork and Lewisham* (London: Institute of Psychiatry).

Goldie, N. (1974) 'Professional processes among three occupational groups within the mental health field', unpublished PhD, City University, London.

Goldie, N. (1977) 'The division of labour among mental health professionals – a negotiated or an imposed order?', in M. Stacey and M. Reid (eds), *Health and the Division of Labour* (London: Croom Helm).

Goodwin, S. (1992) *Community Care and the Future of Mental Health Service Provision* (Aldershot: Avebury).

Gough, I. (1979) *Political Economy of the Welfare State* (London: Macmillan).

Gournay, K. and Brooking, J. (1994) 'Community psychiatric nurses in primary care', *British Journal of Psychiatry*, 165, pp. 231–8.

Gove, W. (1984) 'Gender differences in mental and physical illness: the effects of fixed roles and nurturant roles', *Social Science and Medicine*, 19(2), pp. 77–91.

Gove, W. and Geerken, M. (1977) 'Response bias in surveys of mental health: an empirical investigation', *American Journal of Sociology*, 82, pp. 1289–317.

Granshaw, L. (1989) 'Fame and fortune by means of bricks and mortar: the medical profession and specialist hospitals in Britain 1800–1948' in L. Granshaw and R. Porter (eds), *The Hospital in History* (London: Routledge).

Green, J. (1988) 'Frequent rehospitalisation and non-compliance with treatment', *Hospital and Community Psychiatry*, 39, pp. 936–66.

Greenslade, L. (1992) 'White skin, white masks: psychological distress among the Irish in Britain', in P. O'Sullivan (ed.), *The Irish in the New Communities* (Leicester: Leicester University Press).

Grohmann, R. Schmidt, L., Speiss, K. and Ruther, E. (1989) 'Agranulocytosis and significant leucopenia with neuroleptic drugs', *Psychopharmacology*, 99(109), p. 112.

Gunn, J. (1978) *Psychiatric Aspects of Imprisonment* (London: Academic Press).

Haafkens, J., Nijhof, G. and van der Poel, E. (1986) 'Mental health care and the opposition movement in the Netherlands', *Social Science and Medicine*, 22, pp. 185–92.

Habermas, J. (1971) *Toward a Rational Society* (London: Heinemann).

Hagen, J.L. (1990) 'Designing service for homeless women', *Journal of Health and Social Policy*, 1, pp. 1–16.

Ham, C. (1985) *Health Policy in Britain* (London: Macmillan).

Hamid, W. (1991) 'Homeless people and community care: an assessment of the needs of homeless people', unpublished PhD thesis, University of London.

Hamilton, M. (1973) 'Psychology in society: end or ends?', *Bulletin of the British Psychological Society*, 26, pp. 185–9.

Hammer, M. (1968) 'Influence of small social networks as factors on mental hospital admission', in S.P. Spitzer and N.K. Denzin (eds), *The Mental Patient* (New York: McGraw-Hill).

Hannay, D. (1979) *Health and Lifestyles* (London: Routledge).

Hardt, R.H. and Feinhandler, S.J. (1959) 'Social class and mental hospital prognosis', *American Sociological Review*, 24, pp. 815–21.

Hare, E. (1988) 'Schizophrenia as a recent disease', *British Journal of Psychiatry*, 153, pp. 523–5.

Harrington R.C. (1993) *Depressive Disorder in Childhood and Adolescence* (Chichester: Wiley).

Harrison, G., Owens, D., Holton, A., Neilson, D. and Boot, D. (1988) 'A prospective study of severe mental disorder in Afro-Caribbean patients', *Psychological Medicine*, 11, pp. 289–302.

Hearnshaw, L.S. (1964) *A Short History of British Psychology* (London: Methuen).

Heginbotham, C. and Bosanquet, N. (1995) 'A promise of better things to come' *Health Service Journal*, 27, July, 26–7.

Heginbotham, C. and Ham, C. (1992) *Purchasing Dilemmas* (London King's Fund College).

Hemmenki, E. (1977) 'Polypharmacy among psychiatric patients', *Acta Psychiatrica Scandinavica*, 56, pp. 347–56.

Hemsi, L. (1967) 'Psychiatric morbidity of West Indian immigrants', *Social Psychiatry*, 2, pp. 95–100.

Herman, J.L., Perrey, J.C. and vander Kolk, B.A. (1989) 'Childhood trauma in borderline personality disorder', *American Journal of Psychiatry*, 146, pp. 490–5.

Hill, R. and Leiper, R. (1992) 'Evaluation of mental health services: some quality assurance models', *International Journal of Nursing Studies*, 29, pp. 289–99.

Hirsch, S.R. (1986) 'Clinical treatment of schizophrenia', in P.B. Bradley and S.R. Hirsch (eds), *The Psychopharmacology and Treatment of Schizophrenia* (Oxford: Oxford University Press).

Hitch, P. (1981) 'Immigration and mental health: local research and social explanations', *New Community*, 9, pp. 256–62.

Hitch, P. and Clegg, P. (1980) 'Modes of referral of overseas immigrant and native-born first admissions to psychiatric hospital', *Social Science and Medicine*, 14A, pp. 369–74.

HMSO (1926) *Royal Commission on Lunacy and Mental Disorder* (London: HMSO).

HMSO (1984–5) *House of Commons Select Committee Report on Community Care* (London: HMSO).

HMSO (1986) *Mental Health Enquiry* (London: HMSO).

HMSO (1989) *Caring For People: Community Care in the Next Decade and Beyond* (London: HMSO).

HMSO (1990) ('The Griffiths Report') *Community Care: Agenda for Action* (London: HMSO).

HMSO (1993) *Inpatients Formally Detained in Hospitals under the Mental Health Act 1983 and other Legislation Year ending 31st March 1990* (London: HMSO).

Hoenig, J. and Hamilton, M. (1969) *The Desegregation of the Mentally Ill* (London: Routledge & Kegan Paul).

Hoggett, B. (1990) *Mental Health Law* (London: Sweet & Maxwell).

Hogman, G. and Melzer, D. (1992) 'Talk – don't inject', *Nursing Times*, 88, pp. 62–3.

Hollingshead, A. and Redlich, R.C. (1958) *Social Class and Mental Illness* (New York: Wiley).

Horwitz, A. (1977) 'The pathways into psychiatric treatment: some differences between men and women', *Journal of Health and Social Behaviour*, 18, pp. 169–78.

Horwitz, A. (1983) *The Social Control of Mental Illness* (New York: Academic Press).

Hoyt, M.F. and Austad, C.S. (1992) 'Psychotherapy in a staff model maintenance organisation', *Psychotherapy*, 29, pp. 119–29.

Hughes, E. (1971) *The Sociological Eye: Selected Papers* (Chicago: Aldine Atherton).

Humphrey, M. and Haward, L. (1981) 'Sex differences in recruitment to clinical psychology', *Bulletin of the British Psychological Society*, 34, pp. 413–14.

Hunt, S.M. (1990) 'Emotional distress and bad housing', *Health and Hygiene*, 11, pp. 72–9.

Hunter, R. and MacAlpine, I. (1964) *Three Hundred Years of Psychiatry* (Oxford: Oxford University Press).

Huxley, P. (1990) *Effective Community Mental Health Services* (Aldershot: Avebury).

Hyndman, S.J. (1990) 'Housing, dampness and health among British Bengalis in East London', *Social Science and Medicine*, 30, pp. 131–41.

Ingleby, D. (1983) 'Mental health and social order', in S. Cohen and A. Scull (eds), *Social Control and the State* (Oxford: Blackwell).

Islington Mental Health Forum (1989) *Fit for Consumption? Mental Health Users' Views of Treatment in Islington* (London: IMHF).

Jenkins, R. (1990) 'Towards a system of mental health outcome indicators', *British Journal of Psychiatry*, 157, pp. 500–14.

Jodelet, D. (1991) *Madness and Social Representations* (London: Harvester Wheatsheaf).

Johnstone, L. (1992) *Users and Abusers of Psychiatry* (London: Routledge).

Jones, G. and Berry, M. (1986) 'Regional Secure Units: the emerging picture', in G. Edwards (ed.), *Current Issues in Clinical Psychology* (London: Plenum Press).

Jones, K. (1960) *Mental Health and Social Policy: 1845–1959* (London: Routledge & Kegan Paul).

Jones, K. (1972) *A History of the Mental Health Services* (London: Routledge & Kegan Paul).

Jones, K. (1988) *Experience in Mental Health: Community Care and Social Policy* (London: Sage).

Jones, L. and Cochrane, R. (1981) 'Stereotypes of mental illness: a test of the labelling hypothesis', *International Journal of Social Psychiatry*, 27, pp. 99–107.

Jones, M. (1952) *Social Psychiatry* (London: Tavistock).

Jones, R. (1991) *Mental Health Act Manual*, 3rd edn (London: Sweet & Maxwell).

Kane, J.M. (1985) 'Compliance issues in outpatient treatment', *Journal of Clinical Psychopharmacology*, 5, pp. 220–70.

Kay, D., Beamish, P. and Roth, M. (1964) 'Old age mental disorders in Newcastle upon Tyne, part 1, a study of prevalence', *British Journal of Psychiatry*, 110, pp. 146–8.

Kellam, A.M.P. (1987) 'The neuroleptic syndrome, so called: a survey of the world literature', *British Journal of Psychiatry*, 150, pp. 752–9.

Kendrick, T., Sibbald, B. Addington-Hall, J., Brenneman, D. and Freeling, P. (1993) in the *British Medical Journal*, 307, pp. 544–6.

Klassen, D. and O'Connor, W. (1987) 'Predicting violence in mental patients: cross validation of an actuarial scale', Paper presented at the annual meeting of the American Public Health Association.

Klassen, D. and O'Connor, W. (1988) 'A prospective study of predictors of violence in adult male mental patients', *Law and Human Behaviour*, 12, pp. 143–58.

Kowarzik, U. and Popay, J. (1988) *That's Women's Work* (London: London Research Centre).

Lacey, R. (1991) *The MIND Complete Guide to Psychiatric Drugs* (London: Ebury Press).

Laing, R.D. (1967) *The Politics of Experience* (Harmondsworth: Penguin).

Laing, R.D. and Esterson, A. (1964) *Sanity, Madness and the Family* (Harmondsworth: Penguin).

Langer, T.S. and Michael, S.T. (1963) *Life Stress and Mental Health* (Glencoe: Free Press).

Lapouse, R., Monk, M. and Terris, W. (1956) 'The drift hypothesis and socioeconomic differentials in schizophrenia', *American Journal of Public Health*, 46, pp. 968–86.

Larkin, E., Murtagh, S. and Jones, S. (1988) 'A preliminary study of violent incidents in a special hospital', *British Journal of Psychiatry*, 153, pp. 226–31.

Lebow, J. (1982) 'Consumer satisfaction with mental health treatment', *Psychological Bulletin*, 91(2), pp. 244–59.

Le Grand, J. and Robinson, R. (1981) *The Economics of Social Problems: The Market versus the State* (London: Macmillan).

Leigh, C. (1994) *Everybody's Baby: Implementing Community Care For Single Homeless People* (London: CHAR).

Lemert, E. (1951) *Social Pathology* (New York: McGraw-Hill).

Lemert, E. (1967) *Human Deviance, Social Problems and Social Control* (Englewood Cliffs, NJ: Prentice-Hall).

Levine, M., Toro, P.A. and Perkins, D.V. (1993) 'Social and community interventions', *Annual Review of Psychology*, pp. 525–8.

Light, D. (1980) *Becoming Psychiatrists: The Professional Transformation of Self* (Chicago: W. Norton)

Light, D. (1985) 'Professional training and the future of psychiatry', in P. Brown (ed.), *Mental Health Care and Social Policy* (Boston: Routledge & Kegan Paul).

Little, J. (1990) 'Can health be promoted?', in J. Martin and L. McQueen (eds), *Readings for a New Public Health* (Edinburgh University press).

Littlewood, R. and Cross, S. (1980) 'Ethnic minorities and psychiatric services', *Sociology of Health and Illness*, 2, pp. 194–201.

Littlewood, R. and Lipsedge, M. (1982) *Aliens and Alienists* Harmondsworth: Penguin).

216					*Bibliography*

Lomax, M. (1921) *Experiences of an Asylum Doctor, with suggestions for Asylum and Lunacy Law Reform* (London: George Allen & Unwin).
Main, T. (1957) 'The ailment', *British Journal of Medical Psychology*, 30, p. 29.
Maloy, K. (1992) *Critiquing the Empirical Evidence: Does Involuntary Outpatient Commitment Work?* (Washington DC: Mental Health Policy Center).
Mangen, S. and Paykel, E., Griffith, J., Burchell, A. and Mancini, P. (1983) 'Cost effectiveness of community psychiatric nurse or outpatient psychiatrist care of neurotic patients', *Psychological Medicine*, 13, pp. 401–16.
Manthorpe, J. (1994) 'The family and informal care', in N. Malin (ed.), *Implementing Community Care* (Buckingham: Open University Press).
Marks, I. (1992) Innovations in mental health care. *British Journal of Psychiatry* 160 589–597.
Marmor, T.R. (1973) *The Politics of Medicare* (Chicago: Aldine).
Martin, D. and Lyon, P. (1984) 'Lesbian women and mental health policy', in L.E. Walker (ed.), *Women and Mental Health Policy* (London: Sage).
Martin, J.P. (1985) *Hospitals in Trouble* (Oxford: Blackwell).
Mayer, J. and Timms, N. (1970) *The Client Speaks* (London: Routledge & Kegan Paul).
McGovern, D. and Cope, R. (1987) 'The compulsory detention of males of different ethnic groups with special reference to offender patients', *British Journal of Psychiatry*, 150, pp. 505–12.
McIntyre, K., Farrell, M. and David, A. (1989) 'What do psychiatric inpatients really want?', *British Medical Journal*, 298, pp. 159–60.
McMillan, I. (1995) 'Reviewing the review', *Nursing Times*, 91 (3 May) 18.
Means, R. and Smith, R. (1994) *Community Care: Policy and Practice* (London: Macmillan).
Mechanic, D. (1969) *Mental Health and Social Policy* (Englewood Cliffs, NJ: Prentice-Hall).
Medawar, C. (1992) *Power and Dependence* (London: Social Audit).
Meltzer, H., Baljit, G. and Petticrew, M. (1994) *The Prevalance of Psychiatric Morbidity Among Adults Aged 16–64 Living in Private Households in Great Britain*, Bulletin No. 1 (London OPCS Social Survey Division).
Mental Health Foundation (1994) *Creating Community Care* (London: Mental Health Foundation).
Miller, P. (1986) 'Critiques of psychiatry and critical sociologies of madness', in P. Miller and N. Rose (eds), *The Power of Psychiatry* (Cambridge: Polity Press).
Miller, P. and Rose, N. (1988) 'The Tavistock programme: the government of subjectivity and social life', *Sociology*, 22(2), pp. 171–92.
Mills, E. (1962) *Living with Mental Illness* (London: Institute of Community Studies/Routledge & Kegan Paul).
Mills, M. (1992) *SHANTI – A Consumers-Based Approach to Planning Mental Health Services for Women* (London: SHANTI Women's Counselling Services).
Monahan, J. (1973) 'The psychiatrization of criminal behaviour: a reply', *Hospital and Community Psychiatry*, 24(2), pp. 105–7.
Monahan, J. (1981) *Predicting Violent Behaviour* (Beverly Hills: Sage).
Monahan, J. (1992) 'Mental disorder and violent behaviour perceptions and

evidence', *American Psychologist*, 47(4), pp. 511–21.

Morris, B.S. (1949) 'Officer selection in the British Army', *Occupational Psychology*, 23, pp. 219–34.

Murphy, E. (1993) 'Mental illness and community care', paper presented at the Conference of the Association of Social Service Directors, Solihull, October.

Myers, J. (1974) 'Social class, life events and psychiatric symptoms: a longitudinal study', in B.S. Dohrenwend and B.P. Dohrenwend (eds), *Stressful Life Events: Their Nature and Effects* (New York: Wiley).

Myers, J. (1975) 'Life events, social integration and psychiatric symptomatology', *Journal of Health and Social Behaviour*, 16, pp. 121–7.

Myers, J. and Bean, L. (1968) *A Decade Later: A Follow Up of Social Class and Mental Illness* (New York: Wiley).

Newton, J. (1988) *Preventing Mental Illness* (London: Routledge).

NHSME (1994) *Guidance on the Discharge of Mentally Disordered People and Their Continuing Care in the Community* (HSG (94)27) (London: Department of Health).

NHSME Mental Health Task Force (1994) *Black Mental Health – A Dialogue for Change* (London: Department of Health).

Nicolson, P. (1989) 'Counselling women with post-natal depression', *Counselling Psychology Quarterly*, 2, pp. 123–32.

Nicolson, P. (1992) 'Gender issues in the organisation of clinical psychology', in J. Ussher and P. Nicolson (eds), *Gender Issues in Clinical Psychology* (London: Routledge).

Nilbert, D., Cooper, S. and Crossmaker, M. (1989) 'Assaults against residents of a psychiatric institution: residents' history of abuse', *Journal of Interpersonal Violence*, 4(3), pp. 342–9.

Norris, M. (1984) *Integration of Special Hospital Patients into the Community* (Aldershot: Gower).

Nuffield Provincial Hospitals Trust (1994) *Housing, Homelessness and Health* (London: Nuffield Provincial Hospitals Trust).

O'Brien, J. (1992) 'Closing the asylums: where do all the former long-stay patients go?', *Health Trends*, 24(3), pp. 88–90.

Offe, C. (1984) *Contradictions of the Welfare State* (London: Hutchinson).

Olfsen, M. (1990) 'Assertive community treatment: an evaluation of the experimental evidence', *Hospital and Community Psychiatry*, 41, pp. 634–41.

Oliver, M. (1987) *The Politics of Disablement* (London: Macmillan).

Onyett, S., Heppleston, T. and Bushnell, D. (1994a) 'A national survey of community mental health team structure and process', *Journal of Mental Health*, 3, pp. 175–94.

Onyett, S., Heppleston, T. and Bushnell, D. (1994b) 'Job satisfaction and burnout in community mental health team members', unpublished paper.

OPCS (1977) *Mortality Statistics* (London: HMSO).

OPCS (1994) *National Psychiatric Morbidity Survey* (London: HMSO).

Oppenheimer, M. (1975) 'The proletarianisation of the professional', *Sociological Review Monograph*, 20.

Orwell, G. (1986) *Down and Out in Paris and London* (Harmondsworth: Penguin).

Ostamo, A. and Lonnqvist, J. (1992) 'Parasuicide rates by gender in Helsinki,

218		*Bibliography*

1988–91', poster paper at Joint Conference of the British Sociological Association Medical Sociology Group and the European Society of Medical Sociology (Edinburgh).

Palmer, G. (1978) 'Social and political determinants of changes in health care financing and delivery', in A. Graycar (ed.), *Perspectives in Australian Social Policy* (Melbourne: Macmillan).

Palmer, G. and Short, S. (1989) *Health Care and Public Policy: An Australian Analysis* (Melbourne: Macmillan).

Parker, E. (1985) 'The development of secure provision', in L. Gostin (ed.), *Secure Provision* (London: Tavistock).

Parker, M.M. (1992) 'Post-modern organisations or post-modern organisational theory?', *Organisation Studies*, 13(1), pp. 1–19.

Parkhouse, J. (1991) *Doctors' Careers: Aims and Experiences of Medical Graduates* (London: Routledge).

Parry, G. (1992) 'Improving psychotherapy services: applications of research, audit and evaluation', *British Journal of Clinical Psychology*, 31, pp. 3–19.

Parry, N. and Parry, G. (1977) 'Professionalism and unionism: aspects of class conflicts in the National Health Service', *Sociological Review*, 25(4), pp. 823–40.

Patmore, C. and Weaver, T. (1991) *Community Mental Health Centres: Lessons for Planners and Managers* (London: Good Practices in Mental Health).

Paykel, E. (1990) 'Innovations in mental health care in the primary care system', in I. Marks and R. Scott (eds), *Mental Health Care Delivery* (Cambridge: Cambridge University Press).

Peay, J. (1989) *Tribunals on Trial: A Study of Decision-Making Under the Mental Health Act 1983* (Oxford: Oxford University Press).

Peck, E. and Cockburn, M. (1993) 'Comparative costs of adult acute psychiatric services', *Psychiatric Bulletin*, 17, pp. 79–81.

Perring, C., Twigg, J. and Atkin, K. (1990) *Families Caring for People Diagnosed as Mentally Ill* (London: HMSO).

Pilgrim, D. and Rogers, A. (1993) *A Sociology of Mental Health and Illness* (Buckingham: Open University Press).

Pilgrim, D. and Rogers, A. (1994) 'Something old something new: sociology and the organisation of psychiatry', *Sociology*, 28(2), pp. 521–38.

Pilgrim, D. and Treacher, A. (1992) *Clinical Psychology Observed* (London: Routledge).

Popay, J. (1992) '"My health is all right, but I'm just tired all the time": women's experience of ill health', in H. Roberts (ed.), *Women's Health Matters* (London: Routledge).

Porter, R. (1987) *Mind Forged Manacles* (Harmondsworth: Penguin).

Prior, L. (1991) Mind, Body and Behaviour: Theorisation of Madness and the Organisation of Therapy Sociology 25(3) pp. 403–22.

Privy Council Office (1947) *The Work of Psychology and Psychologists in the Services: Report of an Expert Committee* (London: HMSO).

Punch, M. (1979) 'The secret social service', in S. Holdaway (ed.), *The British Police* (London: Edward Arnold).

Rack, P. (1982) *Race, Culture and Mental Disorder* (London: Tavistock).

Ramon, S. (1985) *Psychiatry In Britain: Meaning and Policy* (London: Gower).

Ramon, S. (1986) 'The category of psychopathy: its professional and social context in Britain', in P. Miller and N. Rose (eds), *The Power of Psychiatry* (Cambridge: Polity Press).

Ramon, S. (ed.) (1991) *Beyond Community Care* (London: Macmillan).

Read, J. and Wallcraft, J. (1992) *Guidelines for Empowering Users of Mental Health Services* (Banstead: COHSE).

Ritchie, J., Dick, D. and Lingham, R. (1994) *The Report of the Inquiry into the Care and Treatment of Christopher Clunis* (London: HMSO).

Rochefort, D. (1988) 'Policy making cycles in mental health: critical examination of a conceptual model', *Journal of Health Politics, Policy & Law*, 13(1), pp. 129–51.

Rogers, A. (1990) 'Policing mental disorder: controversies, myths and realities', *Social Policy and Administration*, 24(3), pp. 226–37.

Rogers, A. (1993) 'Police and psychiatrists', *Social Policy and Administration*, 27(1), pp. 33–58.

Rogers, A. and Pilgrim, D. (1986) 'Mental Health Reforms: contrasts between Britain and Italy', *Free Associations*, 6, pp. 65-79.

Rogers, A. and Pilgrim, D. (1989) 'Citizenship and mental health', *Critical Social Policy*, 26, pp. 25–32.

Rogers, A. and Pilgrim, D. (1991) '"Pulling down churches": accounting for the British mental health users' movement', *Sociology of Health and Illness*, 13(2), pp. 129–48.

Rogers, A. and Pilgrim, D. (1993) 'Service users' views of psychiatric treatments', *Sociology of Health and Illness*, 15(5), pp. 612–31.

Rogers, A. and Rassaby, E. (1986) 'Have you opted out? Social work under the Mental Health Act', *Community Care*, 696, pp. 20–2.

Rogers, A., Pilgrim, D, and Lacey, R. (1993) *Experiencing Psychiatry: Users' Views of Services* (London: Macmillan).

Rose, N. (1986) 'Law, rights and psychiatry' in P. Miller and N. Rose (eds) *The Power of Psychiatry* (Cambridge: Polity Press)

Rose, N. (1990) *Governing the Soul* (London: Routledge).

Rose, S.M., Peabody, C.G. and Stratigeas, B. (1991) 'Undetected abuse among intensive case management clients', *Hospital and Community Psychiatry*, 42(5), pp. 235–50.

Rosen, G. (1968) *Madness in Society* (New York: Harper & Row).

Rosen, G. (1979) 'The evolution of scientific medicine', in H. Freeman, S. Levine and L. Reeder (eds) *Handbook of Medical Sociology* (Englewood Cliffs, NJ: Prentice-Hall).

Rosenhan, D.L. (1973) 'On being sane in insane places', *Science*, 179, pp. 250–8.

Roth, M. (1973) 'Psychiatry and its critics', *British Journal of Psychiatry*, 122, p. 374.

Rothblum, E.D. (1990) 'Depression among lesbians: an invisible and unresearched phenomenon', *Journal of Gay and Lesbian Psychotherapy*, 1, pp. 67–87.

Royal College of Psychiatrists (Scottish Division) (1973) *The Future of Psychiatric Services in Scotland* (London: Royal College of Psychiatrists).

Rwgellera G.G.C. (1977) 'Psychiatric morbidity among West Africans and West Indians living in London', *Psychological Medicine*, 7, pp. 317–29.

Saks, M.(1983) 'Removing the blinkers? A critique of recent contributions to the sociology of the professions', *The Sociological Review* 2, pp. 1–21.

Samele, C. (1993) 'The impact of law 180 on women carers', unpublished Phd thesis, University of Kent.

Samson, C. (1992) 'Confusing symbolic event with reality: the case of community mental health in the USA', paper presented at the Conference of the British Sociological Association Medical Sociology Group and the European Society of Medical Society.

Samson, C. (1995) 'The fracturing of medical dominance in British Psychiatry', *Sociology of Health and Illness*, 17(2), pp. 245–69.

Sashidharan, S.P. (1986) 'Ideology and politics in transcultural psychiatry', in J.L. Cox (ed.), *Transcultural Psychiatry* (London: Croom Helm).

Sayce, L. (1989) 'Community mental health centres – rhetoric and reality', in A. Brackx and C. Grimshaw (eds), *Mental Health Care in Crisis* (London: Pluto).

Sayce, L. (1990) 'Care reforms dislocated', *OpenMind*, 46, p. 5.

Scheff, T. (1966) *Being Mentally Ill: A Sociological Theory* (Chicago: Aldine).

Scott, J., Normanton, M. and McKenna, J. (1990) 'Developing a community orientated mental health service', *Psychiatric Bulletin*, 16, pp. 150–2.

Scott, R.D. (1973) 'The treatment barrier, part 1', *British Journal of Medical Psychology*, 46 pp. 45–53.

Scull, A. (1977) *Decarceration: Community Treatment and the Deviant – a Radical View* (Englewood Cliffs, NJ: Prentice-Hall).

Scull, A. (1979) *Museums of Madness* (Harmondsworth: Penguin).

Seagar, C.P. (1991) 'Management of district psychiatric services without a mental hospital', in P. Hall and I. Brockington (eds), *The Closure of Mental Hospitals* (London: Gaskell/Royal College of Psychiatrists).

Sedgwick, P. (1982) *Psychopolitics* (London: Pluto Press).

Shaikh, S. (1985) 'Cross-cultural comparison, psychiatric admissions of Asian and indigenous patients in Leicestershire', *International Journal of Social Psychiatry*, 31, pp. 3–11.

Sheppard, M. (1990) 'Social work and psychiatric nursing', in P. Abbott and C. Wallace (eds), *The Sociology of the Caring Professions* (London: Falmer Press).

Sheppard, M. (1991) 'General practice, social work and mental health sections: the social control of women', *British Journal of Social Work*, 21, pp. 663–83.

Showalter, E. (1985) *The Female Malady* (London: Virago).

Sibbald, B., Addington-Hall, J., Brennerman, D. and Freeling, P. (1993) 'Counsellors in English and Welsh General Practices: their nature and distribution', *British Medical Journal*, 302, pp. 28–33.

Skultans, V. (1979) *English Madness: Ideas on Insanity, 1580–1890* (London: Routledge & Kegan Paul).

Snow, D. Baker, S., Anderson, L. and Martin, M. (1986) 'The myth of pervasive mental illness amongst the homeless', *Social Problems*, 33, pp. 407–23.

Spicker, S. (1993) 'Going off the dole: a prudential and ethical critique of the health fare State', *Health Care Analysis*, 1, pp. 11–16.

Steadman, H., Monahan, J., Applebaum, P., Grisso, T., Milvey, E., Roth, L., Clark Robbins, P., and Klassen, D. (1994) 'Designing a new generation of risk assessment research', in J. Monahan and H. Steadman (eds), *Violence and Mental Disorder: Developments in Risk Assessment* (Chicago: University of Chicago Press).

Stein, L. and Test, M. (1980) 'Alternative to mental hospital treatment', *Archives of General Hospital Psychiatry*, 37, pp. 392–7.

Stone, M. (1985) 'Shellshock and the psychologists', in W.F. Bynum, R. Porter and M. Shepherd (eds), *The Anatomy of Madness, Vol. 2* (London: Tavistock).

Strathdee, G. and Williams, P. (1984) 'A survey of psychiatrists in primary care: the silent growth of a new service', *Journal of the Royal College of General Practitioners*, 34, pp. 615–18.

Szasz, T.S. (1961) 'The uses of naming and the origin of the myth of mental illness', *American Psychologist*, 16, pp. 59–65.

Szasz, T.S. (1963) *Law, Liberty and Psychiatry* (New York: Macmillan).

Szasz, T.S. (1971) *The Manufacture of Madness* (London: Routledge & Kegan Paul).

Taylor, P.J. and Gunn, J. (1984) 'Violence and psychosis 1: risk of violence among psychotic men', *British Medical Journal*, 288, pp. 1945–9.

Teasdale, K. (1987) 'Stigma and psychiatric day care', *Journal of Advanced Nursing*, 12, pp. 339–46.

Teplin, L.A. (ed.) (1984) *Mental Health and Criminal Justice* (New York: Sage).

Thompson, D. (1987) 'Coalitions and conflict in the National Health Service: some implications for general management', *Sociology of Health and Illness*, 9(2), pp. 127–53.

Thornicroft, G. and Strathdee, G. (1991) 'Mental Health', *British Medical Journal*, 17 August, pp. 410–12.

Thornicroft G., Brewin, C. and Wing, J. (1992) *Measuring Mental Health Needs* (London: Gaskell).

Titley, M., Watson, G. and Williams, J. (1992) 'Working women, including older women, in the mental health services', paper presented at the London Conference of the British Psychological Society.

Titmuss, R. (1958) *Essays on the Welfare State* (London: George Allen & Unwin).

Tomes, N. (1988) 'The great restraint controversy: a comparative perspective on Anglo-American psychiatry in the nineteenth century', in W. Bynum, R. Porter and M. Shepherd (eds), *The Anatomy of Madness: Essays in the History of Madness* (London: Routledge).

Tomlinson, D. (1991) *Utopia, Community Care and the Retreat from the Asylums* (Buckingham: Open University Press).

Trent Regional Health Authority (1992) *Trent Health GP Fundholding Initiative Price List: Final Version 1992/3*, Nottingham Trent RHA 1992.

Tudor, K. (1991) 'One step back, two steps forward: community care and mental health', *Critical Social Policy*, 30, pp. 5–23.

Turner, B.S. (1990) 'The interdisciplinary curriculum: from social medicine to post-modernism', *Sociology of Health and Illness*, 12(1), pp. 1–23.

Turner Crowson, J. (1993) *Reshaping Mental Health Services* (London: King's Fund Institute).

Veblen, T. (1925) *The Theory of the Leisure Class* (London: Routledge).

Vernon, P.E. and Parry, J.B. (1949) *Personnel Selection in the British Forces* (London: London University Press).

Wagenfeld, M. (1983) 'Primary prevention and public mental health policy', *Journal of Public Health Policy*, 4(2), pp. 168–80.

Walker, N. and McCabe, S. (1973) *Crime and Insanity in England, Vol. 1* (Edinburgh: Edinburgh University Press).

Warner, R. (1985) *Recovery from Schizophrenia: Psychiatry and Political Economy* (London: Routledge).

Webster, C. (1988) *The Health Services Since the War (Vol. 1)* (London: HMSO).

Weissman, M. and Klerman, G. (1978) 'Epidemiology of mental disorder: emerging trends in the US', *Archives of General Psychiatry*, 35, pp. 705–12.

Weller, B. and Weller, M. (1989) 'Prison – the psychiatric dumping ground', *New Law Journal*, 6 October, p. 1335.

Weller, M. (1985) 'Freirn Hospital: where have all the patients gone?', *The Lancet*, 1, pp. 569–70.

Westermeyer, J. and Kroll, J. (1978) 'Violence and mental illness in a peasant society: characteristics of violent behaviours and "folk" use of restraints', *British Journal of Psychiatry*, 133, pp. 529–41.

Whiteley, J. (1955) '"Down and Out in London": mental illness in the lower social groups', *The Lancet*, 1, pp. 553–4.

Williams, J., Watson, G., Smith, H., Copperman, J. and Wood, D. (1993) *Purchasing Effective Mental Health Services for Women: A Framework for Action* (Canterbury: University of Kent).

Williams, P., Tarnopolosky, A., Hand, D. and Shepherd, M. (1986) Minor psychiatric morbidity and general practice consultations: the West London Survey', *Psychological Medicine Monograph Supplement*, 9.

Williamson, C. (1993) *Whose Standards?* (Buckingham: Open University Press).

Wing, J.K. (ed.) (1985) *Health Service Planning and Research: Contributions of Case Registers* (London: Gaskell).

Wing, J.K. and Freudenbergy, R.K. (1961) 'The response of severely ill chronic schizophrenic patients to social stimulation', *American Journal of Psychiatry*, 118, p. 311.

Winnicott, D.W. (1958) *Collected Works* (London: Hogarth Press).

Wolfe, J. and Tumin, S. (1990) Prison Disturbances 1990 (The Turin Report) London HMSO, CMND 1456.

Wootton, B. (1959) *Social and Science and Social Pathology* (London: George Allen & Unwin).

World Health Organisation (WHO) Regional Office for Europe (1985) *Targets for Health for All Copenhagen* (WHO).

Index

226 *Index*